Top Coaches Talk About
Coaching Basketball Successfully

''Morgan is such a great teacher. He has always amazed me with his ability to organize and teach. *Coaching Basketball Successfully* will help coaches, players, and fans gain a greater appreciation of our game.''

Mike Krzyzewski
Head Basketball Coach, Duke University

''Every so often a book comes along that is special, and that's the case with Morgan Wootten's *Coaching Basketball Successfully*. Outstanding effort! Not to be missed . . . ''

Chuck Daly
Former Head Coach, Detroit Pistons, New Jersey Nets
Head Coach, 1992 U.S. Olympic Men's Basketball Team

''All of us in coaching should be grateful that Morgan Wootten has made his tremendous experience available to us in this book. . . . ''

Bob Knight
Head Basketball Coach, Indiana University

''Coaches, players, and fans will enjoy and learn from Wootten's engaging and information-filled book. He has set the standard for many years to come. . . . ''

Dean Smith
Head Basketball Coach, University of North Carolina

''When someone refers to basketball greatness they mean men like Morgan Wootten. *Coaching Basketball Successfully* is about greatness. This book should be every aspiring coach's bible.''

Pat Riley
Head Coach, Miami Heat

''Morgan Wootten has made a tremendous contribution to the coaching profession through his book *Coaching Basketball Successfully* . . . a must-read book for many years to come.''

Lute Olson
Head Basketball Coach, University of Arizona

''This is the most comprehensive [Coaching basketball successfully by Wootten, Morgan] ead. Coach Wootten covers every aspect of establi [...] cessful basketball program and reveals the essenti [...] al success.''

Rick Pitino
Head Basketball Coach, Universi [...]

COACHING BASKETBALL SUCCESSFULLY

Morgan Wootten
DeMatha Catholic High School

With Dave Gilbert

Leisure Press
Champaign, Illinois

Library of Congress Cataloging-in-Publication Data

Wootten, Morgan.
    Coaching basketball successfully / Morgan Wootten with Dave
Gilbert.
        p.   cm.
    Includes index.
    ISBN 0-88011-446-0
    1. Basketball--Coaching.   I. Gilbert, Dave, 1964-   . II. Title.
GV885.3.W67   1992
796.323'077--dc20

91-21041
CIP

ISBN: 0-88011-446-0

Acquisitions/Developmental Editor: Ted Miller; **Assistant Editor:** Dawn Levy; **Copyeditor:** Vickie West; **Proofreader:** Stefani Day; **Indexer:** Barbara E. Cohen; **Production Director:** Ernie Noa; **Typesetters:** Yvonne Winsor and Kathy Boudreau-Fuoss; **Text Design:** Keith Blomberg; **Text Layout:** Tara Welsch; **Illustrations:** Gretchen Walters; **Interior photos:** Yearbook Associates, Bowie, MD; **Printer:** Versa Press

On the Cover: Vaughn Jones (#30) of DeMatha scores the winning basket over Johnny Rhodes (#15) of Dunbar with 12 seconds to play in the 1991 Washington, DC, title game played at the University of Maryland's Cole Field House. DeMatha coach Morgan Wootten (in photo to right) called this 16-point second-half comeback victory one of the greatest in his remarkable career. His 1990-91 team finished the season with a 30-0 record, ranked in the top 10 in every national poll.

Cover photos contributed by Lon Slepicka of the *Prince George's Journal* and Yearbook Associates.

Printed in the United States of America   15   14   13

Human Kinetics
Web site: www.humankinetics.com

United States: Human Kinetics, P.O. Box 5076, Champaign, IL 61825-5076
800-747-4457
e-mail: humank@hkusa.com

Canada: Human Kinetics, 475 Devonshire Road, Unit 100, Windsor, ON N8Y 2L5
800-465-7301 (in Canada only)
e-mail: orders@hkcanada.com

Europe: Human Kinetics, Units C2/C3 Wira Business Park, West Park Ring Road
Leeds LS16 6EB, United Kingdom
+44 (0) 113 278 1708
e-mail: hk@hkeurope.com

Australia: Human Kinetics, 57A Price Avenue, Lower Mitcham, South Australia 5062
08 8277 1555
e-mail: liahka@senet.com.au

New Zealand: Human Kinetics, P.O. Box 105-231, Auckland Central
09-523-3462
e-mail: hkp@ihug.co.nz

Dedication

This book is dedicated to my number one team of all time—my wife, Kathy; our children, Cathy, Carol, Tricia, Brendan, and Joe; and our grandchildren, who are adding quality depth to our team.

Contents

Foreword

It has long been my expressed opinion that Morgan Wootten is one of the finest coaches in the sport of basketball. And he might be the best.

This feeling is not based on his remarkable winning percentage, but on the manner in which his teams execute the basic fundamentals and the fact that almost every one of his players has received a college scholarship upon graduation. He is a great teacher, whether it be in the classroom or in the sports arena. Every parent should be pleased to have a child under his supervision.

Therefore, it is no surprise that his book, *Coaching Basketball Successfully*, is as fine a teaching aid on the development of a high school basketball team and program as I have ever read; and I have studied almost every book that has been written about this sport. I can also state, without fear of valid contradiction, that it can be invaluable to a coach on any level.

Morgan's approach to the sport goes far beyond teaching the proper and quick execution of the fundamentals at each end of the court. He also has a way of getting each player to accept and execute his role to the best of his ability, to maintain proper physical, mental, and emotional balance, and to keep the welfare of the team ahead of personal desires. But perhaps most importantly, Morgan has managed to keep winning in proper perspective by never permitting it to take precedence over the Lord, his family, or the maturation and education of his players.

John Wooden
Former UCLA Head Coach

Acknowledgments

I could not begin this book without acknowledging the deep debt I owe so many people for so many reasons:

All the fine young men I have had the privilege of teaching and coaching.

The great coaches who have coached with me and against me.

That special group of coaches who gave so much of their time and wisdom to teach me the game of life as well as basketball: men like John Wooden, Red Auerbach, Joe Gallagher, Jim Kehoe, Vic Bubas, Dean Smith, Ken Loeffler, Bud Millikan, John Ryall, and so many others.

My mother, for passing to me her intense drive and love of competition; and my father, for teaching me to tell the truth and to be myself—always.

My sisters, Clare and Helen Lee, and my brother, Angus, who all helped in so many ways.

My Uncle Jack and Uncle Robert, who were like second fathers to me.

To four physicians and friends, Doctors Gaffney, Sullivan, Scalessa, and Lavine.

To the parents of all the young men I have had the privilege of teaching and coaching.

To John Moylan, one of the nation's most respected high school principals, and his outstanding staff.

To all the great men and women who were my teachers from the first grade on.

The three men who coached me in high school and college, Reno Continetti, Tony Creme, and Frank Rubini.

The Holy Cross nuns who gave me my start as a coach.

The Christian Brothers, who gave me my start as a teacher and enabled me to advance my career as a coach.

The Trinitarians and all the DeMatha family, for their help and support through the years.

And to so many other people, too numerous to mention, who touched my life and inspired me to touch others' lives.

Author Notes

I would like to recognize the efforts of two gentlemen, *Dave Gilbert* and *Pat Smith*, who helped me prepare this book for publication. Dave, a sport journalist and announcer in Washington, DC, assisted me in preparing the manuscript. Pat, a former captain of DeMatha and Harvard basketball teams and presently my top assistant coach, helped me with the nearly 200 diagrams in the book.

Also, I want to explain two things concerning my manner of expression in this book. First, the editors asked me to use the pronoun *I* instead of the collective pronoun *we*. At clinics and during everyday conversations, I always say *we* because I am part of a team that includes my assistants as well as my players. The use of *I* throughout the book in no way diminishes my acknowledgment of the valuable roles my assistants fulfill or my appreciation of the outstanding jobs they do. Second, although I use male pronouns and terms such as "him" and "man-to-man," the book's content applies to coaches and players of both sexes. I hope that these expressions would not offend females, who have contributed to basketball in so many ways.

Introduction

When I was approached by the fine people at the American Sport Education Program about writing such a complete book about coaching basketball, several thoughts went through my mind. Should I do it? Could I write anything that I hadn't already written in other books? Would it be too time-consuming? Would it be worth the effort?

I decided it would be time-consuming, and it would be a lot of work. But I also decided I should do it, and that it would be worth the effort. What convinced me to go ahead with the book was my desire to pay at least some portion of the debt that I owe to the game of basketball, which has been such a big and rewarding part of my life.

I figured if there was some small way that I could give something back to the game that has been so good to me, I should do it. I figured if I could play a part in other coaches' lives the way that so many coaches have played a part in mine, it would be worth it.

I have strong feelings about basketball and the valuable role it can play in a young person's life. I felt this book would be an excellent forum from which to share some of those feelings. And I thought this book would also be an opportunity to relate my philosophy about the proper role of basketball in young people's lives, and our roles as teachers and coaches, and how we can positively influence the lives of those young people who come under our care.

We, as coaches, are some of the luckiest people in the world. We get up in the morning truly excited about our work. We look forward to teaching in the classroom and then coaching after school. Why are we so excited about what we do? I think it's because we have the blessed opportunity to work with, to positively influence, and to learn from the world's most valuable resource—its young people.

We are with our student-athletes when they are most impressionable. In the glow of victory, when they are at their emotional peaks, we are there. In the disappointment of defeat, when they are at their emotional depths, we are there. It is in these instances that young people are most pliable. What an opportunity to be a force for good in so many lives in a way that will stay with these young people as long as they live!

But it's more than an opportunity; it's also a responsibility. Of those to whom much is given, much is expected. Any coaching job must be undertaken with this in mind. I believe the best way to make sure we are a positive influence on the young people we work with is to treat them as we would treat our own children. And in many ways, they are our children.

The great Notre Dame football coach, Knute Rockne, was once asked about a just-completed season, "How do you think the season went?" To me, his answer embodies the true spirit of coaching. Rockne responded by telling the questioner to check back with him in 10 or 15 years. Then, he said, he would know what kind of young men he had produced and what kind of citizens they had become. Only at that point and judging by that standard, said Rockne, would he be able to evaluate his season.

It is my wish that all of us would approach every season with that same attitude. If we do, we will never lose. It's nice to be successful in terms of wins and losses. But it's the values we instill in young people through the vehicle of athletics that will continue to be a positive influence long after we've named our last starting lineup.

After all, the real game is the game of life. And it's the one game we cannot afford to lose.

Part I

Coaching Foundation

Chapter 1

Developing a Basketball Coaching Philosophy

So, you want to be a basketball coach?

I know of no more rewarding, satisfying, and fulfilling job than working with young people on the basketball court, as I have done for the last 34 years at DeMatha High School in Hyattsville, Maryland. There is nothing else I would rather be doing.

The first and perhaps most important step toward becoming a successful basketball coach is developing a basketball coaching philosophy. Without a philosophy, you will lack the road map and direction necessary to achieve your goals. This is true in any endeavor that you undertake in life.

Defining Your Philosophy

A coaching philosophy is established in many ways and over many years, beginning with personal experiences as a player. Yours began forming from the first time you picked up a basketball. It grew as you observed games in person and on television. And it will continue to grow as you learn more about the game and how to work with players. To ensure that the philosophy you develop is a positive one, examine the approaches taken by successful coaches. Talk with them, read their books, and attend their clinics. Books and clinics are especially important to your growth and development as a coach.

Reading books allows you to find out what other coaches think, what they've done through the years, and what has worked for them. All types of publications are helpful, but a book—because of its depth—provides real insight into a coach's philosophical approach.

Attending clinics is an absolute necessity. Not only do you hear for yourself what respected coaches think, but you also have a chance in private sessions to talk with them, ask questions, and receive feedback about your own ideas. These gab sessions will contribute significantly to your philosophical development and growth as a coach.

So what is a philosophy? Well, when you take your experiences as a player, the information you've gained through observing games, the lessons you've learned through reading, and the ideas you've picked up by listening and asking questions at clinics, then add your own personality, you have all the ingredients of your own coaching philosophy. But don't be mislead; more playing experience, observation, reading, and listening does not guarantee you'll have a better coaching philosophy. The quality of your experiences and how you implement your philosophy are equally important in determining your success.

Philosophical Foundation

Elements of your philosophy will continue to evolve through the years. These will be primarily tactical elements that change with your personnel and with the game itself (a recent example of which is the institution of the 3-point shot). But there is a core to every sound philosophy that is virtually unchanging, and I call this the philosophical foundation. Many fundamentals of basketball fall into this category, such as the proper way to shoot the ball, the proper defensive stance, the proper rebounding position, and the proper physical conditioning. Even more important, however, is a coach's value system. What do you emphasize—winning a basketball game or winning in life? What priorities do you have regarding the development of your athletes as people, not just as basketball players?

Be Yourself

In determining where your philosophical foundation rests, keep in mind that you *must* be yourself. You can't be John Wooden, Red Auerbach, Mike Krzyzewski, or Dean Smith—you have to be you. It's all right to adopt certain ideas from other coaches, but if you try to be somebody you're not, you'll be inconsistent in your thoughts and actions, your players and assistants will question your honesty, and you will not be as successful as you could be. If you try to be someone else, the best you can do is only second best.

One of my favorite sayings is "I am me, and I want to be the best me that I can be." If all of us try to be the best we can be, we will be successful.

My favorite definition of success comes from John Wooden, the now-retired coaching legend from UCLA. He said, "Success is a peace of mind which comes as a direct result of knowing that you did the best you could to be the best you are capable of becoming."

John Wooden is just one of the many fantastic teachers I have been fortunate to learn from throughout my career. I have been eager to learn and have actively sought advice from people I respect, but to all this information I've added my own approach to life and to basketball. I felt it was important to be my own coach and person, not try to emulate someone else. Although I may take certain suggestions or attributes from a particular coach, I've always tried to be the best me I could be and to do what I felt was right.

Positive Influences

Over the years, I've developed my own coaching philosophy under the positive influence of a number of other coaches. My philosophical development got off to a great start with my high school coach, Tony Creme. He was an excellent coach who stressed fundamentals and communicated well with his players, almost as a father figure. That was my first real contact with an established coach, and he was a real gentleman, the kind of man you would want your own child to play for.

Later, in my first coaching job at St. Joseph's Orphanage, I was fortunate to meet Ken Loeffler, the brilliant former head coach at LaSalle University who is now in the Hall of Fame. I believe he was 25 or 30 years ahead of his time in many areas, including the development of the 1-4 offense, which we started using at DeMatha in 1956.

Another man who influenced me greatly is Red Auerbach, the legendary coach and general manager of the great Boston Celtic teams. He taught me the importance of having the feel of the game, of observing closely and knowing what was happening out on the court rather than just being a spectator from the bench. He also was influential in the development of my conviction that each player has a certain role on a team, and that the ideal team consists of players who understand and fulfill their roles.

John Wooden also has been a dear friend for many years. He has unselfishly shared many, many hours with me, all the while helping me determine where I am, where I'm going, and how I should get there. I've often said that when Dr. James Naismith invented the game of basketball and perhaps dreamt of the perfect coach, the dream became a reality when John Wooden came along.

The many hours North Carolina coach Dean Smith has spent with me have been some of the most valuable for expanding my knowledge of the game of basketball. His ideas on trapping defenses, four-corner offenses, foul-line huddles, and changing defenses are just a few elements of the game with which he has helped me. In addition to considering Dean a great friend, I also consider him one of the greatest coaching innovators the game has ever known.

Many other people have helped me at different points in my career, and not all of them have been basketball people. Jim Kehoe, the long-time athletic director at the University of Maryland, taught me the importance of discipline, of getting things done ahead of time, and of doing things well and doing them wholeheartedly. It was Coach Kehoe who told me, "If you don't have time to do it right the first time, you better make sure you have double the time to do it the second time."

Duke coach Mike Krzyzewski has also been a great help to me. And Mike is a good example of a coach who has adopted much of what he learned from others, then adapted those teachings to fit his own special style. Bob Knight, the Indiana University coach whom Krzyzewski played for and coached under while at West Point, has been instrumental in Mike's career; Mike's great Duke teams have reflected many of the principles he learned from Knight. But Mike also added his own beliefs and experiences to come up with an approach to the game that is uniquely his. For example, Coach Knight will not run set plays designed to get the ball to his outstanding players, for he believes everything comes from within the structured offense itself. "Coach K," however, feels you should have a special play to get the ball into the hands of a great player.

Louisville coach Denny Crum is another example of a coach who has developed a unique approach. He played under Coach Wooden at UCLA and his high-low post offense and fullcourt trapping defense are all reminiscent of Coach Wooden's UCLA teams. But there are also many things that Denny Crum's teams do that Coach Wooden's teams did not.

I met many of these men who influenced me so greatly at different clinics and basketball functions. Because of my respect for them and my desire to be the best coach I could possibly be, I frequently took the initiative to approach these men and pick their brains in an effort to increase my expertise. Not once was I disappointed by their knowledge or their kindness.

Be Eager to Learn

It is important, then, to seek as much advice and knowledge from other coaches as you possibly can. But being willing to learn is not enough—you must be eager to learn.

When I speak at clinics, coaches frequently come up to me and tell me what they are doing. I appreciate them sharing their approaches, but they don't *ask* me anything. When they merely tell me what they do I may learn from them, but they won't learn from me without seeking my feedback. Remember, learning stops when you think you have all the answers.

And don't limit your learning to clinics, books, and discussions with other head coaches. Chances are you may have great resources right in your own building in the form of one or all of your assistant coaches. I have had the privilege of working with and learning from some great assistant coaches. In fact, over a dozen former DeMatha coaches or players are now college coaches—I believe this is an all-time record. What an opportunity I would have missed had I not been alert enough to learn from these talented people.

Touch People's Lives

As coaches, we are extremely fortunate to have the opportunity and ability to work with and positively influence young people. That is why I suggest following this rule of thumb: Be the kind of coach that you would want your own sons and daughters to play for. That is a good basis from which to evaluate and correct yourself. All of us should be determined to be that kind of coach.

It is of the utmost importance in developing your coaching philosophy to *never* lose sight of the tremendous impact you are having on young people's lives. We are with young people at their emotional heights and their emotional depths, the times when they are most impressionable. Teachers of other subjects would love to have the classroom situation that we do, for we have a class that young people are pleading to get into and be a part of. It is our moral responsibility, then, to use this unique opportunity in a positive manner to help prepare our young people for life.

As a coach, you must always be aware of that influence you have on your players. Because of their keen interest and emotional involvement in sport, your athletes will be hanging on every word you say. Many times, you may not think you're reaching them, but what you say to them in practice can determine how good their dinner will taste and how well they will sleep that night. An incidental cutting remark, which you forgot about as soon as you said it, can stay with that young person and be a source of pain for a longer time than you may ever know.

 WOOTTEN VS. THE CHAMP

My first job as a basketball coach was at St. Joseph's Orphanage in Washington, DC. At that time, Rocky Marciano had just won the heavyweight boxing championship, and we were fortunate to have him visit the orphanage not too long after he had won the title. Marciano gave a nice talk and then took questions from the youngsters. Some of the questions were quite astute, such as whether he would recommend boxing as a career, or how his mother felt when he had decided to become a boxer. Of course, there were also the typically humorous questions and one of those almost got me killed. I cringed when one of the fourth graders at the orphanage asked, "Rocky, do you think you could beat Morgan?"

Fortunately for me, Rocky Marciano was a kind man. He looked at the youngster and said, "Well, I think it would probably be the toughest fight I've ever had, and I don't know which way it would go. If I won, it would probably be because I'm a little bigger than he is." Since then, I've always told people I'm the only person Rocky Marciano didn't say he could definitely beat. But what made me cringe even more than the boy's question was his comment on Marciano's answer. He said, "I think Morgan would kill you."

At that point, I realized just how much of an impact I was having on these youngsters and the tremendous responsibility that goes along with that. We as coaches will touch our athletes' lives by what we say, what we do, and even by what we think because the athletes can read us. We must never forget the impact we're having, even when it is not readily visible.

At St. Joseph's, one of my best athletes was leaving the eighth grade and was destined to be sent to a trade school. But I felt he had too much talent for that, so I brought him home to stay with the Wootten family. The young man went on to St. John's College High School in Washington, DC, where he had an outstanding career both academically and athletically. He continued on to college, and today is a successful sales executive. I was truly honored when, years later, he asked me to be the best man at his wedding and then to be godfather to his first son.

In fact, I have been asked to be in the weddings of about 10 of my former athletes and have been godfather to many of their children.

 BUILDING FUTURES

One of my former players, Johnny Herbert, was a point guard who came to DeMatha when I did in 1956. He helped me introduce the tactic of taking a charge for an offensive foul. (The Basketball Rules Committee was forced to change the rules four times to cope with this defensive innovation.) Johnny went on to captain the basketball team at Georgia Tech and is now a successful builder. He named a son after me, and the main street in one of the subdivisions he built is called "Morgan Drive."

If you as a coach take the influence you have on young people's lives seriously, then you too will have former athletes coming back to you many years later to tell you how you enhanced their lives. They'll thank you for the time you took to work with them—and you will share with them the special and everlasting bond of coach and player.

Establishing Objectives

Once you have developed your general philosophy, you can then establish objectives for your players, your team, and yourself. The most important of these steps is establishing objectives for your athletes. Always keep in mind that the game is for the players, and that they are the most important part of any program. Yes, the coach provides the leadership, but it's the athletes who must be the main focus. As much as we may hate to admit it, it's not the coach.

Player Objectives

A fundamental job of a coach is to help the athletes get their priorities in order. At De-

Matha, we encourage our players to devote themselves to four things.

1. God
2. family
3. school
4. basketball

Everything else must come after. Show me young people who have their priorities in order, and I'll show you players who have the best chance of getting the most out of their lives, both on and off the court.

These priorities are one element of my coaching philosophy that has not changed over the years. These four cornerstones came as a result of stepping back and taking a look at the characteristics I wanted in a player.

My primary emphasis on a strong spiritual commitment results from experience; those with such a conviction are better able to meet life's challenges than those without one. Second, I have found that young people who are loyal and devoted to their families are more capable of becoming loyal and devoted members of a team. Third, academics are the purpose of school; a student who is willing to work hard toward that purpose is more likely to work hard toward becoming a better basketball player and helping the team. And fourth, basketball is the sport the athlete is playing, so obviously a strong commitment to that is necessary as well.

Players who demonstrate these priorities are far superior to those with equal talent who do not have such objectives. Because I have seen much less talented teams with the proper priorities beat more talented teams, I love to play against teams whose players are only interested in individual statistics and scoring their 25 points. That kind of player is not the player for me.

Instead, give me a Bill Bradley, former New York Knick and now a U.S. Senator for New Jersey. Bradley was capable of scoring 50 points a game, a feat he performed on several occasions. But Bradley did not care if he scored only two points, as long as his team won. Give me a dozen such players, and I'll be happy because that team will be successful, regardless of the level of talent.

Kids today want the same things as kids did when I started coaching almost 40 years ago. They seek guidance, discipline, and

people who are interested in them. We as coaches must be both teachers and guides, for they sometimes have no one else to help them establish priorities. To reach these young people, I demonstrate to them what the proper priorities should be and give them examples of the kind of positive results such objectives can produce. I then try to make sure that they taste success when they attempt to put things in the proper order. Because once they've seen it work, they're convinced.

 PRIORITIES PAY OFF

In the summer of 1990, one of the guest speakers at my summer basketball camp was Jerrod Mustaf, a former player of mine who had gone on to the University of Maryland and become a first-round draft choice of the New York Knicks. He told the young campers that the main reason he had been successful was his realization that he had to have his priorities in order before he had any chance of reaching his potential.

Another former DeMatha player who wound up in the NBA, Danny Ferry, also spoke at the camp. He too said that the proper priorities, stressed first at DeMatha and then at Duke, were instrumental in his success as a player and as a person.

And one of the most flattering moments in my life came when Adrian Dantley spoke at the camp. One of the campers asked him, "Who is the best coach you ever played for?" and I kind of gulped. But Adrian pointed at me and said, "That man sitting right over there." I was touched when I thought of all the great college, Olympic, and pro coaches for whom Adrian had played. However, the camper tried to burst my bubble by telling Dantley, "You're just saying that because he's sitting there."

"No," Dantley replied. "I'm saying that because he taught me two things. He taught me the importance of priorities, and he taught me the fundamentals of the game of basketball."

I use success stories like these to help convince young people that their priorities must be in order. Once they see how these personal objectives have helped other players I've had (especially the likes of a Dantley, Ferry, and Mustaf), they quickly understand the importance of proper priorities in their own lives.

Team Objectives

After your athletes establish their priorities and have a good idea where they're head-ing, then you must establish objectives for the team. Our team objectives are very simple, and they never change.

- We're going to play hard.
- We're going to play smart.
- We're going to have fun.

How a team approaches the game makes all the difference in the world. A team can take the floor with one of three perspectives:

Team A goes out on the court feeling it must win at all cost, which places an unbelievable pressure on the athletes. This team will very rarely play anywhere near its potential.

Team B comes into games with a fear of losing. Therefore, the players play the game trying not to lose rather than trying to play their best. Again, this is an unhealthy attitude that will inhibit the players on the team from playing up to their potential.

Team C enters a game with the attitude that I stress: Play hard, play smart, and have fun. This is the best approach because it promotes maximum effort from all members of the team while allowing them to enjoy the thrill of competition. In this situation, the players aren't burdened by the pressure of winning at all cost, nor do they fear losing. Rather, they simply try to give their best effort and to have fun, and, as a result, they play up to their potential.

Play Hard

When I tell our players to "play hard," I want them to give everything they have to every second out on the basketball floor. If they give anything less than 100%, then they are not getting the most out of their abilities. You cannot reach your potential without putting your maximum effort into everything you do.

Play Smart

By encouraging smart play, I try to get each player to work within the team offense we spend so much time on in practice, to play within his own physical limitations. To me, these are both part of "playing smart." As a general rule, I do not want inventors out there. I tell the players to just make the basic plays and let the overall flow of the play take care of itself. When all five players are performing within the team offense and their own physical limitations, then you have a team that is playing smart.

Have Fun

When I stress that the players "have fun," I merely want them to remember that basketball is a game, and that their primary reason for participating in the sport is simply for the pleasure they experience while playing it. But they won't get any enjoyment if they play a game feeling afraid to lose, or feeling that they must win at all cost. I want my players to play with this mindset: Basketball is just a game, it's supposed to be fun, and we can have fun while we are busy playing hard and playing smart.

Practice as You Play

The best way to get your athletes to enter games with the proper perspective is to help them approach each practice with a positive mindset. Stress that the players should play hard, play smart, and have fun while practicing. Conduct your practices in an upbeat manner. Your practices should move quickly and emphasize the proper execution and repetition of fundamentals.

One of the commandments of coaching is, "As you practice, so shall you play." Because my players follow this advice (I believe we practice as hard as anybody in the country), our teams are as well prepared as they can be when going into a game. The players, consequently, enter the game with a feeling of confidence that inspires them to really get after the task at hand. They take the floor knowing that they will not beat themselves.

Throughout my coaching career, I've observed that more teams lose because they have beaten themselves than for any other reason. Conversely, players who take the floor with confidence will believe they can win the game—if they play hard, play smart, and have fun.

As you develop a winning tradition, your players will learn that maximum effort, intelligent play, and enjoyment of the game are the keys to the success of the program. And, after all, success is the greatest motivator; players who see what previous teams have done to be successful respond to the challenge, because they want to be successful too.

A Winning Effort

One of the all-time great sportswriters, Grantland Rice, once wrote, "It's not whether you win or lose, but how you played the game." And there is a lot of truth in that. Therefore, I never talk to my players about a game in terms of winning it. For example, I'll never say in a pregame talk, "Let's go out and win this game."

> Adrian Dantley recalls a pregame talk I gave before we played St. John's one year for the league championship. According to Dantley, the only comment I made was "Everyone knows what DeMatha does in big games. Let's go." I did not tell the team to go out, win the game, and win the championship. Still, Dantley says that remark really fired him up.
>
> And what does DeMatha do in big games? We hope, more than anything, to give a winning effort.

The first time we played against Power Memorial High School and their All-American center Lew Alcindor (now Kareem Abdul-Jabbar), we lost by three points. But we had played as well as we possibly could have. Even though we lost, we had still made a winning effort, the only aspect of winning that I stress.

We keep score during games so that the team with the most points at the end is recognized for its achievement. And, without question, I want each game to go in the books as a "W" as much as anybody. But winning has a prominent place in my coaching philosophy only if it is accompanied by winning *effort*. A winning effort is more important than the actual outcome. When we can look back at a game and know we did the best we possibly could, then we know we made a winning effort. That is all any coach can ask of his players, his assistants, and himself.

A trap every coach must avoid falling into is evaluating the success of the program in terms of wins and losses. It could result in the old cycle: If you win, everything is wonderful; if you lose, everything is terrible. But, again, if you and the players evaluate performance strictly on winning and losing, the team will not reach its potential. You will never acknowledge the mistakes made in the games you win, so you won't work to correct them. Conversely, the only thing you'll think about after losses is how poorly the team played. Then the players' confidence is bound to suffer. As a result, the task of improving seems overwhelming because the players see and hear no glimmer of hope for a turnaround.

What you should keep in mind and stress is that sometimes you can learn more from a loss than a win. The players may be more motivated to improve, and they may be more receptive to the constructive criticism that will help them do so. So maintain an even keel. Work on the mistakes you make even in a win, but also praise the successes even in the games you lose.

Coaches' Objectives

Once we've established objectives with our athletes as individuals and with the team as a whole, we must then look at ourselves. What is it that you want to accomplish through coaching?

I believe the biggest personal goal that I as a coach must have is to do the best I can to have my team as well prepared as possible. You owe this to your school, your assistants, your players, and their parents.

From a professional point of view, we, like our players, should work hard to become the best that we can possibly be. We need to continue to add to our knowledge of the game through

- reading as many books as we can get our hands on,
- attending as many clinics as possible,
- exchanging information freely with fellow coaches, and
- asking intelligent questions of the right people.

Over the years, I have found that basketball is full of nice people, and that coaches at every level are ready and willing to share information. Whether you're doing the talking or the listening, you will become a better coach by discussing this great game with wise and experienced counterparts.

 THE BIG UPSET

I've taken advantage of other people's knowledge on many occasions. When we were getting ready to play Power Memorial High School from New York City (undefeated with their star Lew Alcindor), I went to an old friend, Ken Loeffler, for advice. Ken, who had been former President Gerald Ford's roommate at Yale Law School, was then coaching at LaSalle University. I told him we were playing against Alcindor, who was 7 ft 3 in. tall, and discussed what a tough task it was going to be. Leoffler said in response, "No problem. Just put a 7-footer in front of him and a 7-footer in back of him."

But, I told him, we didn't have a couple of 7-footers hanging around the DeMatha gym.

"Still no problem," he said. "Do it with a couple of 6-10 guys."

"But I don't have a couple of 6-10 players either," I responded. This went on until I finally admitted the best I could come up with was a 6-6 player. It was then Ken asked the question I had already been contemplating, namely "Why are you playing the game?"

That little bit of kidding aside, he then sat down and helped me devise the strategy that resulted in one of the biggest upsets in basketball history. Power Memorial's 71-game winning streak was to be snapped, and DeMatha High School was on its way to national acclaim.

Summary

The best ways to develop your own coaching philosophy and to help your players and your teams reach their full potential are as follows.

- Be eager to learn, and work hard to be as up-to-date as possible by reading, attending clinics, and talking with fellow coaches.
- Be yourself, and strive to be the best you that you can be.

- Never lose sight of the impact you are having on young people's lives.
- Teach your players the importance of proper priorities that allow for maximum personal, academic, and athletic development.
- As a coach, make it your goal to have your team as well prepared as possible.
- Make it your team objective to play hard, play smart, have fun, and give a winning effort in games and practices.
- Evaluate wins and losses objectively, focusing more on effort and execution than on the outcome of the game.

Chapter 2

Communicating Your Approach

It's said that effective communication takes place in any successful relationship or organization, whether it be a business, marriage, or team. Conversely, if you have a failing business, marriage, or team, it's often because of a lack of communication.

Obviously, no one way of communicating is successful for everyone in all situations. That being the case, the most important aspect of effective communication is to use the style that fits you. And that means communicating in a manner consistent with your personality and coaching philosophy.

If you are a vocal, fired-up kind of person, then be that kind of coach. Never abuse the players, but feel free to be animated if that's what you're all about. If you're a relaxed,

father-figure kind of person, then be that kind of coach. Perhaps you are somewhere in between. Whatever the case, your style of communication should be based on who you are and what your philosophy is. That's what you will be most comfortable with, so that's what will make your communication most effective.

Although styles of communication will and should vary from coach to coach, the one common ingredient should always be enthusiasm. Nothing worthwhile has ever been accomplished without enthusiasm. You can be laid back or animated and still be enthusiastic; so be enthusiastic in your teaching, preparation, and individual and team work with your players.

Communication—An Open Door Policy

I have found that it is important to keep open the lines of communication with coaches, players, and parents. I constantly remind them that my office door is always open and encourage them to come see me about any problem.

I tell every player that I want to treat them exactly the way I want to be treated myself. I never want them to feel that I am embarrassing them or treating them improperly in any way. I wouldn't want them to embarrass me, and I have no desire to embarrass them. And if they do feel that I'm unfair, I want them to come and talk to me about it. Good communication can help prevent problems.

Try to remind players every week that they may come and talk with you about any problems they might have. And explain to them that if you seem a little harsh at times, it is simply because of your enthusiasm to see them become better players and people.

Communicating With Players

In communicating with the players on the court, I find it extremely helpful to precede constructive criticism with praise. I use what I like to call the "sandwich technique": First, I compliment an aspect of the player's performance, then I slip in the constructive comment, and then I top it off with more praise.

An example of this is, "Hey, Bill, great rebound! But you didn't look up. And if you had, we had someone wide open who could have triggered the break. But you did a great job of protecting the ball, and that at least assured us of the possession."

The two things people like to hear the most are the sound of their own name and a compliment—preferably together. So when talking to your players, if you call their name and pay them a compliment, you know you're going to have their full attention. And that is communication at its best.

Honesty and humility are also important. A coach is not expected to know every single thing about basketball, and you should never be afraid to admit to a player that you aren't sure of an answer to the player's question. For instance, sometimes a player will ask me for the best way to guard another player in a particular situation. I might say, "I'm not sure. Let's look at a couple of ways and see which one seems to work the best for you."

So don't assume that you must have an instant answer to every question. No one ever does, yet many coaches feel they have to. When coaches sometimes start inventing answers, they lose a certain degree of integrity with the players, and thereby reduce the effectiveness of their communication.

Never Humiliate

My style of communicating to players on the court is not one of hollering or screaming. I may get a little loud sometimes, but I tell my players at the first meeting that when I get loud, it's because I'm enthusiastic. Humiliating players by screaming at them has no place in coaching, not only because it is wrong, but also because it will not achieve the desired results. We need to treat our players as the young men and women they are, and we need to treat them with the dignity they deserve. Also, though you may never intentionally humiliate your players, be careful that you aren't doing it unwittingly.

 GETTING THE MESSAGE

One day after practice, Chris Gildea, a player on the team, asked to see me. On the verge of tears, Chris told me, "Coach, you're really embarrassing me in practice. You're constantly harassing me to rebound stronger and to get more rebounds. I know you're doing this to help make me a better player, but it's having the opposite effect and driving me into a shell. I think the quiet type of encouragement will work better with me."

I thanked Chris for letting me know how he felt, and I made a conscious effort to provide more of that "quiet type of encouragement." Chris eventually became the team's leading rebounder and went on to a fine career at the University of New Hampshire. I learned a lesson from Chris and became more convinced than ever that the "open door policy" is the best policy for players and coaches.

The Chris Gildea example also illustrates the importance of flexibility. An "open door policy" is only a facade if you are not willing to learn from the talks you have with the players and to make the necessary changes.

Instruct, Don't Dictate

We, as coaches, must be teachers. So your style of communicating on the court should be the same style of communicating you would use in a classroom. When you work with your team, think of yourselves as teachers working with students. Give some direction, but promote an atmosphere of interaction and self-discovery.

When Wilt Chamberlain was traded to the Los Angeles Lakers, a reporter asked him if he thought Coach Bill van Breda Kolff could handle him. Chamberlain's answer was, "No one handles Wilt Chamberlain. They work *with* him." When communicating with players, we must remember these words. We're not handling our players. We're working with them, helping them to become the best they can be.

Game Communication

Communication on the court during an actual game is also very imporant. A head coach has to be able to send messages to and receive messages from the players on the floor and the players observing from the bench.

 CODE RED

During the first year the 3-point shot was in effect, we played conference rival Bishop McNamara High School in a game that would help determine the league champion. With 8 seconds left in the game, we had a 2-point lead as McNamara brought the ball down the court. Obviously, I did not want them to hit a 3-pointer and steal a victory from us, but, I must confess, I had not thoroughly covered all of the aspects of stopping the 3-pointer.

So, when McNamara's best 3-point shooter got the ball, I thought it best to foul him and only give up two free throws. The worst that could happen would be overtime, and I felt we had the better team and would prevail if an overtime period was necessary. The problem, however, was telling my players what to do. If I yelled to my players to commit the foul, the referees might then call it a deliberate foul, and McNamara would get two shots as well as possession of the ball.

Fortunately, in our "time and score" repertoire (which I will discuss later), we have a color call, "Red," for extreme danger; it indicates that we must immediately steal the ball or stop the clock with a foul. With a 2-point lead in this game, I hollered out to our floor captain, Reggie Veeney, "Red! Red! Red!" He glanced my way

in disbelief, knowing we had a 2-point lead. But he went for the ball anyway, and the official called a foul. McNamara made its first free throw and missed the second. We grabbed the rebound and sealed the victory.

Your players have to be prepared to accept what you say without question, particularly in the crucial moments of big games. The groundwork for this effective communication is laid through the trust they develop toward you and preparation in practices. Reggie Veeney may have thought I was a few cards short of a full deck, but he reacted to the communication instead of questioning it. In a tight game when time is a crucial factor, communication from the coach and reaction from the players can be the difference between winning or losing.

Communicating Off the Court

Perhaps the most important off-court communication between coaches and players is during the off-season. After the last game, we can't just tell our players, "So long, see you next year." It doesn't work that way.

Frequent off-season communication with players is important from an academic point of view, but it's also important in building rapport with your players. Coaches should ask their players how their lives are going, maybe talk about college choices with juniors, and certainly work hard with seniors as they prepare for college. Constant communication between the players and the coach during the off-season helps to build a strong bond, which in turn builds strong teams.

Whether you offer a friendly smile when passing one of your players in the hall, say a simple "hello" to acknowledge a player's presence, or show interest when an athlete comes to you with a problem, you can—through effective communication—help build enduring relationships that will last long after players have finished playing for you. In fact, one way to determine whether you've been a successful communicator and coach is by the achievements of your former players and by whether they seek to remain in touch with you. The legendary coach Joe Lapchick once told me that the greatest thrill in coaching came when a player returned some years later and, with a big smile, said, "Hi, coach!" Nothing else needs to be said.

It disturbs me when I hear players say that they can't talk to their coaches, or that they're difficult to sit down and ask questions to, or, worst of all, "My coach doesn't really care about how I'm doing in school, or whether I have a chance to play college ball." I am always saddened by such stories of a lack of communication because we have so much to give to our players, and, in turn, to receive from them.

In the long run, player-coach communication off the court is more important than on the court. Many players will remember the coach's pep talk that helped them get better grades long after they've forgotten the one on how to handle a zone press.

Communication Failures

No matter how hard we try to be great communicators, there will be times when we fail. But we should always strive to stay in touch with our players, coaches, and everyone connected with the success of our basketball teams.

 A CAPITAL MISCOMMUNICATION

At the end of the 1990 basketball season, our championship team was invited to the White House to help President Bush kick off May as Physical Fitness Month. Basketball was to be one of 10 sports represented on the South Lawn of the White House when President Bush made the rounds to view each sport. What a great honor for DeMatha High School to be the only high school team included in this gala affair!

However, try as I did to change it, the organizers told me that I could only bring 10 players from our 13-man team. Three of our players were seniors; one had already been to the White House 2 years prior to meet President Reagan when he greeted our City Championship team of 1988, and all three had secured college scholarships as a reward for their athletic and academic efforts in high school. So I thought the fairest approach would be to take the 10 underclassmen, and I assumed the three seniors would understand that they were victims of the numbers game.

The mistake I made was that I failed to talk to each senior individually, and I found out later that there were some hurt feelings. I then met with the seniors and explained to them how hard we had tried to get permission to bring all 13 players, but that we just could not. The seniors understood, and the problem was resolved, but better communication on my part could have avoided the problem in advance.

You're always going to have some communication problems, but the key is to head off as many of them as possible. Learn to anticipate problems, and address them quickly and directly when they occur. Most of them then will remain manageable.

Communicating With Your Assistants

It is essential that you communicate with your assistant coaches so that they are prepared and comfortable with their roles. As part of your practice planning (which I will discuss in chapter 6) include a prepractice meeting with your coaching associates. At that meeting, seek their input and make them aware of what you want them to do, such as when they should step in and correct mistakes. Good advance communication with your coaches will prevent misunderstandings and will improve the efficiency of your staff.

A coach that is followed by "yes men" will never grow beyond a certain point. Encourage your assistants to interject their ideas and to offer any constructive suggestions they might have. Even if we don't use a particular idea from our assistants, we need to let them know we appreciate that they've taken the time and made the effort to come up with the idea.

One year at DeMatha, I suspected one of my assistants of being disloyal to the program. I never thought he was doing so deliberately, but I felt certain that he was giving others the wrong impression. So I arranged a meeting, the two of us sat down, and we worked everything out. Today we are the greatest of friends. From that incident, though, I started a tradition of passing out a poem titled "Loyalty" at the first staff meeting every year.

 AN ASSISTANT'S ASSIST

During our 1990 championship season, we had to beat the two best teams in our league within a 3-day period to win the league title. Then, if we did that, we would move on to play the #10 team in the nation for the Washington, DC City Championship. In one of our coaches' meetings, our junior varsity coach, Mike Hibbs, said, "I would love to be playing on DeMatha's team this week. They have a chance to do something here that no DeMatha team has ever had the opportunity to do."

That comment helped me get my players focused on what they could accomplish that week. On Tuesday, we beat a fine Carroll team by a decisive score. Two days later, with Vice President Dan Quayle and Washington Redskins coach Joe Gibbs looking on, we won the league title at sold-out Georgetown University. Then, on Sunday, 12,000 people saw us play one of our best games of the season for the City Championship, even though we lost at the buzzer by 2 points. I am convinced that one reason we performed so well in those three games was because of the perspective provided by our junior varsity coach.

So promote an environment in which your coaches feel free to give their comments. They'll like their jobs more, and your program will benefit from their input.

Communicating With Officials

Basketball is the hardest game in the world to officiate. I can make that claim with confidence because I was an official for 10 years. It is a thankless job, yet this great game would not be what it is without the dedicated officials who work night after night and do their job so well.

It is very important that you and your staff maintain effective communication with officials. And it is not that difficult to do, for the same communication philosophy that applies to players and coaches also works for officials: Treat them with the proper respect, and they will treat you the same way.

Sure, in a moment of heat you might say something to an official that you regret later, but that should be the exception rather than the rule. Coaches who bait, scream, and holler are not enhancing their relations with officials (or their team's chances). On the other hand, the coach who treats officials with respect will have a good relationship with them.

One of the best and most respectful ways to get a point or two across to the officials is in the pregame chat. This is an opportunity to generate some good will between yourself and the officials, and perhaps get a message to them. For example, you can talk about a play in a previous game and say something like, "Can you imagine the official in this situation awarding two free throws for that kind of foul?" Most of the time, the officials will respond, "He must not have known the rules."

Pregame talks are an opportunity to subtly remind officials about the certain elements of the game you feel could become important in that particular contest. DeMatha is a pressing team, and one of the rules that figures into many of our games is the inbounds rule. The rule states that a player must pass the ball inbounds within 5 seconds or the team loses possession. The official who hands the players the ball is required to give a visible hand count of each of the 5 seconds. So, in the pregame chat, I will frequently tell the officials about a game in which another official told me that he did not have to give the hand count, and that the ball did not have to be inbounded within 5 seconds. I encourage you to use the pregame situation in a similar manner.

Above all, however, treat officials with the respect they deserve. It's both morally right and strategically more effective. Basketball can sometimes bring out the best and the worst in all of us; we need to strive to bring out the best, especially in our behavior toward officials. It's better not only for those who officiate, but for our players, ourselves, and our sport.

Communicating With Parents

We must make ourselves available to the parents of our young athletes. Set aside time to talk with them individually or collectively. Remember, parents are rightfully involved in the progress of their children, and it is our duty to speak with them and patiently answer all of their questions.

We sometimes expect parents to be a problem. And the problems that do arise often stem from parents' unrealistic views of their children's athletic abilities. However, if you tactfully and positively communicate a more realistic assessment of their child's talent, you can usually keep the problems under control, if not entirely eliminate them. That's important, because parents can be tremendous assets to your program.

We must remember that each young person we are coaching is the most precious thing in the world to his or her parents. Consequently, it is very hard for parents to be completely objective. For this reason I often start conferences with parents by saying, "Look, I know this is an emotional subject. I promise you that I will treat you with respect, and I expect you to treat me with the same respect. Let's work hard together to do what is best for your child." During a parent conference, I've found it helpful to always keep an open mind and to remember the words "You can disagree without being disagreeable."

A PARENT SOLUTION

I have had good luck with parents, with only a few exceptions. One of those exceptions first became evident at a tournament in a neighboring state during two games I had had to miss (something I have only had to do five times in my career). My assistant, Jack Bruen, now the head coach at Colgate, took the team to the tournament and brought them home with two victories. As I was congratulating him on the terrific way he had started his coaching career, he said, "Morgan, everything went great except during time-outs. Only four players would sit on the bench and listen to me. One of the fathers would actually come over and grab his son and talk to him during the time-outs." I found it hard to believe that any parent would do that, and I realized that I was in for a year-long problem if I didn't do something to correct the situation.

During the first time-out of our next game, all five of the players sat down on the bench to face me as they are supposed to do. However, this one young man's father, sitting in the first row behind the bench, jumped up and started hollering instructions to his son. I stood up, looked the father dead in the eye, and said, "If you're going to coach your son, you're going to have to find a team for him to play on. Because

you're not going to coach him here." I then went back to the huddle and started talking to the players. I never had a problem with that parent again.

I want to emphasize that my desire in this situation was not to embarrass the young man, but to solve a problem that I felt could only become more harmful to the player and the team if allowed to continue. If you don't address such problems immediately, all they do is get worse.

Getting Things Off to a Good Start

Generally, we should view parents the same way we view the players—as part of the team. And good communication will help make them positive contributors. So I try to make the parents feel a part of the program early in the year.

Once the team is selected, I invite the parents to come to the school after regular practice for a team Mass. After Mass, we have a social hour in which we all get to know each other a little bit better, followed by a dinner. At the end of the dinner I generally give a short speech. I talk about the rules the players have voted on, encourage the parents to be active participants with the team, and emphasize that we are all part of the team and must work together to make it a successful year. I also take this opportunity to stress to the parents, as well as the players, that my door is always open any time they feel the need to come and talk to me.

I have found over the years that this preseason gathering is a great way to start the year on a positive note. It allows the parents to meet each other as well as the coaches who will be working with the children. And it helps begin building the team unity among the coaches, players, and parents that is so essential to any successful basketball program.

Communicating With School Faculty

I stay in constant contact with the teachers of our players. Every teacher in your school can help your program in some way, even if it's just by coming to the games and showing support. You'll be amazed at how many people are eager to help your program if you only ask.

For years, all of our games at DeMatha were filmed by Rocco Manella, the head of our computer programming department. As a technician and as a friend, his interest was invaluable to me and to our program. Other teachers have kept statistics for us, and the art department makes posters for our games.

The faculty supports us because they know I do not put basketball ahead of academics. They know that I pass along this philosophy to my players: The classroom is more important than the basketball court. They see our players taking the same course load as every other DeMatha student. And they know that I do not expect them to give our athletes any special treatment; they appreciate that I will allow players to miss practice for tutoring or to take an exam. Our coaching staff demonstrates its willingness to work with the faculty and reinforces the priority of academics over athletics. If you take the same approach, every teacher in your school will support your program.

Monitoring Academics

Every 2 weeks, my players take a form to all of their classes. The teachers are asked to provide the student's current grade and any other comments that are relevant. This allows me to closely monitor our players' academic standing. This way, there are no surprises when report cards are distributed at the end of the term.

Any time a bad grade shows up on a 2-week report, I have a personal chat with the teacher to find out what I can do to help the situation. And because the lines of communication between myself and the faculty are open, the reverse is often true. I have teachers come to me and ask me to talk with a player who may be having trouble in a certain subject.

I also monitor the kinds of courses the players register for every year to insure that they are taking the core courses required by DeMatha High School. Fortunately, these school-mandated courses are in accordance with NCAA bylaws regarding eligibility for college athletic scholarships.

Also to help players meet the NCAA standards, I have every player take their college entrance exams in the spring of their junior year. At DeMatha we are fortunate to have a teacher who is an expert on the Scholastic Aptitude Test (SAT). Every spring, Dr. Charles "Buck" Offutt conducts an SAT preparation course for basketball players and anyone else who wants to attend.

We have had tremendous success in preparing athletes to play in college through our close monitoring of their academic standing and our strong recommendations that our players take the SAT prep course. It is a coach's moral obligation to ready players for life after school. If you do not, then you are using your players.

That's why you need to make the faculty part of your basketball team. Let them know they are important and that you appreciate their contribution. I love it when a teacher comes up to me and says, "Hey, I saw where we won a big one last night." Everyone likes to be part of a good team—one whose players are good people, have their priorities in order, and represent the school in the right way.

The same system works for other extracurricular activities, such as the school's band. Our school has one of the finest music programs in the nation, and I am extremely proud of it. I, the basketball coach, constantly brag about the band's accomplishments. Whether it's the school's basketball or music program, faculty members will support you if you put academics first. And, along with that, you must keep the lines of communication with them wide open.

Communicating With the Student Body

From what I have said, you can see that I encourage my players to take active roles as members of the student body. I encourage them to go to the school's other athletic events, support the school teams, and interact with the other students. One year I called off practice so the whole team could watch our soccer team play in a championship game.

 BROADCASTING APPEAL

James Brown, now a network sportscaster for CBS, made our basketball team as a sophomore. He did not play much that year, but at almost every home game the crowd would chant, "We want James! We want James!" The reason everybody loved James is that he always had a big smile and "hello" for everyone he met in the hallway, from the littlest freshman to the biggest senior.

While you are encouraging your players to get involved in the activities of the rest of the student body, also make an effort to keep the student body informed about the basketball team. Urge them to come out and show their support in the proper way. Ask them to cheer for your team, not boo or harass the opponent. Then, when they really turn out and support the team positively, show your appreciation. For example, during morning announcements we sometimes have our players come on the loudspeaker and thank the students for their support at the previous game.

Finally, and perhaps most importantly, let all of the students know that the students who participate in the basketball program will receive no academic favors. The student body will be more supportive when they find that the basketball players do not get special treatment. Consequently, there is little or no jealousy or animosity from other students toward the student-athletes.

Communicating With Community Members

I am proud that so many community-minded people in Hyattsville, Maryland have chosen to be a big part of our teams over the years. A large part of our success can be attributed to the local automobile dealer, restaurateurs, and many other business people, service organizations, and clubs in the area.

For instance, during the summer of 1977, I had an opportunity to take the team to compete in Brazil. With little prompting on my part, the community helped us raise the necessary funds to give our young athletes an experience of a lifetime. That team went on to become one of the five national champions we have had at DeMatha. Without question, the community played an important role in that team's success.

Communicating With the Media

Whether it's on a regular basis or only a couple of times a season, you will at some point have to communicate with the local media. It can mean a great deal to your program if you make yourself available for interviews and take the time to courteously answer all of the media's questions. Demonstrate to the reporters your understanding that they have a job to do, and that you view their job as important. Keep your answers to questions positive, and remember to promote the team and your players, not yourself.

Also, try not to give preference to one reporter or to one media outlet over another. Several media sources cover our games, from small local papers to *The Washington Post*. I make myself equally accessible to reporters from every news organization that shows an interest in the basketball program. I believe accessibility to the media can help your program attract more coverage. And I believe equal treatment of all reporters can help insure that your program receives fair coverage from the press.

I also make the players available to the media. I do not believe in shielding or hiding the players; in fact, I encourage reporters to talk with them. I think part of their education as basketball players (even at the high school level) is to learn to speak with members of the press. The only rule I have for players speaking to the media is that they keep their comments as positive as possible. I don't think it serves any purpose to be negative toward other people through the media.

Because many media organizations have limited staffs to cover the high schools, I will sometimes go to them with a story that

I feel they might be interested in. One such story involved Tracy Bergan, a former point guard at DeMatha.

 A TALE WORTH TELLING

Tracy was from a family that consisted entirely of deaf-mutes, and he was the only exception. Tracy's family frequently came to our games to support him and the team. During stoppages of play, Tracy would use sign language to communicate with his family and inform them about what was happening on the court. This story was picked up by several news organizations, and I know they appreciated my effort to come to them with the idea.

In short, make the media your ally. Keep the lines of communication open with reporters by taking the time to be available to them, and by making the effort to initiate contact with the media when you have a good story idea.

Summary

The keys to communicating effectively as a basketball coach can be summed up as follows.

- Communicate your approach in a style that fits your personality and philosophy, and is comfortable to you.
- Learn to anticipate problems, and correct them quickly through good communication.
- When offering constructive criticism, use the "sandwich technique." (Compliment, criticism, compliment.)
- Be enthusiastic but not overbearing in your communication. Never intentionally embarrass a player.
- Be honest when communicating, even if it means admitting you don't know something.
- Be friendly with your players off the court. Show interest in their lives beyond basketball.
- Always keep your door open to your players, their parents, your assistants, faculty members, and individuals from the community. Treat all groups as an important part of your program.
- Treat officials with the respect they deserve. Use the pregame chat to your benefit.
- Be accessible and accommodating to members of the media. Promote the team, not yourself or only one or two players.

Chapter 3

Motivating Players

A motivated player or team will attain greater results than a player or team that is simply going through the motions. When your team does not play well, it may have nothing to do with the offense or defense you're using; rather, it may be because your players lack the necessary desire, enthusiasm, and eagerness to achieve. In other words, they may not be motivated. Your ability to increase their level of motivation will go a long way toward determining how successful your team will be.

So where do you begin? Before we get into that, let me first issue a word of caution against using the packaged approach. Do not try to treat all of your players the same because they are not the same. Just as they stretch differently to warm up for practice, some will react differently in terms of motivation. Some are self-starters; others need a push. But the one area in which every coach should remain consistent is in applying rewards and punishments fairly.

Let's first consider when and what you should reward and punish, both on and off the court. I try to reward whenever possible; players love to hear compliments, so rewards really grab their attention. And I try never to punish, but instead to use discipline to teach. In the rare instances when I do punish, it is for violation of a team rule or improper conduct.

As for what to reward, an obvious choice is good performance. But perhaps more importantly, always try to reward players who are working hard and putting forth a good effort, both on and off the court.

Once you know when and what to reinforce, you need to know how to go about it. The remainder of this chapter describes the approaches that have worked best for me.

Verbal Reinforcement

The most effective means of reward on the court is a simple one: verbal reinforcement. You can praise this player for the outstanding pass or that player for the great defensive play. But if you praise only for the show of athletic skill, how are you going to reward the less athletically inclined players who give great effort? Chances are, you wouldn't, which is an obvious mistake. So keep in mind the different abilities of players and praise them for demonstrating hustle just as much, or more than, skill.

A player feels especially rewarded when his coach praises him in front of the rest of the team. Therefore, when a player makes an outstanding effort I stop practice and single out the individual. Over time, the message that effort draws my praise spreads throughout the team; the players become motivated to earn that praise, and a greater team effort is the result.

Emphasis on Emphasis

I've often said that it is not so much what you coach but what you emphasize that really counts. Your coaching philosophy will tell you what you want to emphasize, but remember that your players will react to what you are emphasizing. In their eagerness to please, they will try to do what they know is important to you.

For example, if you believe defense is important, your players will pick up on that by what you say and by what you reward. Every year I tell my players, "I don't know who will start this year, but I do know the best defensive player will. And I'm not sure that the second best defensive player won't also start. If it's a close call between two players as to who will start, the better defensive player will get the nod." This straightforward talk sends a clear message to my players about the importance I assign to defense. It doesn't just motivate my top two defensive players to excel, it motivates all the players to become better defensively, which means we will play better team defense. I also tell my players that the best rebounder will be in the starting lineup. And, as a result, everyone attacks the boards in our practices.

All players want to play, and they want to play as many minutes as possible. I will frequently use this desire as leverage when I talk to the team about what I want them to do. I may then say, "If you noticed the other night, Joe played 3-1/2 quarters. He's consistently been our defensive stopper. He's dived for every loose ball. He's our blue-collar worker. And we know that every good team has some blue-collar guys."

Right away, the players know what's important to me. If you take the same approach, pretty soon you will see more and more of your players playing better defense and diving for loose balls. It becomes contagious.

The opposite is also true. Your players will know what not to do and what is unimportant to you by what you de-emphasize. If you don't glorify the 3-point shooter, or if you don't play a member of the squad who never passes the ball, the team will realize that the long shot is of little importance, whereas passing is very important to you.

Remember this: Players pick up on everything you say and do. I have seen teams that come out and shoot around for warm-ups with no organization or structure whatsoever. Somewhere along the line, the coaches of those teams have communicated to the players (perhaps unintentionally) that warm-up is not very important.

I let my players know that the pregame warm-up is significant, and that they must go about it properly. On the other hand, hardly any of our players ever warm up before the second half. That's because I tell them that they can warm up if they wish, but it's not essential; I let each player determine what he feels most comfortable with. So most of my players sit on the bench and get mentally prepared for the second half. And if anyone gets the impression that halftime warm-ups are not that important to Morgan Wootten, they would be absolutely correct.

Discipline to Teach

On the opposite end of the spectrum from positive verbal reinforcement is punishment. I don't even like the word "punishment." Yet some coaches punish more than they praise.

I strongly suggest that you *never* discipline to punish; rather, discipline to *teach*. This will allow you to complement your use of rewards with a disciplinary system that leaves no doubt as to what is unacceptable in terms of effort, conduct, and court decorum. And it won't cause your players to be so frightened of the consequences following a miscue that they become hesitant or refuse to even try.

Off-Court Behavior

I tell my players that I am responsible for their physical conditioning and behavior on the court. However, I also tell them that for the remaining 22 or so hours in the day, it is their job to keep themselves in shape and to conduct themselves appropriately.

One way I've found to have a positive impact on players' off-court behavior is simply through brief team meetings at the end of almost every practice. I use these meetings to talk about how the just-concluded practice went. And I also use the time to cover any other points that I feel to be important, such as the rules the team has voted on.

These postpractice discussions serve three purposes. First, they remind the players of their own team rules. Second, they allow me to emphasize to them what I feel is acceptable or unacceptable behavior. Third, they help to establish a certain amount of control through peer pressure.

My teams traditionally spend much of their social time together. Consequently, the players tend to monitor each other in these off-court situations. I don't mean to suggest that they spy on each other, but rather that they keep each other focused on their goals and reinforce the proper behavior to achieve those goals.

I encourage players to come talk to me if they see improper behavior from anyone on the team. However, I do not ask them to tell me either the name of the player violating the rules or the specifics of the incident. I am careful not to create the unhealthy situation in which teammates are squealing on teammates. The players feel comfortable coming to talk to me because they know the conversation will be kept in confidence, and they will not be getting a specific teammate in trouble.

If a player feels the need to talk to me about such a situation, he will usually say something like, "Coach, can you make a general statement to the team regarding smoking?" That's all I need to know—no names, dates, and phone numbers. I'm not conducting a police investigation.

I will then use one of the meetings after practice to send a message to the team. "It has come to my attention," I will say, "that a few of you are not abiding by the curfew that the team set." Or, "We know we have a no smoking rule on this team, and apparently some of you have forgotten that." They usually get the message.

Individual Attention

One of my favorite means of reaching young people is through motivational, thought-provoking poems. Some of my greatest players, such as Adrian Dantley and Danny Ferry, have told me how much some of these poems have helped them. I have included a few of my favorites in Appendix A.

But perhaps the best way to motivate a young person to reach his potential is through one-on-one talks. Occasionally take a player aside, pat him on the back, and let him know he is special to you and the team. Praise his effort, and encourage him to give an even better effort. You'll be amazed at how much a seemingly small talk can do. It can work wonders.

 AN MVC: MOST VALUABLE CONVERSATION

During Adrian Dantley's senior year at DeMatha, we went to Cumberland, Maryland for the Alhambra Tournament, the most prestigious Catholic high school tournament in the country. By the time we reached the finals to play St. Leo's, an undefeated team from Chicago, it had become fairly evident that our senior guard, Billy Langloh (who later went on to start for 4 years at Virginia), would probably be voted the outstanding player in the tournament. Dantley had won the MVP trophy the year before, but this particular year he had been slowed by a knee injury and forced to wear a knee-wrap for the first time in his life. Understandably, he was discouraged.

On the afternoon of the championship game, I took Adrian aside in the hotel lobby and spoke to him for about 5 minutes. I told him that I thought Langloh would be the MVP, but I also reminded him that this was his own last high school game. "Why don't you go out like the All-American you are?" I asked him.

That night, Dantley showed up for the game without the knee-wraps. He scored 38 points and grabbed 22 rebounds in 16 minutes, and we beat undefeated St. Leo's by a record margin for that tournament. It was the only loss of the year for St. Leo's, who went on to win the Illinois State Championship.

This example is living proof of what a one-on-one talk can accomplish. Of course, I had a big advantage with Adrian Dantley, the kind of player who had that competitive fire burning in him all the time. But even the best of us needs a boost at times.

I believe coach-player talks prompt more positive responses because players like being dealt with individually. It demonstrates to them that they are important to you as individuals, and they appreciate your willingness to help them solve their individual problems.

 LIGHTENING THE LOAD

In the mid-1970s, we were locked in a tight race for the Metro Conference championship. We were two games down with four to play after a loss to Carroll High. We had played very well, but our opponent had made an unbelievably high percentage of low percentage shots. After the game I told the team, "Fellas, we couldn't have played any better. You did a magnificent job. And at the worst we are going to tie for this title and get a playoff because they cannot rely on that kind of shooting to win games."

Then I had a one-on-one talk with Pete Strickland, our point guard, who was in the midst of a shooting slump. During the course of our conversation, I discovered that Pete felt that the DeMatha dynasty was resting squarely on his shoulders and that he had to do everything. But I was able to convince him that all anybody asked of him was to play smart, play hard, and have some fun. I told him his responsibilities were no greater than anyone else's, and to just go out and enjoy playing the game. I reminded him that basketball was just a game.

After that talk, Pete Strickland went on to average 26 points a game down the stretch. We won both the Conference Championship and the City Title game, in which Pete was without a doubt the finest player on the floor. He went on to a fine career at the University at Pittsburgh and today is the assistant coach at Old Dominion. Even today, Pete will occasionally remind me how important that talk was to him.

A lot of coaches are skeptical about how much a simple talk can mean to a player and a team. Instead they focus their energies on looking for that secret offense or that magic defense that will win games. But I feel individual communication is far more important, and I encourage you to give it a try. I think you'll find these one-on-one interactions will prove far more helpful to the team, both on and off the court.

Nonverbal Rewards

In addition to verbal forms of motivation, I use a system of behavioral rewards called "permissions." The system is based on the amount of effort and the quality of performance demonstrated during practice. Outstanding efforts and accomplishments earn players permissions, which allow them to get out of a certain amount of running at the end of practice. Failure to put forth total effort or to remain alert throughout the practice, however, may result in extra running.

At the end of practice, we add up the permissions to determine how many double suicides each player must run. (A suicide involves running the length of the floor in short sprints from foul line to baseline, half-court to baseline, the other foul line to baseline, and finally baseline to baseline. A double suicide involves completing this sequence twice.)

Another way permissions are granted is through our three foul-shooting sets during the practice:

1. Players shoot 10 free throws at the start of practice.
2. Halfway through, players shoot 5 two-shot fouls.
3. And at the end of practice, players shoot 5 one-and-ones.

If a player makes 9 or 10 free throws in any of the sets, he will pick up a permission. If he shoots below 7, he will pick up a double suicide.

We assign permissions and double suicides to other elements of our practices as well, such as the halfcourt offense (which will be discussed in chapter 10). We make a game out of it; the winning side picks up a permission, the losing side gets a double suicide.

You can assign permissions or suicides to any activity during practice. This will encourage your players to concentrate and practice as hard as possible, which is essential to player development. Coaches who have watched our workouts are amazed at the effort put forth by the players. I think this reward system is one of the major reasons why the players work so hard.

I also encourage hustle by allowing players to reduce their running at the end of practice in ways independent of permissions and double suicides. Most of our conditioning work is done during the practice itself, so the amount players run at the end of practice varies with how much conditioning I feel the players actually got during practice. If, for example, we're running 20 sprints in 2 minutes, I may decide that the leader after 10 will get to drop out, then the leader after 12, and so on.

At the end of practice, some players have more permissions than double suicides and do not have to do the extra running at all. Those who have the extra running try to borrow permissions from the players who have a surplus by offering to stand in line for the teammate's lunch, carry his books, or shovel snow off his car. But any player who does finish in a deficit will have to run at least one double suicide.

It always works out that we issue more permissions than double suicides, however. So most players who end up running only run one double suicide, which they must complete in 1 minute. But I do not view this extra running at the end of practice as a punishment; rather, I tell the players that it is an opportunity for them to get in a little better condition.

The system of permissions is actually designed for training more the mental, than the physical, condition of players. Players' awareness of permissions and double suicides increases their concentration and effort during practice. They perform with maximum intensity because they know it can result in permissions. Additionally, the bartering between players who have extra permissions and those who need them increases the camaraderie among the players and invariably leads to some of the more amusing moments of practice.

Addressing Problem Behaviors

The permission-suicide system works well on the court in practice. But how do you administer rewards and punishment relative to compliance with or violation of team rules?

Because I believe that the team is not my team, but rather the players' team, I let the players make the rules. However, I do encourage the team to set as few rules as possible. And I've learned not to fall into the trap of designating exactly what punishments will be applied if the rules are broken. If you announce what the punishment is before an infraction occurs, you'll paint yourself into a corner. Any situation that arises should be dealt with in the context of its own circumstances.

 FLEXIBILITY A MUST

When I was a young coach, I asked the players to set the night curfew for a road trip. When the curfew was established, I foolishly announced that anyone missing the curfew would be off the team.

Wouldn't you know it, my 6-8 star center, Sid Catlett, and a young sophomore named Billy Hite missed the curfew by 15 minutes. At the team breakfast the next morning, I announced that both of them were off the team because I had said that would be the penalty.

But after talking to the two players individually, I found out that they had had a legitimate reason for being late. Now my problem was to solve the bad situation that I had created by announcing a penalty without extenuating circumstances in advance.

The next school day, I called a meeting of the team and had both Sid Catlett and Billy Hite attend. I told the rest of the players that if Catlett were kicked off the team, all the colleges who were recruiting him would think he was a bad person, and we all knew that wasn't true. I could not, I said, put myself in the position of playing God and possibly ruining a young man's future. I told them that Sid would be reinstated, and that, because Sid was being reinstated, Billy Hite had to be brought back as well.

Sid went on to a great career at Notre Dame. Billy had a great football career at the University of North Carolina and is now the associate head football coach at Virginia Tech.

You can, as I almost did, ruin or at least damage future athletic and academic careers when you paint yourself into a corner by announcing penalties in advance. Penalties can only be fairly arrived at after all the facts have been weighed.

This lesson has also affected my approach in the classroom. When I start a year, I introduce myself, say we're going to have a great year, and get right into the subject matter. Inexperienced teachers who walk in and distribute a set of printed rules and the exact consequences of violating them sometimes have a tough time.

For less serious infractions that come up along the way, you have to use your good judgment. If a player is slightly late for practice, I merely say, "You've missed some of your conditioning. But don't worry. At the end of practice, we'll let you catch up." That usually drives the point home.

Suspending or Cutting Playing Time

One punishment I do not believe in is reducing a player's minutes in a game. If the penalty is worthy of suspension, then the player should miss the whole game. Conversely, if a player dresses for the game, he should be allowed to play as much as he is needed.

If you try to punish a player by limiting his minutes, you are getting into murky waters. First of all, the ever-changing conditions in games never really allow you to predict how many minutes a particular player will be playing. A second problem is that you may send the wrong message to the player about his role on the team.

 CURFEW ON DISCIPLINE

During the 1989 season, we played against a team on which some of the players had broken curfew. Before the game, their coach announced that those players would not start, and none of them played in the first half while we built a lead. But the coach allowed the curfew violators to play in the second half, and because they did, their team was able to pull out

a victory. To me, the only thing this team's coach proved to his players was, "We can't win without you." The original intent of the punishment was lost, and the players suffered no negative consequences from their actions.

Talking One-on-One

If a player ever has an unexcused absence, a good one-on-one talk generally assures that it will not happen again. Of course what is said in these talks will vary depending on the circumstances, but one of the main points you want to emphasize to the player is that his behavior reflects what kind of person he is. Ask him, "Is this the person you want to show to the rest of the world? Your message to everybody else is 'I'm totally out of shape, I can't run up and down the floor, and I don't come to practice on time.'" Tell him that people, including college representatives, will be forming opinions of him based on the image he presents on the court.

In addition, I remind players that they also represent their families and their school. In these situations, try and appeal to their sense of loyalty, pride, and commitment.

People often ask me if kids are as easy to coach and as good today as they were 30 years ago. I think kids today are as good as ever. They need the same things kids needed 30 years ago: discipline, love, and attention. They need adults in their lives who care for them, treat them as human beings, take the time to work with them, and give them constructive criticism. Coaches should provide all of these—not only because we feel we should, but also because we want to better our young athletes.

Choosing Good People

One of the best ways to prevent problems from ever happening is to pick good people for your team. The only way to develop the best team possible is to put good people on it, so choose players who want to come to practice, are unselfish, and are dedicated to their studies. I don't care how talented the player is; a player of lesser ability with a greater attitude will do better in the long run.

Talent is only about seventh or eighth on the list of what I look for in a player. Don't get me wrong—talent is nice. But other things are more important.

I ask, "What kind of person is the player?" A good person? Loyal? Dedicated? Does he get along well with people? Is he eager to sacrifice for the good of the team? Will he solve instead of create problems? Is he emotionally balanced? Is he conscientious about schoolwork?

If the answers to all of these questions are "yes," only then do I start to consider the player's physical talent and basketball skills. By picking good people this way, you'll find that you don't have to worry about punishment. You'll be too busy using your reward system instead!

 CHARACTER VS. TALENT

A player who had been one of our top substitutes during his junior year was earmarked to be a starter his senior year. However, he worked very little on his game the summer before his senior year, and he reported to practice completely out of shape, thinking himself the star of the team. And so, even though I gave him every opportunity, he did not make the final cut.

On the other hand, there is the uplifting story of a young man named Billy Mecca, whom I kept as the 16th player his junior year. The only reason I kept him was because he was a great kid and possessed all the personal qualities I like to see. He could be an inspirational leader for us, I thought; he could improve the team's chemistry with his attitude and his closeness to the rest of the members of the team. But because Billy was only 5-5 and had limited abilities, I told him he probably would have a tough time making the team as a senior.

Billy proved me wrong his senior year (and I was never so happy to be wrong). He became our starting point guard, won a full scholarship to Niagara University, and today is the head basketball coach and assistant athletic director at Quinnipiac College in Connecticut.

Invariably, every 4 or 5 years, these situations repeat themselves. Some player I'm counting on will fall backwards because he no longer works to improve his game; some other player will improve dramatically, emerge almost out of nowhere, and become an established star. Such disappointments and surprises are not unique to DeMatha. If you'll recall, Michael Jordan once got cut from his high school basketball team. So keep an open mind about the potential of your players. The projected starter may not pan out, but the player you put in his place may be the next Michael Jordan!

Summary

The following are the most effective ways to motivate your players to become the best they can be on and off the court.

- Be fair in applying rewards and disciplinary actions.
- Praise your players whenever possible, especially for an outstanding effort.
- Emphasize in your speech, actions, and reward system what is important to you. Your players will react to what you emphasize.
- Never discipline to punish; discipline to teach.
- Take the time to talk with your players individually to motivate them and to work out problems.
- Use inspirational poems and clever sayings to motivate players.
- Never announce penalties for rule violations in advance.
- Partial suspensions (reducing playing time as punishment) can send the wrong message to a player.
- Choose quality people for your team.

Chapter 4

Building a Basketball Program

It is not uncommon for coaches to ask me how they should build their basketball programs. I'm flattered when they do, but I think they expect me to possess some magic formula. If I did, I would be more than happy to pass it along. But unfortunately, there isn't one. Or at least I haven't found it.

Although top basketball programs achieve a similar level of success, they don't do it the same way. Your efforts to build a program will bear fruit only if you target them to your particular needs. So, although DeMatha basketball is recognized as one of the finest high school programs in the nation, the system we use may not be for you. Instead, look to build your own DeMatha using a variation of our approach that suits you best. In this chapter,

I'll give you some general guidelines for developing and implementing a system that you can tailor to the specific elements of your program.

Developing a System

The first and most important step in building a basketball program is developing a system, a style of play. Your philosophy and knowledge of the game will shape that system. But don't get too set in your ways. Be flexible so you can change your system to best utilize the abilities of your players.

In high school, we cannot recruit players as do college coaches. Nor do we have the

31

luxury of keeping the same players for several years as do coaches in the NBA. Therefore, we must be flexible enough to adapt our system each year to maximize the attributes of the players on the team.

I have seen coaches do very well with mediocre players, yet when they have had some of their best players, those same coaches haven't been as successful. Other coaches seem to excel with a superstar, but don't fare as well with a good all-around team. These situations happen because some coaches stick with the style of play that they like, no matter what. They may modify it slightly from year to year, but the same basic style of play emerges because it's the one they are most comfortable with. What these coaches fail to consider or acknowledge is that certain systems are more successful with certain kinds of talent. A coach who stays primarily with one system will only be successful during those years when his talent matches his system.

For example, a coach who is married to a zone defense that best suits a taller, slower team may find himself coaching a team that lacks size but is extremely quick. It would not make a lot of sense for the coach to play his favorite zone with such a team. That coach should switch to a pressing defense that would take advantage of the team's quickness and create turnovers. But the reverse can also be true, as it was one year at DeMatha.

A MISMATCH

The varsity team was small and quick, and excelled in a fullcourt pressure defense. Our junior varsity, in contrast, was one of the biggest we've ever had. It featured 6-7 Kenny Carr, who would later make a name for himself at North Carolina State and with the Portland Trailblazers.

When the junior varsity returned from its first game, I asked the coach how much he'd won by. "We got beat," he replied.

"You got beat? How?"

"Well, we were pressing all over the court," he answered, "and they just kept zipping through us. Our big guys just couldn't stay up with them."

I then understood the problem and its correction. "You don't have a pressing team," I replied. "A team with that size should do no more than just play solid halfcourt defense because no one will ever get a second shot against you."

The coach of that team, Marty Fletcher, took my advice, and that team never lost another game. Marty is currently the head basketball coach at Southwest Louisiana University, one of the emerging powers in the South.

To be a consistent winner, the coach and the system must be flexible enough to bring out the best in the players as individuals, and to capitalize on those strengths for the good of the team. Your coaching philosophy should allow for such flexibility. Although the system that fits that particular team may not be your favorite or the one you know best, it may be the one that gives your team its chance to become the best it can be. And providing that chance is the essence of coaching.

If you bend the system to fit the ability of the players, you can then take it one step further and design a system that will get the ball into the hands of your best players most frequently. I like to have at least one special play to accomplish this purpose. If you're blessed with two or three highly skilled players, then it is wise to have a play for each of them. To keep all the players happy, some coaches have a play isolating each position. Whatever the approach, a coach needs set plays that allow the team to go to its money players in the clutch.

Having advocated flexibility, let me now issue a word of caution: Make sure your system is *intelligently* flexible. Remember, there is no progress without change, but change does not necessarily mean progress. Study your system, and change only when the talent you have dictates that it is beneficial to do so.

Gaining Administrative Support

The better your players work together on the court, the better your basketball team will be. Similarly, the off-court success of your basketball program depends on the amount of support it receives from, and how well you work with, your school's administration.

The principal must fully support the objectives of your program. Take the time to talk with your principal and discuss your philosophy, your goals, your approach to the players and assistant coaches, and your belief that the basketball team is an important part of the school's total educational experience.

Top administrators know interscholastic sports are important and, therefore, will want to support your program. You can receive and maintain that support through effective and frequent communication with your school's administration. Let them know of your willingness to cooperate and of your need for their backing. But be careful not to abuse the program and its role in education, or that support will quickly erode.

At DeMatha, we are extremely lucky to have one of the nation's great principals in John Moylan, who has always been 100% behind our basketball program. He feels that a good basketball program is good for the whole school, and I think a primary reason he supports us is that he agrees with the priorities we stress to our young athletes: God, family, school, and then basketball. We also tell our players that the basketball team is not bigger than the school, but merely a part of it like any other extracurricular activity. And it is the school's basketball team, not mine. I am just the coach. This philosophy also makes it easy for the administration to support the program.

John's support has extended into every facet of the program. He even helped us plan for what, to date, has been the biggest victory in DeMatha's history, the win over Power Memorial with their player Lew Alcindor. It was John who suggested to me that our tallest players use tennis racquets in practice so our guys would get some idea of what it would be like shooting over the 7-2 Alcindor. It was a great idea, and there's no question that we were a better prepared team because of it.

If you ever have trouble with administrative support, take a step back and evaluate your conduct. Ask yourself if you or anyone else in your program has committed any wrongs, or if you have failed to promote the positive values of your program. Then talk to the principal and find out what the problems are and what can be done to correct them. He might think you are practicing too long, or he may not like you closing your practices to the student body. But any good administrator is going to want a good, solid basketball program and should be willing to hear you out. So discuss the problems openly with key administrators and ask them for the opportunity to correct the problems to their satisfaction.

Gaining Student Support

In addition to support from the school administration, your basketball program will benefit from the backing of the entire school. Nothing beats having a large, loud, and vocal student section cheering the team on at games. And because the basketball team represents the school, players should know that their peers are behind them 100%. This will give players extra confidence and inspiration.

Remind players to fulfill their responsibility of representing their families, their school, and themselves with dignity and class. They should exhibit exemplary behavior, of which their school's students and faculty can be proud.

Gaining Community Support

Support and enthusiasm from community members can make a big difference in the success of your program. Take the time to meet people, send them schedules and information about your team, and invite them to be your guests at games and practices. Positive community relations can do much to enhance your basketball program.

Implementing the System

Once you've developed your basketball system and have the school and community fully behind you, you are then ready for the final step in building a basketball program: implementation.

The Feeder System

Most of the kids that come to DeMatha go to local Catholic grade schools or junior high schools in the Washington, DC area. My staff and I conduct free clinics for the coaches and players at these schools, and we also work with the local boys' clubs. We also invite area coaches and players to attend our clinics at DeMatha, and we frequently include our players in these clinics to demonstrate basketball fundamentals. We talk to the kids about the importance of studying hard and preparing for high school. Obviously, all of the kids we work with at clinics are not going to come to DeMatha, but we feel the clinics are a nice community gesture and good for everyone involved.

If you have a feeder system within your school (freshman and junior varsity teams), it is important that you spend time with the coaches of these teams. Talk with them about your philosophy, objectives, and the type of basketball you like to emphasize. Treat these coaches as if they are members of your own staff, and always make yourself available to them.

At DeMatha, we have two younger teams that feed into the varsity, a 9th-grade team and a junior varsity (JV). The JV team consists mostly of 10th graders and, occasionally, an outstanding freshman. I rarely place juniors on the JV; I would rather have them on the varsity if we feel they are going to help us in any way. However, I have made three exceptions to that rule since I've been coaching at DeMatha. In all three cases, the exceptions were made because the athletes were terrific kids, exhibited potential, and provided us with some size when the program was lacking in big men.

 FROM JV TO NFL

The most recent exception to the rule was a young man named Mike Graybill. Mike played on the JV team as a junior and then made the varsity his senior year. He won a basketball scholarship to Boston University, where he continued to get bigger and stronger. While a junior there, he decided for the first time to use his much larger physique on the football field.

The next thing I knew, Mike was being drafted as an offensive lineman by the Cleveland Browns. I'm glad we kept him in our program his junior year, and it's a lesson to all of us about what can happen when a young person is given a chance.

I spend a significant amount of time with our JV and freshman coaches. I invite them to sit in on all of our varsity coaching meetings, encourage them to see the team play as much as they can, and ask them for their input whenever possible. By the same token, I make it a point to watch their teams play whenever I get the chance. This is important to those coaches and helps to make them feel like the integral part of the program that they are. Plus, younger players feel special when the varsity coaches show their support and interest.

Setting the Rules

No basketball program is complete without some sort of structure, the primary component of which is team rules. As I mentioned in chapter 3, our players make the rules for the team every year. I believe that if the players truly feel it is their team, they will take better care of it.

The Rule-Setting Process

Once our team is selected, we take all of our players to a classroom for a meeting on the team rules. They vote on each issue by Australian ballot, meaning the players do not have to sign their names to their votes. At the meeting, I ask the players what the team rules will be on the following subjects:

- Smoking
- Use of drugs
- Drinking
- Curfews
- Dress code to and from games
- Bringing dates to games

You, as the coach, can have your players vote on anything you feel is appropriate. Frequently, while the players are voting on the rules, a new player on the team will ask me what previous teams have done. This is my opportunity to say, "Well, I can tell you what the National Championship team with Danny Ferry voted for as its rules." Funny thing, more often than not the current players will vote the same way.

After the results are tallied, we then call another meeting and I announce to the players, "These are the rules that you have selected for the season. Because they are *your* rules, I know there will be absolutely no problems."

The Final Tally

Some people may feel that it is a problem to have teenagers vote on sensitive issues or that the athletes are not yet responsible enough to determine their own rules. I have not found this to be true. Almost without exception, this is the way our teams vote.

- No drugs, because they are illegal. (The only dissention to this came in the 1960s when one player voted that using marijuana was okay, as long as you were smart in the way you used it. He was voted down.)
- No drinking, with the possible exception of family holidays like Thanksgiving or Christmas where families sometimes serve a glass of wine with the holiday meal.
- Seniors should set the curfew. So, the day before a game when we gather at the end of practice, I'll ask the seniors what the curfew for that night will be. I've found that they're generally tougher with the curfew than I would have been. On a Friday night before a Saturday game, the seniors will frequently announce that it's all right to go watch a local college game, but that everyone must come right home and have the lights out by 11:30 p.m.
- Players must wear a coat and tie to all games. The athletes are aware that college coaches and recruiters will be judging their performances before and after the game, as well as when they are on the floor. We tell our players in our meetings, "You only have one chance to make a first impression." A coat and tie can help make that first impression a good one.
- Team members may not drive a date to the game (unless she has no other way of getting there). However, a player may take her home afterwards. The reason I have players vote on bringing girls to the game gets back to the matter of priorities; I want them to be completely focused on the game.

It is very rare that we get any real dissenting votes from a player. And if we do, the player will usually feel compelled to go along with the rules because his peers chose them. The rules weren't just handed down from on high by the coaches. When I sometimes ask former players how effective the team rules were they invariably confirm this impression. The players will say, "Coach, we really kept them because we knew they were our rules."

But when I ask about the teams we have played, teams for which the coaches made the rules, I usually find that their players rarely obeyed the rules. Their players felt it was not their team, but the coach's team. After all, it's just human nature that people will take better care of their own car than of a rental car. And so it is with players—they will take better care of their team if they truly feel it is their team.

 THE LAST TO SURRENDER

One year when I coached football at DeMatha, we were leading in a championship game 7-0. However, the opposing team had first and goal on our 2-yard line, and time was running out. Then one of our linebackers, Ricky Cook, called time-out and had a team meeting right out there in the middle of the field. Not one of the players came over to the bench during the entire time-out. When play resumed, we made one of the greatest goal line stands I've ever seen and won the game, 7-0.

After the game, I asked Ricky why he had called time-out and what had gone on in the huddle. He said he had told the players, "Fellows, for 10 weeks now we have been Spartans. We have worked our butts off. We've gone to parties where people from other teams have been sitting around drinking, but we haven't had a drop. We've sacrificed, and we've given up a lot. These two yards right here in front of us represent our sacrifice. We know these guys coming at us have not made the same sacrifice we have. Now let's find out if our sacrifice has been worth it." That incident verified for me the truth of a statement made by Vince Lombardi: "Those who have invested the most are the last to surrender."

The Coach's Input

Even though the players vote on the rules, I nevertheless have certain expectations. Primarily, I expect them to act as gentlemen at all times. I tell our players they will never hear profanity from the coaching staff, and we don't expect to hear it from them.

I constantly remind our players whom they are representing—themselves, their families, and the school—and of the responsibilities that accompany that. I also tell them they will *always* be a DeMatha player. For that reason, I give all of our athletes a letter entitled "The DeMatha Player" and share with them a short poem called "Players as Models" (see Appendix A). These written passages remind the athletes that they are always in the public eye and should therefore conduct themselves in a manner reflecting positively on those they represent.

For the off-season, I don't stress rules so much as individual improvement. In the spring, I hold a meeting to talk about which players will be playing on what summer league teams. At the meeting, I have each player complete a written evaluation of his playing to date and what he thinks he needs to work on.

Providing Medical Services

As with any sport, basketball injuries are a reality and cause for a coach's concern. How you prevent injuries and deal with them must be a part of your basketball program. Whenever possible, all our coaches complete a certified Red Cross first aid course, and I always try to have a certified trainer at our practices. A qualified student trainer also is always on hand.

Our student trainers are developed in a fashion similar to our athletes. They come up through the system through the freshman, junior varsity, and varsity levels. We pay tuition costs for these students to attend summer training courses that help them become proficient in all areas of athletic training. A student trainer is invaluable for providing immediate attention to an injury. For example, if a player turns an ankle, the student trainer is there to treat it right away, in the right way. This immediate medical attention can reduce the time missed by the player by several days.

 CHAMPIONSHIP TRAINING

Three days before one of our championship games, one of our players, Pete Reese, turned an ankle in practice. One of our trainers was there immediately putting ice on the ankle, getting it elevated, and taping it to stop the swelling from spreading. I took one look at the ankle, though, and said Pete would never play in the game on Sunday.

But Pete followed the therapy prescribed by our team physician, and, wouldn't you know, he was ready to go by the championship game! Our trainer's immediate response was the key factor in reducing the injury's severity and promoting such a rapid recovery.

Incidentally, my concern with ankle injuries in particular is such that I require all of our players to wear high-top athletic shoes. Properly laced high-tops provide good support for the ankles and eliminate the need for taping uninjured ankles. If a player does request taping, the trainer will provide it, but we prefer not to rely on the tape. Some college and pro players have their ankles taped regularly—but notice that they are usually the ones wearing low-cut sneakers. Low-cuts are good for only two things: spraining your right ankle and spraining your left ankle.

Having a certified trainer on hand does not free a coach from his responsibility to be well-versed in training techniques. I am responsible for the players' physical conditioning on the court, so I make all the decisions with regard to their training. The players themselves are responsible for their conditioning off the court, and I make that very clear to them. The players are also responsible for informing me when they are injured. I don't want them trying to be heroes, and then missing even more time by aggravating an injury. I never want an injured player to play, but occasionally a player can play with a minor injury or a little soreness. In these instances, I speak with both the trainer and the player, and all three of us decide whether the player can go. If there is any doubt, he sits out.

Instilling Pride

Looking out for players' physical needs is only half the battle. We must be concerned with their mental vitality as well. Specifically, a coach must develop team pride and spirit, those intangibles that, unlike the players, can remain with a program through the years.

As the leader of the team, the coach must work hard to develop that team pride and spirit. Intangibles, like pride and spirit, can be major benefits to your program. The sense of great pride found at DeMatha is a big reason why the basketball program has thrived over such a long period of time.

Starters and Nonstarters

One of the biggest threats to team spirit is the selection of a starting lineup. If the selection process is handled improperly, nonstarters may feel dejected, an attitude that can be contagious and harmful to your team.

For example, you might say, "Joe, if you beat out Bill, you'll be the starter." In a player's eyes this is the equivalent to saying, "Joe, you can be the winner and make Bill the loser." Thus, in a player's mind, you have five winners and five losers among your top ten players, an obviously unhealthy situation.

But part of being a good teacher-coach is the ability to sell. So, when dealing with the issue of starters and nonstarters, you have to sell your players on the fact that being in the starting lineup or on the bench is not a win-lose situation.

Instead, you can create a win-win atmosphere. To make the previous example a win-win situation, say, "Joe, you're doing a great job, and we're going to start you at the guard position." Immediately afterwards, take Bill aside, and tell him, "Bill, this team is really going to count on you because you're the kind of guy that can come off the bench and spark us."

I always tell my team, "We can only start five players, but we need a lot of finishers. Any one of you may be called upon to finish a game because of injuries, foul trouble, or any number of situations that may develop." I think this approach increases nonstarters' appreciation of their role on the team, and thus builds depth. It's a big reason why we often have 8 to 10 players we are comfortable putting on the floor when the game is on the line.

 THE MOST FAMOUS SIXTH MAN

Our 1973 National Championship team featured Adrian Dantley as our star player. Also on that team was a young man named Ronnie Satterthwaite, who, although an outstanding player, did not figure to start. Before the start of that season, I had taken Ronnie aside and said, "Ronnie, I don't think you're going to start, but you're going to be our sixth man, and you're going to be the most famous sixth man in America. I'm going to make a rule with you now. If I don't put you in any game in the first quarter, come to me at the end of the quarter, ask me who you should go in for, and I will put you in the game. You can tell your mother, father, grandparents, girlfriend, and everybody to come to the game because you're going to play in every game. And the latest you're going to get in is the second quarter."

Ronnie's face lit up when he heard me say that, and he was happy as could be. He went on to have a terrific season for us and wound up with a scholarship to William and Mary, where he was eventually named Southern Conference Player of the Year. I think this is the perfect example of creating a win-win situation with starters and nonstarters. By taking Ronnie aside and talking to him, I avoided having him sitting on the bench as a disgruntled sixth man who felt he should have been a starter.

Unhappiness and disenchantment can grow like a cancer. Players who are unhappy will practice with less enthusiasm, and that inhibits team development. But by creating win-win situations, you can diffuse some of these situations before they become problems.

Captains

Another method I use to build team unity is to rotate the appointment of two captains—a game captain and a bench captain—for each game. The game captain is chosen from among the five starters, and the bench captain from among the nonstarters.

These two captains have the responsibility of meeting with the other team's captains and the officials before the game. During the game, the game captain takes on the traditional roles associated with a captain, and the bench captain is given the job of keeping the bench full of team spirit. By the end of the year, every player has been a captain several times over. This creates more of an attitude of team unity among the players than would the appointment of one or two captains for the entire year.

Former Players

Whenever one of our former players returns to DeMatha for a visit, I always ask him to talk to the players. This, too, develops team pride. More than 125 of our players have gone on to play at the college level. When these veterans visit the school and communicate their personal experiences and "DeMatha Pride," it helps instill that pride in the younger players.

Certain stories become part of a basketball program's folklore and help to carry on the school's tradition as they are passed down from team to team. One such story at DeMatha involves our 1988 team, which was invited to the White House to meet the President.

  ONE FROM THE GIPPER

We met President Reagan at the South Gate as he was preparing to depart to Camp David for the weekend. Each member of the team got to shake hands with the President, and he was presented with a DeMatha letter jacket. President Reagan took a few minutes to talk to the team and even told a few humorous stories that the team enjoyed. He finished by saying, "Congratulations on your victory over Coolidge [High School] for the City Championship. I just knew you would be the team that would be here."

Such an event and the subsequent stories told about it help link the current team with the past teams who've visited the White House. Furthermore, the stories provide an incentive to duplicate the previous teams' accomplishments. Now, whenever I tell my players this story, I say, "If the President of the United States expects DeMatha to win the City Championship, why shouldn't you?"

A Class Operation

A picture I have on my office wall shows two penguins standing on the ice. One penguin is saying to the other, "I cried because I had no feet, until I met a man who had no class." Above all else, team pride is developed by being positive and by emphasizing that the team must carry itself with class. Any program can take pride in itself, win or lose, when the players and coaches behave with class and give their best effort to get the most out of their abilities.

You can be a model for your players to follow by organizing spirited practices, by being optimistic in what you say and do, by treating your young people as you would want your own child to be treated, and by responding positively to both victory and defeat. Your players will draw upon your example and learn from it. If you teach them well, the athletes who graduate from your program will be better players and people than they were when they entered it.

Summary

The keys to creating and maintaining a successful program are

- implementing a sound system or style of play that fits the players you have available;
- setting up and nurturing a feeder system;
- getting administration, faculty, student, parent, and community support;
- instituting a structure of roles to which the players are committed; and
- instilling pride in every player who is issued a uniform.

Part II
Coaching Plans

Chapter 5

Planning for the Season

All of us would rather work on our zone press than press our players to return their insurance forms, but such tasks are a necessary part of our planning for the basketball season. They may not be the fun part of coaching, but we have to address these many important responsibilities:

- Medical Screening and Insurance
- Conditioning Your Athletes
- Making Up a "Master Plan"
- Planning for Medical Care
- Scheduling Games
- Scouting Opponents
- Helping Players With Their College Plans
- Providing Proper Equipment
- Traveling to Games

Medical Screening and Insurance

Before beginning physical conditioning and practice sessions, you must make sure that every candidate for the team has passed a complete medical examination and has a physician's permission to try out. We have a doctor come to DeMatha in early August to give complete physicals at a reasonable rate for athletes on all of our teams. No student is allowed to try out for a sport without providing a completed health exam form (see Figure 5.1).

A related requirement involves insurance coverage for athletes. Because the school insurance on every student is minimal, we

Athletic Participation Health Examination Form

(Cooperatively prepared by the National Federation of State High School Athletic Association and the Committee on Medical Aspects of Sports of the American Medical Association.) Health examination for athletes should be rendered after August 1 preceding school year concerned.

(Please print)   Name of student _____   City and school _____

Grade_____   Age _____   Height _____   Weight _____   Blood pressure _____

Significant past illness or injury _____

_____

Eyes _____ R 20/ _____ ; L 20/ _____ ; Ears _____ Hearing R   /15; L   /15

Respiratory _____

Cardiovascular _____

Liver _____   Spleen _____   Hernia _____

Musculoskeletal _____   Skin _____

Neurological _____   Genitalia _____

Laboratory: Urinalysis _____   Other _____

Comments _____

Completed immunizations: Polio _____   Tetanus _____
                                            Date   Date

Other _____

"I certify that I have this date examined this student and that, on the basis of the examination requested by the school authorities and the student's medical history as furnished to me, I have found no reason which would make it medically inadvisable for this student to compete in supervised athletic activities, EXCEPT THOSE CROSSED OUT BELOW."

BASEBALL	GOLF	SOFTBALL	VOLLEYBALL
BASKETBALL	GYMNASTICS	SWIMMING	*WRESTLING
CROSS COUNTRY	LACROSSE	TENNIS	OTHERS _____
FOOTBALL	SOCCER	TRACK	_____

*Estimated desirable weight level: _____ pounds

Date of examination: _____   Signed: _____
                                                                Examining physician

Physician's address _____   Telephone _____

Figure 5.1   Athletic participation health examination form.

have the parents of our candidates complete a form indicating that their child will be covered under the family's medical insurance. This form, shown in Figure 5.2, includes the parents' insurance information, their permission for the child's participation in school athletics, and their authorization for the coaches and qualified medical personnel to make on-the-spot decisions in emergency care situations.

Conditioning Your Athletes

For the best basketball team possible, your players must be in top physical condition by the start of the season. Conditioning, therefore, must be a year-round process for athletes. Conscientious players will never get out of shape.

DE MATHA CATHOLIC HIGH SCHOOL

Trinitarian Fathers

4313 MADISON STREET
HYATTSVILLE, MARYLAND 20781-1692

Office of the Principal   Fall, 1991   301-864-3666

Dear Parent:

Participation in high school athletics has many rewards and can provide tremendous enjoyment. However, it is important for both the participant and his parents to realize that an element of physical risk is present when one is involved in athletics. The purpose of this letter is to clarify the school's position in terms of insurance coverage and to obtain your permission to secure the quickest medical assistance possible if your son should be injured.

DeMatha's insurance coverage, like that of all schools, *does not cover personal injury that is the result of athletic participation.* It is most important that you check with your own insurance carrier to be certain that athletic injury for your son would be covered by your own policy, especially if he is participating in a contact sport such as football or lacrosse.

The school's insurance policy does cover injury that would result from an accident incurred with school transportation going to and from practice or game sites. Students who choose to provide their own transportation *must carry their own insurance coverage.* Likewise, students and/or parents who volunteer to transport others to and from practice and/or game sites *are not covered by school insurance.*

Please complete the bottom portion of this letter and return it immediately to the school main office. If you have any questions, you may call the school business manager (864-2339) or the associate athletic director, Mr. William McGregor (864-2755).

John L. Moylan, Principal

Please complete and return immediately to the school main office.

Student name _____   Present grade _____   Sport(s) _____

_____

Parent home phone _____   Emergency phone _____

Parent whose policy covers student/athlete _____

Health insurance carrier _____

Policy number _____

I hereby give permission to the proper authorities at DeMatha Catholic High School to seek the appropriate medical assistance for our son in the event of any injury. I likewise understand that DeMatha Catholic High School is not liable for the payment of the medical costs in the event of injury sustained in athletic participation. I assure DeMatha Catholic High School that I am duly authorized to execute this document.

_____   _____
Parent's signature   Date

Figure 5.2   Athletic participation insurance form.

It's important that all our players are working as hard in the summer and fall as they are during the actual basketball season. Therefore, I set up off-season as well as in-season conditioning programs.

Before the summer leagues start, I meet with each player individually and discuss the player's written evaluation. At the same time, I give him my own evaluation, detailing what I feel he should concentrate on in his personal off-season workouts. I also issue our Daily Summer Workout forms, one for post players (see Figure 5.3) and one for perimeter players (see Figure 5.4). These evaluations and suggestions give the players specific ideas for improving their skills.

Summer Workout for Post Players

Ballhandling	Drills without dribbling (5 minutes)		
	Drills with dribbling (5 minutes)		
	Drills with two balls (5 minutes)		
Foot quickness	Jump rope	- for endurance	5 minutes at 3/4 speed
		- for quickness	right foot 15 seconds
			left foot 15 seconds
			alternate 15 seconds
			both 15 seconds
		Do 3 repetitions of each with 30 seconds rest between each minute of quick jumping.	
	Run steps	- up to build leg strength	
		- down to build foot quickness (6 repetitions of 15-20 seconds)	
	Run hills	- jog down and sprint up (6 repetitions of 15-20 seconds)	
	Intervals	- on a track, sprint straightaways and jog curves (alternate sprint/jog up to 1 mile)	

*To build additional quickness and leg strength run backwards or sideways, picking your feet up and putting them down as quickly as possible.

*Build to running 2-3 miles a day at 6-1/2- to 7-1/2-minute miles, with a timed mile once a week. Above reps should be increased as player becomes more well-conditioned.

	Post moves	- without thinking of scoring, establish foot quickness in the post through repetition of the moves	
Passing	All types with both hands—especially outlet, flick, and bounce pass		
Rebounding	Six and in	(4 repetitions from each side of the basket)	
	Superman	(4 repetitions of 8)	
	Tap Drill	(4 repetitions of 10 each hand)	
	Hook Drill	(4 repetitions of 10 or 30 seconds)	
	Second Effort	(4 repetitions of 12 with last one as many as possible)	
	Blocking Out	- work on foot work (reverse pivot) and holding contact	
Shooting	Low Post	- drop step both ways	(3 sets of 15 shots each way)
		- pivot and shoot	(3 sets of 15 shots each way)
		- jump hook	(3 sets of 15 shots each way)
		- up and under off jump hook and pivot (4 sets of 15 shots)	
		- outside pivot to make room (4 sets of 15 shots)	
	High Post	- stationary moves for baby J or power layup (5 sets of 10 shots)	
		- shot off the pass (5 sets of 10 shots)	
		- outside pivot to make room (5 sets of 10 shots)	
		- step off high and low post for J (5 sets of 10)	

*Work the shot fake into every third set of shots, either on the move or at the end.

*Shoot free throws in between sets to rest—otherwise, GAME SHOTS AT GAME SPEED!!

Figure 5.3 Summer workout for post players.

At the end of the summer, I evaluate each player's performance in the summer leagues. When school starts, I will again meet individually with each varsity candidate and share my thoughts on where he stands and how far he needs to go in the 2 months remaining before varsity tryouts. During the season, our practices are structured to insure that our players remain in top condition.

Weight Training

I am a firm believer in weight training as an important element of a basketball player's overall physical conditioning. But it must be a certain kind of weight training. The weight lifter who is trying to develop bulk and the All-American body may get stares on the street, but he will not help himself as far as basketball is concerned. I advocate

Summer Workout for Perimeter Players

Ballhandling Drills without dribbling (5 minutes)
Drills with the dribble (5 minutes)
Moves on the move - Make a move at the free throw (FT) line, the midcourt line and the FT line, and in for the layup. Do each of the seven twice up and down the floor.

Foot quickness

Jump rope	- for endurance	5 minutes at 3/4 speed		
	- for quickness	right foot	15 seconds	
		left foot	15 seconds	
		alternate	15 seconds	
		both	15 seconds	

(Do 3 repetitions of each with 30 seconds for rest between each minute of quick jumping. Build to more repetitions over time.)

Run steps   - up to build leg strength
   - down to build foot quickness (6 repetitions of 15-20 seconds)

Run hills   - jog down and sprint up (6 repetitions of 15-20 seconds)

Intervals   - on a track, sprint straightaways and jog curves (alternate sprint/jog up to 1 mile)

*Build to running 2-3 miles a day at 6-1/2- to 7-1/2-minute miles with a timed mile once a week. Above repetitions should be increased as player becomes more well-conditioned.

Passing All types with both hands—especially hip pass to feed the wing and post feeds.

Shooting 50 shots off the dribble
   - simulate shooting off the break (pull up quick)
   - move on the move into the shot (especially—crossover, stutter, inside out, inside out crossover)
   - stationary move, putting the defender on his heels and pulling up for the shot
*5 sets of 10 shots at a time with 2 FT in between sets
Repeat 3 times, alternating with other shooting drills.

50 shots off the pass (or self-pass)
   - step into shot, use inside foot, inside and outside pivots to square up
   - if working with someone, always v-cut before coming to the ball
*5 sets of 10 shots with 2 FT in between sets—also repeat 3 times.

30 shots using shot and pass fakes
   - pump fake to shot
   - pump fake to dribble to shot
   - pass fake to shot
*3 sets of 10 shots with 2 FT in between sets—repeat 3 times.

GAME SHOTS, TAKEN AT GAME SPEED—REST BY SHOOTING FT, NOT BY GOING 1/2 SPEED!!

Figure 5.4 Summer workout for perimeter players.

weight work designed to develop the specific muscles that a basketball player uses. The emphasis is on repetition, *not* on the amount of weight used in the exercise. This weight program (see Figure 5.5) has proven successful for us over the years, and I believe it has helped significantly in the prevention of serious injuries.

Making Up a "Master Plan"

Head coaches and their assistants must be on the same page with regard to every as-

pect of the school's program, and that takes planning. In planning for our season, the coaching staff holds four meetings during the month of October. In those meetings, we establish our "Master Plan" for the entire season. This plan includes every tactic that we intend to teach and use during the year:

- Man-to-man offense
- Zone offense
- Pressure offense

Weight Training Program

Key points to remember

* **Diet** - Eat three square meals. You cannot get stronger on a "junk food" diet.
* **Rest** - That is a good night's sleep—plus going into your workout rested. If you play 2 hours of basketball then expect to have a good workout, you can forget it. Shoot around and play after your workout and on days off. Playing and working on your fundamentals is secondary on training days.
* **Buddy system** - Work out with a buddy. This makes it a little competitive, and your partner or partners can act as spotters to make sure there are no accidents while training.
* **Flexibility** - Stretching before and after is just as important as training itself. Injuries occur when athletes start to train before they are loose or warmed up. Just a 10 minute general stretching routine before and after you work out is all you need.
* **Dedication** - Stick with it. Just like working on your basketball fundamentals, it is a daily thing or, in this case, every other day. Results will not show up overnight.
* **Initial soreness** - There will be soreness early. That doesn't mean stop. Stretch and work through it.
* **A balanced body** - Work both sides of a body part to achieve balance. For example, if you work your thighs, you must also work your hamstrings or injury will occur.

Exercises (can be done on free bar, Universal, or Nautilus)

Bench press - Lay flat, and keep your butt down. Push the weight up off of the breast bone and back toward spotter. Grip should not be too wide or too tight.

Bent over rows - Assume a low stance, bent over slightly with head up. Pull the weight toward you.

Curls - Keep the elbows close to the body for a full range of motion. Lean against a wall to keep the back straight.

Lat pulls - Use a Lat machine. Pullups and chin ups are a good substitute for no Lat machine.

Squats - Place the bar across the shoulders, not the neck. Feet should be a little more than shoulder-width apart, and the back should be straight. (A weight belt is really needed for this exercise.) Use a chair at first to touch butt to (do *not* sit), then back up. Leg press machine can be used as substitute.

Leg extension - Use the machine, or use resistance. (Your partner could give resistance.)

Leg curls - Use the machine, or use resistance.

Triceps - Use the machine, or use the free bar. Lay on your back and bring the bar back toward your nose, then push out.

Dips - Work triceps if you cannot get to a machine or free bar.

Sit-ups - With knees bent slightly, rotate your body to work your sides.

Appropriate weight selection

Do not work out with your maximum lifting weights. The first week you will be finding your weight to work out with. For example, if your maximum on bench press is 140, then a good bench press workout would be

1 set 10 repetitions warm-up 100
1 set 10 repetitions   120
1 set 10 repetitions   130

Workout setup

For each exercise, four sets of 10 repetitions is used. For example 1 set of 10 repetitions warm-up; 1 set of 10 repetitions; 2 sets of 10 repetitions. The weight will increase with each set. As you get stronger, the weight used in each set will increase. Rest about a minute between sets.

Workout cycles

The cycle is used over the off-season workout. Sets, repetitions, and weight will change according to how long you have been working out.

Cycles:
Cycle 1 - 6 weeks sets of 10
Cycle 2 - 4 weeks sets of 8
Cycle 3 - 4 weeks sets of 6
Cycle 4 - 3 weeks sets of 5

After Cycle 4, take a couple days off. Then go back to Cycle 2; you will feel stronger and have to increase weight. Remember to increase weight as you feel the need to. Be patient and work up to it.

In-season maintenance program
Bench press 3 sets of 8
Curls   3 sets of 8
Leg press   3 sets of 8
Leg curls   3 sets of 8
Twice a week - no more than 20 minutes

If you have any questions, do not hesitate to ask the coaches.

Figure 5.5 Weight training program.

- Man-to-man defense (including pressure)
- Zone defense (including trapping)
- Foul shot alignments
- Jump ball alignments
- Out-of-bounds plays
- Fast break scenarios
- Our "time and score" codes
- Coaching in special situations
- Pregame, halftime, and postgame procedures
- Time-out procedures

From this Master Plan, we will then build a monthly plan, weekly plan, and finally a daily plan. These planning sessions are often long but are always rewarding, and I encourage you to take the time to plan. Such meetings will help you have everything in place when the season actually starts, will allow you to jump right into the fun part of coaching when practice begins, and also will help prevent running into the unexpected.

One of the favorite sayings of the United States Secret Service, well-known for protecting presidents and other national and international dignitaries, is "Prior proper planning prevents poor performance." And one of my favorites is "Failing to prepare is preparing to fail." Success and rewards don't come to people just by accident. They come as a result of exhaustive, intelligent, and effective planning.

Planning for Medical Care

Some type of medical staff should be present at all your practices and games. In high school, we are limited to some extent in our medical resources. Very few coaches are lucky enough to have a doctor at every practice or every game. In most cases, we must rely on a team physician (usually an orthopedist) to whom players can have quick access. And, because of our concern about our athletes' chances of returning quickly and safely to competition, we should also have a sports medicine specialist in injury rehabilitation available.

You can gain access to competent sports medicine professionals by meeting with local medical experts. Spend time with them, check their backgrounds and references, and select the best and most interested individuals. Then, make them feel a part of the school's basketball program.

Give them season passes and an open invitation to all games and scrimmages. Most physicians take on such positions simply because they love basketball, not to get rich. So let them watch your team perform as much as they want to. The doctors we have worked with usually accept only the insurance money as compensation for their services, and they do not bill the family for the additional cost.

Whenever one of our teams wins a championship, among the first people to be given championship jackets are our team doctor and our sports medicine expert. Without the medical services they've provided, we may never have been champions. So our medical personnel receive any awards given to the other team members. After all, they are part of the team and should be rewarded as such. When people know they are appreciated, they will give you their finest effort.

Student Trainers

Because a physician cannot be present for every game and practice, a regularly attending certified trainer is essential. Ideally, your school will have a certified trainer on its faculty. At the very least, a student trainer should always be on hand. As discussed in chapter 4, I place a great deal of importance on these student trainers, and the school funds their education in summer classes to help them become the best trainers they can be. I also have student trainers work at my summer camps under certified trainers so they may continue to develop their skills.

Student Managers

Any basketball program needs more than just student trainers; it needs managers as well. So recruiting or selecting managers must be part of your preparation for the season.

Good managers are in demand in college as well as high school, and two of our managers have won full scholarships to college. Our managers are often eagerly sought by major colleges because the schools know our young men are good people, hard-working, and well-schooled as basketball managers.

 TRAINING EXCELLENCE

One young man, Jeff Hathaway, came to me as a freshman and informed me that he wanted to be a manager for our basketball team. I told him the usual procedure was to start as a manager for the freshman team, and then perhaps work his way up to the varsity. He asked me if he could try out for the varsity anyway as any other freshman is allowed to do, so I told him yes. Jeff became a 4-year varsity manager *and* trainer for us, and is now an assistant Athletic Director at the University of Connecticut.

We carry four managers for our varsity basketball team: One keeps the scorebook and calls the local media outlets; another keeps statistics; the third, our student trainer, helps out with balls and jackets on the bench; and the fourth manager videotapes all of our games and the occasional practice or drill I want taped. For home games, we add a fifth manager to assist the visiting team in whatever way he can. If we travel to a tournament at the end of the year, we try to take that fifth manager with us.

Those are only the more glamorous of a basketball manager's duties. But good managers can be given these responsibilities:

- Distributing all basketball equipment
- Preparing the gym for practice (mopping floor, pushing in bleachers, taping ankles, having the basketballs ready, etc.)
- Cleaning up after practice (putting basketball and medical equipment away,

making sure everything is locked, turning lights out)
- Making travel arrangements
- Planning team meals, when necessary

In selecting managers, we try to choose students from different classes and bring them up through the system to maintain continuity, much like we do on the basketball court. Any student who is interested is allowed to try out for a manager's position. Most will try out as freshmen and prove themselves with the freshman team, move up to the junior varsity, and then if they are qualified, eventually make it to the varsity team. A few exceptionally talented freshmen, like Jeff Hathaway, have started with the varsity. But I've had fewer freshman managers than players at the varsity level. (Only seven freshman players have made the varsity team in my history at DeMatha.)

Candidates for manager try out in much the same way players do, and I look for the same qualities in a manager as I do in a player. We evaluate a candidate's abilities by giving him jobs to do and then observing the manner in which they are handled. If I have to take the candidate by the hand and remind him of certain things every day, then that person is not likely to get the job. If, on the other hand, I assign a potential manager a task and it's done after the first mention, then I know I've found a good one.

So, when searching for managers, look for responsible, self-starting types who will go ahead and do whatever needs to be done instead of asking the coaches every time.

Mature and responsible managers can be, like an assistant coach or assistant athletic director, an invaluable resource to a coach. They can be given a great deal of responsibility and are well-respected by all members of the team. By relieving coaches of burdensome tasks, managers make it possible for us to spend more time coaching.

Scheduling Games

Another significant part of planning for a season involves scheduling your team's games. High school schedules, to a large extent, are set by school conference administrators. However, most schools are free to schedule some nonconference games on their own. You should have some say in whom and when your team will play. If you work closely with your athletic director, he or she will be willing to try to accommodate your concerns.

I am the associate athletic director at DeMatha as well as the basketball coach, so I make my own schedules for the basketball team. But 99% of the time I go along with what my coaches want when making schedules for their sports. Typically, I let the coaches do their own nonleague scheduling and then come to me for final approval.

Scheduling Fair Competition

I believe the object of high school athletics is to compete against schools with similar athletic philosophies and similar operating conditions, including the size of the talent pool from which the schools may draw. For example, our league prohibits us from using 5-year players, so we never schedule games against high schools that are allowed to have such players on their rosters. If your school has only 300 students from which the basketball team can be chosen, don't make a habit of playing teams that can choose from 1,500 students. In short, schedule games against other schools that are in your school's competitive class.

Keep in mind when scheduling that a program needs successes on which to build. Therefore, do not schedule the most difficult opponents possible for every game. Playing teams you have no chance of beating is not healthy competition, and it can even be damaging to your players' chances of being noticed by colleges. Instead, schedule some games against teams that you have a reasonable chance of defeating.

Some coaches prefer to play the toughest nonleague opponents they can to toughen their players up and prepare them for competition within their league. And I agree that league competition is most important, and that playing better opponents can improve a team. However, if you play only the highest level teams and encounter defeat after defeat, your players will lose the confidence it takes to compete successfully in your own conference.

Never underestimate the importance of proper scheduling. I've been told by successful college coaches that more coaches are fired because of overscheduling than for any other reason. This seems to happen more often at smaller colleges where a coach is trying to bring some recognition to a program, but a loss is still a loss. No matter how good the opponent, and even though the team may be losing to the giants of the game, the team's confidence will begin to erode. This drop in confidence leads to more losses, and, in the end, to the coach's removal.

What you need to strive for in scheduling, then, is a healthy mixture of tough opponents who will make your team better and opponents against whom you have a reasonable chance of gaining confidence-building victories. St. Paul's words of wisdom apply here as they do in all aspects of life: "All things in moderation."

Scouting Opponents

Once your schedule is set, you're going to want to know all you can about your upcoming opponents. And that is why you need to determine how and when you will scout.

Different coaches have different approaches to scouting. Former UCLA coach John Wooden told me he preferred to do very little scouting because he found it either made him scared of the next opponent or lulled him into a feeling of overconfidence. Instead, he wanted to spend most of the time preparing his team to do what it did best. But don't believe for a minute that Coach Wooden didn't know what the other team ran offensively and defensively, or what their strengths and weaknesses were. He did.

I agree with Coach Wooden that you should spend much of your time working on what *your* team does best. But you need to know your opponents' tendencies, strengths, and weaknesses going into games. I believe scouting is crucial in having your team as prepared as possible for a game.

To standardize and simplify the scouting process, I have designed a form for scouts to use (see Figure 5.6). The form includes everything from offensive and defensive formations to inbounds plays and free throw shooting ability. The form also asks for a personal comment from the scout on what he feels we must do to win the game.

Helping Players With Their College Plans

As I've mentioned, a coach has equal responsibility to players off the court as on it. And one of the most important high school coaching duties is working with players who want to go to college.

Virtually every high school player dreams of going on to play basketball at the college level. We all know, though, that as the level of competition increases, the chances of making it at that level decrease. Recent figures show that there are approximately 800,000 high school basketball players, but only 16,000 players at the college level. That means only one out of every 50 high school players will make it in college—roughly one player from every four teams.

The odds are against most high school players, but the efforts of the coach can help a young athlete get the opportunity to play college ball. I'm not saying you can fool colleges into taking a player. You can't. Only the college recruiters know the needs of their particular school. And even if their needs are similar, recruiters are not going to view each player in exactly the same way. But, as a coach, you can get the information regarding your seniors into recruiters' hands, then provide any follow-up information they may need.

 POSTAGE PAID

In my first year at DeMatha, I wrote a letter that included a thumbnail sketch of that year's seniors, a schedule of all our scrimmages and games, and a schedule of all our practices. I sent that letter to over 400 colleges and encouraged each of them to send a representative to see our players in action. In my sketches of the players, I was brief and conservative because I wanted the emphasis to be on getting college representatives to come see the players for themselves.

The results of this first letter were almost immediate. In one of our first games of the season, our point guard, Johnny Herbert, scored 38 points and played an outstanding game. As we were walking off the floor, a gentleman approached me and said, "I'm Coach Byron Gilbreath from Georgia Tech, and I enjoyed the way your team played. I particularly like the way your point guard played. I would like him to visit Georgia Tech, and I feel pretty confident Coach Hyder will offer him a scholarship."

Obviously, I was thrilled. After Johnny had showered, I introduced him to Coach Gilbreath. They talked for a while, the visit was set up, and Johnny went on to become captain of the Georgia Tech team and is now a successful businessman in Georgia. It makes me feel good knowing that the letter I took the time to write may have had something to do with Johnny's successes in athletics and life. I often kid my godson, Steven Morgan Herbert, "Just think, if I hadn't written that letter, there might not be any you." Now, whenever something good happens to the family, Steven just says, "I know. I know. It's the letter."

I recommend this kind of college placement effort to any coach, particularly if a program is just getting started or if you are new to an existing program. Even if none of the players goes on to play in college, the effort is not wasted. The players will appreciate that you are working hard to make colleges aware of them. Don't limit yourself to only Division I schools either. There are plenty of Division II and III schools out there who would love to have a good, hard-working student-athlete.

The Blue-Chippers

The great players will have more than enough scholarship offers, and, in that case, your role as coach is to provide guidance in helping them narrow down the choices. Generally, though, it's the average player you have to work hard to help, and you can do it. As proof of the dividends hard work can yield, *every* graduating basketball player from DeMatha since 1960 has been offered a basketball scholarship to college. With few exceptions, these scholarships have been accepted. (Most of the offers that were turned down were done so by young men wanting to go to Ivy League schools, which only award scholarships based on financial need.)

Sample Scouting Report Form

Team scouted _____   Opponent _____

Personnel and tendencies (height and weight)

1.   6.

2.   7.

3.   8.

4.   9.

5.   10.

First sub—back court: First sub—front line:

Do they have a player who can take over?

Who do we foul?

Pressure offense set:

Halfcourt man-to-man offense set:

Halfcourt zone offense set:

Delay game set:

Inbounds baseline:

Inbounds sideline:

Fullcourt pressure defense:

Halfcourt zone trap:

Man-to-man defensive look:

Zone defensive look:

Defensive look vs. inbounds underneath their basket:

Junk defenses (Box-and-One, etc.):

Match-ups

Us	*Opponent*
1.	1.
2.	2.
3.	3.
4.	4.
5.	5.

How do they play?

What must we do to win?

Figure 5.6 Sample scouting report form.

Once the college representatives begin to show up at your games or practices, it is important that you treat them all equally. Do not give "big name" coaches preferential treatment. They are all college coaches with jobs to do, and they should all be treated fairly. College recruiters know when they come to DeMatha that they will have the same opportunity to talk with a player as would a Mike Krzyzewski, Dean Smith, or Bobby Cremins. The word is out that every college has the same chance at a DeMatha player, and this is the word you should make sure gets out about your program. Why? Because that coach who comes to recruit your star player may end up offering your sixth man a scholarship.

In the case of the heavily recruited players, we have found it is best to have certain rules by which the colleges must abide. These rules are not designed to inconvenience the colleges, but rather to try to control the distractions and pressures that can often be placed on an 18-year-old who is still in high school. Here are our recruiting rules:

- All contacts must be made through the coach's office.
- The student-athlete is never called at home, nor are his parents or any other members of his family. If a recruiter wants to talk with a player, the player will call at his own convenience.
- Any recruiter coming to the school will have the opportunity to meet and talk with any player that he is interested in.
- If the recruiter sparks an interest in the young man, and the young man wants a school respresentative to visit his home, then this will be set up at the convenience of both parties.
- If the school wants the young man to visit its campus, and the young man wishes to do so, then we will set up the visit through the coach's office.
- Visits are allowed in the fall until basketball practice starts and can resume after the season. In-season visits are allowed only if there is a legitimate gap during which time the team is not practicing.

Although I may offer advice and guidance, I make it our policy to let the players make their own decisions about college. I don't tell our players who to marry, and I don't tell them where to go to college—they have to be responsible for their own lives. If you tell a player where to go to college, and things do not work out very well, the player may well blame it on you. But if he makes his own decision, he is the one who has to make it work.

Providing Proper Equipment

Finally, in preparing for the season don't overlook the equipment you will need. Never underestimate the importance of good equipment. From an economic point of view, it is wise to put everything out on bids. Your athletic director and school administration will appreciate the fact that you are looking for the most reasonable deal. Keep in mind, though, that the lowest price is not always the best buy. Compare quality and cost, and then make what you feel is the right decision.

Uniforms

The overall look of a team can be helpful in providing confidence for the players. You want them to look like basketball players. And if they look good, they'll feel good. And if they feel good, they'll play better. This means you will need attractive home and away uniforms.

To offset costs, we try to stagger the purchasing of uniforms so that we are never buying both varsity and freshmen team uniforms in the same year. Also, to help the budget, we try to get 4 years out of a set of uniforms before passing them down to the junior varsity.

Our players are responsible for their other apparel, including their shoes and socks. I recommend that the team decide on a specific high-top shoe so all the players will be dressed alike and further enhance that team look. (We wear the Champion shoe.) Make sure your team uses shoes of the highest quality that are light, durable, and give great ankle support.

Basketballs

Obviously you must include the purchase of basketballs in your equipment for the upcoming season. Every year, our league votes on a basketball to be used in league play. In past years, a MacGregor ball has been selected.

It is imperative that you use the same basketball in practice that you will use in games so the players are used to it. To alter a cliché, familiarity breeds confidence.

First Aid Supplies

Though we try to avoid injuries, we all know they're bound to happen. So your team must be well equipped with medical and first aid supplies for practices and games. Consult the medical personnel who are working with the team as to what type and what brand of equipment they recommend having on hand. Quality cannot be sacrificed for cost. The safety of your players must be a top priority.

Facilities

The school itself establishes the facilities for the season: the gymnasium and baskets. Yet, there are the little things that you don't want to overlook, such as good nets on the baskets and the proper padding on the backboard (which is a rule in most leagues). The nicer a place is to practice in, the better the practice will be. If you want the students to look like players, act like players, and think like players, then they must practice like players. A good practice facility helps distinguish true "players" from their peers on the playgrounds and in rec centers.

I understand that not every high school is going to have a state-of-the-art gymnasium. But, by being a good salesman and a good planner, you can make the best out of any situation.

 TOUGH COURT CASES

The first team I ever coached at St. Joseph's had no gym in which to practice. All we had was an outdoor blacktop playing surface, and a good friend of mine, Johnny Ryall, put up the money to buy two outdoor baskets. When the weather was bad, we would simply shovel the snow off the court. (I hadn't, incidently, learned quite as much about basketball then and did not plan my practices effectively. We spent one third of our practices shooting layups, but that team sure shot layups better than anybody else around.)

When I moved on to St. John's College High School as the junior varsity coach, I had to wait until 6:00 every evening to practice. However, the ambitious freshman team braved the cold and snow and practiced on outdoor courts instead.

Understandably, everyone wants to have the perfect facility, however impossible that may be. One of the buzzwords in coaching today is "innovation," and you can be innovative with your facility. But whatever kind of facility you have, be positive about it—don't play it down; play it up.

Traveling to Games

Finally, in preparing for the season you have to plan how to get your team to its games. The players can arrange transportation to home games on their own, but when traveling to away games, it is far better to travel as a team. Supervision is easier when the team travels as a group. Also, during these trips a greater comaraderie can develop among the players. As the coach, you can set the proper mood on the trip as well as spend the time productively with general discussion about the game.

Today, more high schools than ever take long road trips, particularly during Christmas vacation. End of the year tournaments have become very popular, with some high school teams traveling from coast to coast.

My DeMatha team generally takes three trips a year. The first is right before Christmas, the second is at Christmas, and the third is to a postseason tournament. If traveling is done at the right time of the year, only a very small amount of school time is missed by the student-athletes. We never let basketball get ahead of education. Our moderator, Father Damian, accompanies us on these trips; he checks that the players are keeping up with their schoolwork and provides tutoring when necessary.

On trips of 5 hours or less, I recommend traveling by chartered bus. For shorter distances the bus is quicker than flying because you don't waste time getting to and from the airport and waiting for your luggage. When the trip is more than 5 hours, though, flying makes more sense. Flying is expensive, and the team may have to raise money to be able to take such a trip. But many tournaments now help the participating schools pay some of their transportation costs, so flying becomes an affordable travel option.

I believe that several trips a year are part of the total educational experience. A basketball road trip may be a young person's first flight or trip out of the area. The players will meet people their own age from other parts of the country, and they will share many experiences together that they will never forget.

Before we make a trip, I take the time to emphasize to the players once again that they are representing themselves, their families, and the school. I also tell them that I know their conduct will be exemplary, and stress that they use common sense with regard to their safety.

I also appoint a trip captain from among our seniors. He is in charge of the entire team on the trip. It's an opportunity to place some additional responsibility on a young adult, and it also reminds the players that it is their team, their trip, and their time to remember. Like everything else in your basketball program, your road trips will be only as successful as the care you take in planning them.

Summary

The following items are among the many important plans you need to make before the season.

- Make sure that you have complete medical screenings and insurance coverage for each athlete who tries out for your team.
- Structure in-season practices to provide the necessary conditioning, and provide your players with workout plans for the off-season. Being in top physical shape is a year-round process!
- Institute a weight training program that benefits the muscle groups used specifically in basketball, and that emphasizes strength development rather than muscle definition and bulk.
- Meet with your assistants to develop a Master Plan that includes all the basketball strategies you wish to employ in the upcoming season.
- Develop a relationship with a local doctor and sports medicine staff to provide treatment for and rehabilitation of injuries.
- Have qualified student trainers on hand at all practices and games to provide immediate preliminary treatment to injuries.
- Select responsible, mature student managers to help relieve you of some of the necessary noncoaching tasks.
- Schedule games against teams in your competitive class that you have a reasonable chance of defeating.
- Plan to scout as many of your opponents as possible.
- Work with seniors who want to go to college by actively pursuing college recruiters.
- Help the blue-chippers narrow their choices of colleges, but do not make any decisions for them.
- Put all your equipment purchases out on bids to help you get the most for your dollar.
- Have nice uniforms that the team members will be proud to wear.
- If possible, use the same basketballs in practice that you use in league games.
- Consult medical experts as to the types and brands of first aid supplies to have on hand.
- Be positive about the facilities at your school, even if they are not the greatest.
- Thoroughly plan any traveling the team may do.

Chapter 6

Preparing for Practices

As I mentioned in the last chapter, my assistants and I meet several times before practices start to develop a Master Plan for the season. At those meetings, we identify the offenses we want to run, the defenses we'll use the most, the type of fast break we want to use, our foul shot alignments, and so forth.

Once you draw up an initial Master Plan (see sample in Figure 6.1), you will find that it changes very little from year to year. Obviously, adjustments must be made when rule changes, such as the 3-point shot, are introduced. The actual specifics may (and probably should) vary, but I have found the general nature of a Master Plan allows it to remain fairly consistent through the years.

Before we begin practice, I divide this sea-

son-long plan into five monthly practice plans. Prior to November 8, the date our practices begin, I examine our monthly plan for November and draw up a daily practice plan detailing what we want to cover in each of the sessions. The monthly plan is, then, a chart of the available practice days in November and what we will be working on in those practices leading up to the opener (see Appendix B).

I've talked about flexibility before, and it's important to bring it up again. This monthly plan should not be etched in stone. Conditions constantly change, and you must have the flexibility to change the plan in accordance with conditions. After every practice I meet with my assistants and discuss what we need to work on and why. We

Sample Master Practice Plan

I. Offense
   A. Team
      1. vs. man-to-man
      2. vs. zone
      3. vs. combination
      4. vs. pressure
II. Defense
   A. Team
      1. man-to-man
      2. zone
      3. combination
      4. pressure
   D. Individual
      1. on the ball
      2. away from the ball
      3. pivot or post area
III. Conditioning
   A. Physiological
   B. Psychological
IV. Fundamentals
   A. Footwork
   B. Passing
   C. Shooting
   D. Dribbling
V. Rebounding
   A. Offensive
   B. Defensive
VI. Conversions
   A. Offense to defense
   B. Defense to offense
VII. Free throw situations
   A. Offensive alignment
   B. Defensive alignment
VIII. Jump ball situations
   A. Offensive circle
   B. Midcourt
   C. Defensive circle
IX. Out-of-bounds situations
   A. Defensive end
   B. Sidelines
   C. Offensive end

X. Time and score situations
   A. Delay game for lead protection
   B. Special blitz offense when trailing
   C. Special plays
XI. Player and team evaluation
   A. Our team
      1. charts and stats
      2. scouting reports
      3. films
   B. Opponents
      1. stats
      2. scouting reports
      3. films
XII. Rules
XIII. Game organization
   A. Pregame
   B. Strategy
      1. game plan
      2. bench
      3. time-outs
      4. halftime
   C. Postgame
XIV. Trip organization
   A. Schedule
   B. Players
      1. rules
      2. dress code
      3. curfew
   C. Staff
   D. Guests
   E. Transportation
   F. Lodging
   G. Meals
XV. Public relations
   A. Faculty
   B. Students
   C. Parents
   D. Community
   E. News media
   F. College coaches

Figure 6.1   Sample master practice plan.

finalize the plan for the next practice in these meetings. (For a sample practice plan, see Figure 6.2.)

When formulating your Master Plan, avoid burning your team out by practicing too much. Try to err on the side of caution. It is better to underpractice than to overpractice. For example, two-a-day practices are often too demanding for players at any time of the year. More often than not, two-a-days result in mental and physical fatigue by the end of the season.

You can avoid overpracticing by planning longer practices at the beginning of the year when the players need the extra work and can handle it better. Before the team is selected, our practices run between 2 and 2-1/2 hours. After that point, I try to limit the majority of our practices to 2 hours. The day before a game, though, I limit practice to 90 minutes and do not require any heavy physical work. This helps keep the players rested and sharp for the following day's game.

Sample Practice Plan

Offense	Defense	Other
1/2 ct. man 0 Time—score Shooting	1-1 → 2-2 O-D vs. Wizard 1/2 ct. "D" (22T) 1/2 ct. 0 vs. Zone Trap Individual "0" vs. Dribble	Warm up Big 3 Stations—offensive work Fouls + Sprints + 70%

Time	Drill	Emphasis
10	Warm up	
5	1-1 → 2-2	
5	O-D vs. Wizard	
5	Individual defense vs. Dribbler	- Stay low
10	1/2 ct. "0" vs. Zone Trap	- Ball movement
10	Stations—offensive work	- Perimeter—shallow cuts
10	1/2 ct. Defense (22T)	- Post-shooting
15	Big 3 { 5 2 shot fouls / 3-2 2-1 fast breaks drill / recognition drill }	- Full speed
20	1/2 ct. man "0"	- Patience
5	Time—score	- Down 2—30 sec to go
5	Shooting drill	- Game speed
10	Fouls (5 1-1s) + Sprints	- Reward winner

Comments:

① 1 more practice before next game

② Academic slips due on Friday

③ Stay on the books

Figure 6.2 Sample practice plan.

By January, we are primarily working on fine-tuning various elements of the game, so we may reduce practice time by 10 more minutes. By February, practices are usually shortened by another 5 minutes or so, making the average practice about 1 hour and 45 minutes.

It's also important to give the players at least one day a week off from practicing. Sometimes, I will even give my players two days off. They need this time to rest their bodies and their minds.

Conducting Practice

Our practices generally last about 2 hours, with the time broken down into segments of varying length. Each segment is reserved for a specific purpose. I learned long ago to adhere strictly to this schedule, even if the players perform poorly in one or all of the segments. When I started coaching, my temptation was to stay with a drill until the players were doing it right. Invariably, we would end up spending 20 minutes on the drill instead of the 5 I had allotted for it. What I found was that the longer I stuck with a certain drill, the worse the performance became.

If a certain segment does not go well, I now cut it off after the allotted time anyway. I then call the team together and tell them, "Fellows, the last 10 minutes we really cheated ourselves out of a chance to improve. We didn't do well. But now we have to move on to the next thing, and we have to work hard and work smart because we don't want to cheat ourselves out of any more valuable practice minutes." The players generally pick up the intensity for the next drill, and that higher intensity usually carries over into the remainder of the practice.

Player Preparation

Practices officially start every afternoon at 3:30, or about 30 minutes after the school day ends. However, the players are already out on the floor working in special groups several minutes before the official starting time.

From the time school ends, the players have a half hour to put their books away, get changed, get ankles taped if needed, and prepare for practice by stretching on their own. We do not stretch out as a team because we have our bigger players use one set of stretching exercises, and our smaller players a different set. Also, players with minor injuries may want to take this time for other types of stretching or rehabilitation exercises.

Our players are encouraged to have all of their preparation work done by 3:25, at which time the big men work out individually with their coach, while the perimeter players work on their individual skills and moves.

Off to a Good Start

At precisely 3:30, I blow the whistle and the players *sprint* to where I am standing. I place particular emphasis on the players sprinting toward me, because I believe the way you begin anything will have a direct effect on how well you complete it. Players who take their time and walk over to start practice won't have the enthusiasm neces-

sary to make the practice as productive as it could be. By hustling from the beginning, players establish the proper state of mind to accomplish what we want.

If you have a problem with players not hustling over to you at the start of practice, here's what I would suggest. Once the team is gathered around you say, "You all are supposed to be hustling over here, and I see most of you just walking. You're obviously not warmed up yet. Let's see if we can't get you warmed up a little bit."

At that point, line your team up and maybe have them jog up and down the court a couple of times to loosen up. Then have them run 25 to 30 sprints the length of the gym. Once they've caught their wind and walked around a bit, blow the whistle again and see if they don't hustle over to you this time and, in all likelihood, for the rest of the season. I did this once early in my career, and the players quickly got the message. In subsequent years, the word has gotten out before practices begin, and the players haven't needed any reminders. If you emphasize the importance of hustling at the beginning of practice, your players will do just that. As I said, it's not what you coach, but what you emphasize.

Off to Work We Go

Once the players have sprinted over to me, I will briefly set the tone for the practice. For example, I might say, "Fellows, we have five practices left before our first ballgame. We've got to be ready to make today one of our finest days mentally and physically. Let's go!"

From there, we break into our first drill, which is a fullcourt passing drill in which the players line up at diagonal ends of the court and hand off and throw various passes to their teammates coming from the other end of the floor. This drill helps loosen the players up even more, promotes good conditioning, and also helps improve their ballhandling skills. The fact that we start our practice with this drill emphasizes to the players the importance we place on good passing and catching.

A typical practice at DeMatha proceeds something like this:

1. Fullcourt passing drill
2. Fullcourt layup drill

3. 10 foul shots in a row (If the player makes 9 or 10, he picks up a permission. If he makes 7 or 8, nothing happens. If he makes below 7, he picks up a double suicide.)

4. Defensive footwork and individual defensive work

5. Fullcourt 1-on-1 drills, building to 2-on-2 all the way to 5-on-5

6. Individual station work (We have three baskets in operation, each representing a station at which a different skill is taught and developed. The skills being taught change from practice to practice. The players rotate every 3 minutes, leaving 9 minutes for the entire segment.)

7. Team defensive drills

8. Fast break drills

9. Second set of 10 foul shots (Each player shoots 5 two-shot fouls while rotating from basket to basket. Permission and double suicide rules used in segment 3 apply.)

10. Team offensive drills (These include any teaching that needs to be done, and halfcourt games.)

11. Time and score repertoire (We try to allow 5 minutes at the end of practice to work on special situations. Each practice we work on a different situation—for example, down by 2 points with 30 seconds left to play.)

12. Third set of foul shots (Each player shoots five 1-and-1 situations. Permissions and double suicides again apply.)

13. 20 conditioning sprints

14. Balance the ledger on permissions and double suicides

Effective and Fun

The primary purpose of the Master Plan is to organize your practices from the most general season-long plan all the way down to the most specific daily practice plan. This organization and planning is crucial to making your practices as effective as possible, and it provides the road map to guide your team on its season-long objective of playing up to its potential.

The Master Plan allows you to combine time-management skills with hard-core

---

Tips for Keeping Practices Effective and Fun

- Take the time to prepare and organize your practice in advance. Know exactly what you want to do at the start of each practice.

- Keep your drills and various segments short and snappy. The players' ability to concentrate on one topic decreases the longer you spend on it.

- Keep the attitude upbeat and positive by handing out more praise than criticism. Use the "sandwich technique" that I described in chapter 2 for constructive criticism.

- Have fun yourself, and take advantage of humorous opportunities. If the players see that you are having fun at practice, they will be more likely to have fun themselves.

- Keep everybody involved. If you are going 5-on-5, assign the remaining players to the two teams and let them reap the rewards or suffer the consequences of how their teammates fare. This gives those not physically involved a stake in what happens and keeps them part of the practice mentally and emotionally.

---

basketball instruction and coaching. In devising your practice schedules, never spend a lot of time on one particular drill. Too much time on one thing can lead to laziness and boredom, which in turn can lead to the development of bad habits, exactly what you don't want to happen in practice. Too little time on a certain drill, however, may not promote maximum skill development. As you gain more experience, you will be better able to determine just how much time to spend on a particular drill. In any event, keep your practices moving! Your players will stay sharper physically and mentally if you do.

Also, in organizing your practices, remember to allow for, and even encourage, fun. Never lose sight of the fact that basketball is a game, and that games are supposed to be fun.

The players are out there playing for you because they love the game to begin with, so you as the coach must encourage this, especially in practices. The fun in games will take care of itself, but the fun in practices you can control.

A practice cannot be truly effective if it is not fun. The basketball season is a long one, and if players at any point no longer have fun in practice, their enthusiasm and effort will decrease correspondingly. This lack of mental and physical sharpness can spread like a cancer, and I believe it is why some teams are better in the first part of the season than the last. So keep your practices fun all year long.

The system of permissions and double suicides is one way I keep the fun in our practices. This system helps make practice competitive, and all athletes find fun in competition. Some of our biggest laughs come at the end of practice, when the players with extra permissions and the players with double suicides try to negotiate deals with each other.

To reiterate, my primary objective for the team is to have them play hard, play smart, and have fun. That applies to practices as well as games. And the best way to insure that your team plays that way is for you to be prepared and run a well-organized practice.

Summary

Practices will be only as good as the planning you do before them. Here are the key planning points outlined in this chapter.

- Take time to develop a season-long Master Plan, which can then be broken down into a monthly plan, weekly plan, and daily plan.
- Plan every minute of your practices, and stick to the plan.
- Make your players sprint over to you to begin practice on a hustling, enthusiastic note.
- Keep the fun in practices.

Part III

Coaching Offense

Chapter 7

Basic Offensive Positions, Skills, and Sets

Basketball is unique among sports in that there are fewer specialists or one-dimensional athletes in the game. Each player must be a total player. Football has field-goal kickers, and baseball has designated hitters. But basketball players, although they may excel in certain areas of the game (e.g., 3-point shooting, rebounding, defense), must have a wide array of skills.

Multiple skills are essential to play the game effectively. Every basketball player should be able to

- pass and receive the basketball,
- make the transition from offense to defense and from defense to offense,
- rebound offensively and defensively in relation to their position (a point guard, for instance, is not expected to rebound as much as a post player),
- play good defense, and
- blend in with the other four players.

But a coach should not expect each player to have equal ability in all of these areas. Therefore, you must help players develop and strengthen their abilities, then blend these attributes into the best possible team structure. First you must identify the skills that are needed, then position the players where they will be most effective.

Position Skills

In addition to the universal skills, all five offensive player positions have somewhat different secondary skills and attributes. The following is a rather simplified description of these five offensive spots:

#1 Point Guard
#2 Shooting Guard
#3 Small Forward
#4 Power Forward
#5 Center

Point Guard

Most systems designate a player to run the offense. Often referred to as the point guard or "1-player," this player is usually the best ballhandler on the squad. He should be able to lead the fast break that develops out of any situation, whether it be a steal, a rebound, or a basket by the opponent. If the fast break is not there, he must be able to bring the ball up the floor against pressure defense and set up the halfcourt offense. The point guard does not have to be a big scorer, but should be able to shoot well enough to force defenses to come out and cover him on the perimeter and not sag back into the middle.

The point guard should also be an excellent passer. His ability to hit the open player is very important, as is his ability to anticipate the way a play might develop and to make the pass that sets up the assist pass. He should have the smarts to go to the player with the hot hand, but also the ability to get everybody involved in the offense. He should have the ability to penetrate, attract the defense, and finish the play. By finish the play, I mean that he should make sure that the offense gets a good shot, whether it be on a fast break or through penetration. The 1-player should have the intelligence to read the defenses and adjust the offense accordingly. The

ideal point guard is, in a lot of ways, an extension of the coach on the floor.

Shooting Guard

The second guard is frequently the bigger of the two guards. The "2-player" is generally one of the best outside shooters and, ideally, is the second best ballhandler on the team. He must be a good receiver, because he will frequently get the first pass to start the offense. And, therefore, he must also be a good passer in order to keep the offense moving and take advantage of opportunities to get the ball inside to the post players.

Like the point guard, the 2-player should be able to create and finish the play either on the fast break or by dishing off to an open teammate. The player at the 2 position can also help the team by grabbing offensive rebounds, either by following the shot or by sneaking in from the weak side to get good rebounding position.

Small Forward

The small forward will probably be bigger than the guards, but perhaps not as quick or as good a ballhandler. But the "3-player" should possess many of the same skills as the guards. He should be able to handle the ball well, as he is sometimes called upon to help the guards break pressure defenses. The small forward must also pass the ball well. Sometimes this player can be the best passer on the team, because his slight height advantage over the guards opens up more avenues through which to pass the ball. And he should be able to shoot from the outside to help the 1 and 2 players draw a sagging or zone defense away from the lane area.

Where the 3-player differs from the guards is in the area of offensive rebounding. The small forward must be a good offensive rebounder. From the 3 position a player oftentimes has the best shot at an offensive rebound because opponents concentrate on blocking out the power forward and center.

Power Forward

The power forward should be one of the biggest and strongest players on the team and, therefore, one of your dominant rebounders, both offensively and defensively. The "4-player" should be a physical player. Every team needs a physical presence and, because of his size and strength, the power forward can often provide it.

Like the guards and the 3-player, the power forward should be able to handle the ball well and be a good passer and receiver. This player's size and strength should enable him to post up inside and take the ball to the basket either for an easy shot or to draw a foul.

Center

In many cases, the center will be the heart of the team. Like the power forward, the "5-player" should be either your best, or second best, rebounder. Unlike the perimeter players, the center must be able to play with his back to the basket and be a solid inside scoring threat. Therefore, you must work with your center to develop the fundamental moves that will allow him to score consistently from inside 10 feet.

Because the 5-player often shoots in traffic, he will frequently draw the most fouls. For that reason, the center should be a good free throw shooter (but then again, all your players should be good free throw shooters). Shots taken near the basket are the highest percentage shots, so a good part of your offense should be designed to get the ball inside to the center.

Perimeter and Post

In recent years, I have gotten away from the traditional position designations (i.e., point guard, shooting guard, etc.) just described. I do designate numbers to certain players for alignment purposes when taking the ball out of bounds or setting up the offense. For example, I may want the 3-player to always inbound the ball, and I may want the 1-player to always try to be the first recipient of the inbounds pass. So I do use numbers for alignment and teaching purposes.

But, overall, I prefer to break the players down into two groups: perimeter players and post players. Perimeter players can be defined as any player who has the ability to play effectively while facing the basket.

Post players are defined as those who have the ability to go inside and play with their backs to the basket. As we all know, players today are becoming more and more skillful, and you will find that many athletes have the ability to play both the perimeter and the post. And in today's motion offenses, those versatile players are extremely valuable.

One thing that all of the great players have in common, besides great ability, is the intelligence to play within their abilities. They do what they can do well, but they do not try to do the things they cannot do well. I'm sure you've heard the old coaching cliché that "a player must play within himself." That means we must help our players learn their strengths. We must remind them, "Do what you do best. Don't try to shoot 3-point shots if your range is 15 feet. And try to dunk the ball on the fast break if you can't jump that high."

Teams also must play within their capabilities. A slow team that tries to win with a run-and-gun style will be disappointed. It is up to us, the coaches, to develop a style of play that is within the abilities of our teams.

Offensive Sets

Before getting into much detail regarding offensive sets, I want to point out here that my basic offense is the fast break. In theory, I hope we never have to set up an offense. We strive to take at least one-third of our shots off of the transition game. My rationale for this approach is this: If a team walks the ball up the floor and plays right into the teeth of the defense with every single possession, then that team is in for a long game. That's basically playing 5-on-5 basketball for four quarters.

In any offense, fast break or half court, you always want to create a numbers advantage. With the fast break, a team can create a numbers advantage and through good passing can find an open player for a high-percentage shot. In a halfcourt offense, through good movement, passing, and screens, you can often create a quick 2-on-1 or 3-on-2 matchup that can yield a high-percentage shot.

As much as we would like to, we know we can't run a fast break down the court every time, so we have to be prepared to set up an offense. In these situations, there are two basic sets from which to choose; all offensive formations fall into one of two categories, the one-guard front and the two-guard front.

One-Guard Front

The one-guard front is a good offensive set to use when you have two post players who are effective inside. This set features a true point guard directing the offense from the top of the key. That can be a lonely position against a good pressure defense because the 1-guard is running the show by himself.

The 2-guard is generally on the right wing, and the small forward on the left wing. (I define the wing area as the foul line extended). However, if these players are more comfortable on the left and right wings, respectively, it is wise to play them in those spots instead.

For the post players, you have a few more options. You can use a double low post, with the power forward and the center positioned down low on either side of the basket. Another option is to use a high post and a low post, with the low player down near one block and the high player out near the foul line.

Advantages of a One-Guard Front

A strength of the one-guard front is that it affords more opportunities to pass the ball inside, with the three perimeter players constantly looking to feed the two post players. By emphasizing the inside game, you can sometimes get the opponent into foul trouble. And because your two best inside players are already stationed near the basket, this formation is often the most effective for offensive rebounding.

Disadvantages of a One-Guard Front

Outside shooting ability is the biggest variable in determining whether to play this offensive set. A one-guard front can lose its effectiveness if your perimeter players are not good enough outside shooters to keep the defense honest. Good outside shooters force the defense into making a decision—sag and control the inside game or come out, play tight on the perimeter players, and deny the outside shot. If either your post or perimeter is not a threat, the defense can overplay the strength of your offense.

Another weakness of the one-guard front is that it can put the offense in poor position to get back on defense to prevent the fast break. If you are playing a one-guard front and your opponent is a good fast-breaking team, you must think long and hard about the most effective way to stop the break. You can designate that certain players drop back into coverage whenever a shot goes up (from any offensive set), you can double-team the rebounder to prevent the outlet pass, or you can apply fullcourt pressure on the opponent's ballhandler to slow him down. Whatever way you choose to halt the break, have it ready if you are playing a one-guard front.

Two-Guard Front

The two-guard front is the formation many teams will use when the coach feels the team has only one good inside player to play the post. In this offensive set, both guards are out near the top of the key facing the basket, about 12 to 14 feet apart. The two forwards now become wing players, each stationed on the side where he is most comfortable. The center can set up at the low post (down on the block), medium post (halfway between the block and the foul line), or high post (at the foul line), or the center can rotate among all three spots at various times.

Advantages of a Two-Guard Front

The two-guard offense makes the most sense when you have a good outside shooting team, or if you have only one good post player, and it is in your best interest to spread the defense out. With good screening and ball movement, you should be able to get good outside shots out of the two-guard front. Teams that use this alignment generally will look to the outside shot rather than trying to hammer inside. Unlike the one-guard front, the two players out at the top of the key provide excellent coverage against the fast break.

Disadvantages of the Two-Guard Front

Whereas the one-guard front frees another player to hit the offensive boards, the two-guard front can leave you relatively weak in the rebounding department. In the two-guard alignment, you really have only one player (the center) in good position to go after the rebound.

Court Balance

Many formations can be run out of one-guard and two-guard sets, such as the 1-4, the 1-3-1, the 2-1-2, and so on. But no matter what type of offense your team is running, always try to make sure you have floor balance. By floor balance I mean the offensive players should distribute themselves evenly across the floor, not clustered in one spot.

The object of maintaining court balance is to spread out the defense. Spreading out the defense will allow you better penetration and better shots. This is the reason football teams put a wide receiver on each side. Some football teams even use four wide receivers, two on each side, to further spread the defense.

Good floor balance is particularly crucial once a shot is taken at the offensive end of the floor. You must have the right mixture of players crashing the boards fighting for the offensive rebound, and of others hustling back on defense to prevent the opponent from getting an easy transition basket. I prefer to have three players hitting the boards; but the right mixture of rebounders and defenders depends on your team's capabilities and on your opponent's fast break potential.

Make sure that each player knows what to do in this situation. The one thing you do not want is a player unsure of whether he's supposed to crash the boards or hustle back on defense. When a player is unsure of what he's supposed to do, he often does nothing. And doing nothing is worse than doing the wrong thing. That is why we tell our players to do something, even if it is wrong. We'll correct it later.

Summary

In this chapter, I described offensive player position attributes and skills. I also gave an overview of the general offensive sets that can be used, and their respective strengths and weaknesses. Here are the specific points to remember:

- All players should be able to pass and receive the ball, change ends of the floor, rebound, play good defense, and blend in with their teammates.
- The point guard will be your best ballhandler and one of your best passers. He leads the offense and the fast break.
- The shooting guard is obviously one of your best outside shooters and often your second best ballhandler.
- The small forward should possess the same skills as the guards, but should be big enough to be a more effective rebounder.
- The power forward and center are your biggest, most physical players. They should be able to rebound aggressively and play inside with their backs to the basket.

- I prefer to designate only two positions to players: perimeter and post. The perimeter players are farther away from the basket and play facing it; the post players are closer to the hoop and can play with their backs to it.
- A basic one-guard front offensive set is more effective for getting the ball inside to the two post players. A lack of an outside shooting threat can limit this set's effectiveness by allowing the defense to sag.
- The two-guard front works best if you have only one good post player or excellent outside shooters.
- In any offensive set, teach your players to maintain floor balance to force the defense to spread out to cover them.

Chapter 8

Teaching Offensive Skills

The most effective way to develop basketball skills is to repeatedly practice their proper execution. I call such proper execution of skills the fundamentals of basketball. Skills are given abilities, whereas fundamentals are the execution of those abilities.

I emphasize the fundamentals—the proper execution of skills—at every level of my program, because a coach can build something worthwhile only with a good foundation. It is through learning and repetition of the fundamentals that players will develop their individual skills and, therefore, contribute to the success of a team offense.

I break down the individual skills into two categories: playing with the ball and playing without the ball. Any basketball player

must be able to do both to be a complete player. Playing with the ball includes stationary moves, moves on the move, passing, ballhandling, and shooting. Playing without the ball includes screening and cutting.

Playing With the Ball

A player's individual talent notwithstanding, each one of your players must be a scoring threat while on the court. So the first thing you'll want to teach them is to square up and face the basket upon receiving the ball.

Anytime a player catches the ball, no matter where he is on the court, instruct

Key to Diagrams

All diagrams

———→ = Path of player

– – – → = Path of ball

∿∿∿→ = Dribble

———┤ = Screen

Offensive diagrams

① = Point guard

② = Shooting guard

③ = Small forward

④ = Power forward

⑤ = Center

① = Point guard with ball

X = Defensive player

Defensive diagrams

X1 = Player assigned to 1

X2 = Player assigned to 2

X3 = Player assigned to 3

X4 = Player assigned to 4

X5 = Player assigned to 5

⊗ = Offensive player with the ball

◯ = Offensive player

Drill diagrams

C = Coach
M = Manager

General situations:

◯ = Offensive player

X = Defensive player

Specific situations:

Numbers used when perimeter vs. post distinction is made

Example:

② = Perimeter offensive player, perhaps the shooting guard

X4 = Post defensive player, perhaps the power forward

---

him to immediately get into the triple-threat position. The feet should be about shoulder-width apart and the knees bent. If a player is right-handed, the left foot should be slightly ahead of the right foot, with the left foot acting as the pivot foot. Reverse the footwork for players who are left-handed. In either case, the feet and shoulders should be facing the hoop so that any move made will be in the direction of the basket. From this triple-threat position, a player can dribble, pass, or shoot.

The ball should be protected on the back hip (the right hip for right-handed players), not held out in front where the defense has an opportunity to swipe at it. Stress to your players that they should stay low, a position which allows them to make their moves more quickly and, therefore, gives the defense less time to react.

An offensive player will be most successful if he attacks the defender by moving in a straight line to the basket (see Figure 8.1a).

Discourage your players from taking the "banana cut"—a wide path to avoid the defense (see Figure 8.1b). This path only allows the defensive player more time to recover from the initial move, thereby minimizing the move's effectiveness.

Also, teach your players to "close the gap" (the space between the offensive and defensive player as the offensive player slices to the basket). By that I mean once the dribbler slices by the defender, he should get the defender close to his back, preventing the player from coming between him and the basket. Closing the gap in this manner minimizes the defender's chances of recovering and getting back into the play.

Stationary Moves

After a player has caught the ball and squared up to the basket in the triple-threat position, he is ready to attack the defender.

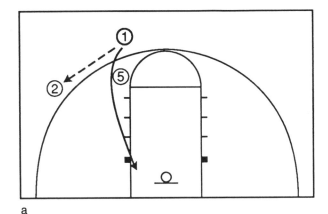

a

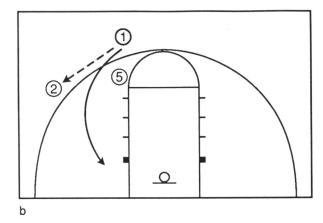

b

Figure 8.1 Straight line (a) vs. "banana cut" (b).

He can do so by using what I call "stationary moves." I use that term because the player makes the initial move from a stationary triple-threat position, before putting the ball on the floor in a dribble.

Strong-Side Drive

After your players catch the ball and get into the triple-threat position, they should execute a jab step. The purpose of the jab step is to get the defense to react. The step should be made with the right foot by right-handed players, and the left foot by left-handed players.

To insure that the offensive player stays balanced, the jab step should be quick and short (only about 6 inches). If the defender does not react quickly enough to the jab step, the offensive player should then take a longer step with the same foot, trying to get his head and shoulders by the defender. The player should then close the gap and explode to the basket with one dribble.

While teaching stationary moves, emphasize to your players the advantages of using their dribble effectively. They must get to the basket using the fewest dribbles possible. This helps prevent their defender or another defender from getting into the play and possibly stopping the drive. Also emphasize to your players the importance of keeping their heads up while dribbling. This will give them the court vision to see both help-side defenders and their own teammates to whom they can dish the ball if the defense collapses when they drive.

Crossover Step

If the offensive player executes a jab step, and the defender responds by sliding over in the direction of that step, the offensive player can then go in the opposite direction with a crossover step. First, a right-handed offensive player jabs with the right foot, forcing the defense to react and take away the strong-side drive. The offensive player then crosses the right foot over to the left side, stepping by the defender's foot and putting the defender on his right hip. (It is important for the player to keep the ball as low as possible as he rolls his shoulders through and steps by the defender.) The offensive player keeps the defender on his right hip, and he puts the ball down left-handed to protect it from the defense.

Once again, the offensive player should attack the defender by going in a straight line to the basket, thus limiting the defender's time for recovery. The fundamentals of effective dribbling, closing the gap, and keeping the head up apply to the crossover drive just as they do to the strong-side drive. When executed properly, either of these moves can lead to a jump shot or power layup, if the defense reacts to the offensive player's footwork.

Jab Step to the Jumper

The defense will eventually adjust to the jab step by taking a retreat step to prevent the offensive player from slicing to the basket. As the defense retreats, the offensive player now has room to go straight up and shoot the jumper (if within shooting range).

To get the shot off, the offensive player must maintain his balance after making the jab step. The player can do so only by keeping the feet shoulder-width apart and staying low. This is why it is important to teach your players to keep the jab step short. A jab step that is too long will force the offensive player to reset, and the defense will be able to recover in time to stop the shot.

Moves on the Move

As opposed to stationary moves, "moves on the move" occur when the offensive player is already dribbling the ball and in motion when he reaches his defender. In each of the following moves, the ballhandler either changes the speed or direction of the dribble to get the defender off-balance and to beat the defender in open court.

Stop-and-Go

The offensive player begins this move by dribbling hard in one direction, all the while protecting the ball with the off hand. The dribbler then comes to a quick stop, and as soon as the defender stops or becomes off-balance, the offensive player then explodes past the defender—pushing the ball out in front of himself, knifing his shoulder by the defender, closing the gap, and keeping the defender behind him.

Once again, it is imperative that the dribbler stay low for maximum quickness and control of the ball. And, as with the stationary moves, the offensive player must attack and freeze the defender. If the move is made too far from the defender, he will have enough time to recover and render the move ineffective.

The dribbler must push the ball out in front to beat the defender. If the dribbler keeps the ball either behind or beside himself, then the defender will have a better opportunity to recover and stop the play.

The complete basketball player will be able to perform the stop-and-go move with the weak hand as well as the strong hand. However, your players may need to work twice as hard and twice as long on perfecting these moves with their weak hand.

Crossover Dribble

If a dribbler cannot change directions, the defense can then force the ball to one side of the court and keep it there. The crossover dribble is an effective way for ballhandlers to change direction.

As with the stop-and-go, the offensive player begins the move by dribbling hard in one direction. To execute the crossover, the offensive player plants the front foot and crosses the ball in front of the body to the other hand, away from the planted foot. He then steps with the opposite foot, pushing off with the plant foot, and slices by the defender.

The danger of the crossover is that the offensive player brings the ball in front of the defender. So to help your players avoid losing the ball, teach them to keep the dribble as low as possible, underneath the defender's hands. Once by the defender, the offensive player should keep the defender on the hip, close the gap, and push the ball out in front.

Reverse Dribble

To execute the reverse, the offensive player plants the right foot (if dribbling left-handed) or the left foot (if dribbling right-handed). The ballhandler then spins around on the planted foot, protecting the ball by keeping his body between the ball and the defender. As the player brings the ball around on the reverse, he should keep it in the same hand until the defender is beaten. After the offensive player has put the defender on the hip, he can then change hands to protect the ball, push it out in front, close the gap, and beat the defender. By keeping the ball in the same hand, the offensive player can avoid palming the ball or leaving the ball behind where defenders can reach in and steal it.

Again, emphasize to your players that they must be as low as possible when making this move. The low position will make them quicker, keep them under control, and enable them to control the ball better.

The biggest difficulty with the reverse comes when the offensive player turns his back to the defense and to his own teammates. A ballhandler performing a reverse could miss an open player cutting to the basket. Also, ballhandlers who turn their backs to the defense are susceptible to traps and to offensive charging fouls if a defender is smart enough to get in proper position.

Fake Reverse Dribble

The fake reverse is almost the same move as the reverse, except that it is only half a spin. A player must stay low with this move and push off the back foot with some strength to get by the defender. Like the reverse, the dribbler should keep the ball in the same hand the entire time, because he is not changing directions but instead is changing speeds.

The fake reverse allows offensive players to have better vision of the court, as they do not fully turn their backs to the basket. However, the dribblers must still protect the ball with their bodies and off hands if they are to be successful with this maneuver.

Dribbling Double-Take

To recap, these are the key points to teach your players about using the dribble to get open:

- Stay low.
- Keep your head up.
- Play under control.
- Attack the defender—don't try to avoid him.
- Go somewhere with your dribble; dribble with a purpose.
- Strengthen the weak hand.
- Keep the defender behind you.
- Close the gap.
- Push the ball out in front.
- Protect the ball with the body and the off hand.
- Change pace and speed.
- Change direction.
- Practice repeatedly in the open court.

Other Moves

The behind-the-back dribble, between-the-legs dribble, pull-back dribble, and inside-out dribble are all very effective in freeing an offensive player from defensive pressure *if* the dribbler attacks the defender and moves forward while performing the moves. Also, teach your players to make something happen after they successfully execute one of these moves. After going to all that work to beat the defender in the open court, the player should be able to experience the satisfaction of finishing the play.

Passing

I emphasize the importance of passing in *every* drill that we do, especially the fast break drills. A team that passes well will have fewer turnovers and create more scoring opportunities. In addition, players must be able to handle fullcourt and halfcourt pressure, and one of the best ways to accomplish that is through effective passing. In the halfcourt offense as well, good, crisp passing can keep the defense on the move and result in an open shot.

Receiving Passes

Even the best pass accomplishes nothing if it is not received properly. Stress to your players the importance of being good receivers as well as good passers.

The first thing I tell my players about being good receivers is to always be prepared to receive a pass. By this I mean that their hands should always be about shoulder-level in anticipation of a pass. Also, players should work hard to get open and make themselves a viable target.

Once the player is open and the pass is thrown to him, he must then receive the ball in the proper way. Proper reception of a pass is executed in three phases:

1. The player must catch the ball with the eyes. He should look the ball all the way into the hands.
2. The player must catch the ball with the feet. He should not wait for the ball to come to him; rather, he should move his feet to go get the ball.
3. The player should then catch the ball with both hands.

Dos and Don'ts for Passing

These are the Dos and Don'ts to emphasize when talking to your players about passing:

DO . . .

- make the easy pass—it doesn't have to be an assist.
- hit the open player.
- use pass fakes to open up passing lanes.
- use the air pass on the break, not the bounce pass.
- use the dribble to create better passing angles.
- feed the post with a bounce pass.
- step into the defender when making the pass.
- feed the post from below the foul line extended.
- follow through on the pass—don't let it float.
- throw with two hands. One-handed passes are difficult to retrieve and often result in a turnover.
- throw away from the defender.
- look at the basket in order to see the entire floor.

DON'T . . .

- throw to a voice.
- jump to pass.
- pass to a player in trouble.
- pass a player into trouble.
- make a pass from the middle of the floor—pick a side.
- overpass—especially on the break.

Ballhandling

All of your players, no matter what position they play, must be able to handle the ball well. Whether they are rebounding, dribbling up court to improve a passing angle, catching the ball in the post or on the break, playing against pressure defenses, or grabbing loose balls, your players' hands must be familiar with the ball to be successful in this game.

Perhaps the best way to increase confidence with the ball is through ballhandling drills. I recommend doing the drills in this order for maximum player development: (1) Start with some basic warm-up drills, (2) move on to nondribbling drills, (3) introduce basic dribbling drills, and (4) hone the skills with advanced dribbling drills.

Have your players begin these drills at about half speed and gradually build to full speed. Also, instruct the players to *keep their heads up* as much as possible during the drills to increase their confidence and to condition them to do the same thing in game conditions. These drills can greatly improve any phase of a player's game, whether it be rebounding, passing, shooting, dribbling, or playing defense. Because these drills are so important, have your players spend 10 to 15 minutes a day on them.

Remind players to concentrate on handling the ball with their finger pads, because that part of the hand is used to shoot, dribble, and pass. The finger pads give the player a higher degree of ball control than he would be able to achieve with any other part of the hand.

Ballhandling Drills

Warm-Up Drills

Ball slap. Players hold the ball in front of them in one hand and slap it with the other hand. Have them switch hands and repeat.

Ball pinch. Hand facing upwards, players start with the ball resting on the fingers, just off the palm of the hand. The players then bring the fingers together, pinching the ball and bringing it to the ends of the fingers.

Ball pat. Players tap the ball back and forth between the fingers of both hands, keeping the ball out in front.

Body circles. Using both hands, players move the ball rapidly in circles around different sections of the body. They should perform several circles around the legs, several more around the midsection, and several more circles around the head.

Corkscrew. Like body circles, but players should circle the legs once, the midsection once, and the head once. Then they repeat in reverse order, going up and down the body.

Figure eights. Players weave the ball between and around their legs.

Football hike. Players put their feet shoulder-width apart and hold the ball in front. They then toss the ball back between the legs and catch it in the back with both hands. Have the players switch from back to front again, repeating the drill to build their quickness.

Side catch. With feet shoulder-width apart, players hold the ball between their feet, with the left hand in back of the left leg and the right hand in front. Players then toss ball up, switch the hands while it is in the air, and catch it before it hits the floor. Have players repeat the drill, trying to improve their quickness.

Socks. Players should start with the legs together and the ball held behind the knees. Have them drop the ball, clap the hands in front, and catch the ball in back before it hits the floor. Have them see how low they can go.

Pockets. Players start with the ball at the midsection. They should drop the ball, slap imaginary front pockets with their hands, and catch the ball before it hits the floor. Have players repeat the drill to their side and back pockets.

Dribbling Drills

Typewriter. Players dribble as low as possible (using the finger tips), alternating hands on the ball, similar to a typist at a keyboard.

Right knee/Left knee. Players dribble around the body and through the legs as they kneel on one knee. Have them switch the knee they're resting on and repeat.

Figure eight dribble. Players dribble the ball between and around legs.

Sit-ups. Players dribble with left or right hand while simultaneously doing sit-ups.

Figure eight dribble while walking. Players dribble the ball between and around their legs as they walk.

Butterfly/Spider dribble. Players start with the ball centered between their legs. They quickly dribble the ball, hitting it with the right and then left hand from the front, then quickly repeating the process from the back. Have players work front to back and back to front, repeating for quickness.

Passing Drills

Figure eight passing. Two players, each with a ball, face each other 10 to 12 feet apart. They begin with the ball in the right hand, complete a figure eight between and around their legs (using both hands), end with the ball in the right hand, and throw an underhanded pass to their partner. The partner simultaneously does the same. Start and pass with the left hand during the next repetition.

Turn and catch. Players pair up. One is a passer and one a receiver. The receiver starts with his back to the passer. The passer calls the receiver's name; the receiver turns, finds the ball, and catches it.

Behind-the-back pass. Two passers, each with a ball, face opposite directions with their sides to each other. Both players simultaneously pass behind the back to each other using the same hand.

Target passing. Two players, each holding a ball, simultaneously make a hip pass with the right hand to the left side of the receiver.

Confidence pass. This is a one-player drill. The player holds the ball above his head with both hands, brings the hands down in front of the body, and bounces the ball hard on the floor between the feet. The player then catches the ball behind the back with both hands.

Two-Ball Dribbling Drills

One knee. Players kneel on one knee with a ball on each side (one for each hand). Players simultaneously pound each ball with the appropriate hand to start the dribble.

High and low. Players dribble two balls simultaneously, one high and one low.

Rhythm. Players bounce a ball in each hand at the same time and at the same height.

Typewriter. Players dribble a ball with each hand. They hit the ball with one finger at a time, rotating through all five fingers. (Like hitting a keyboard).

Sit-ups. Players dribble one ball in each hand while executing a sit-up.

Shooting

Many of the drills we use to practice shooting are found in chapter 10 (on halfcourt offense) and are excellent for getting players to shoot in game-like conditions.

Dos and Don'ts for Shooting

These are the Dos and Don'ts I emphasize to my players when discussing shooting:

DO . . .

- know your range.
- know what a good shot is.
- when receiving a pass for a shot, step into the pass to get the shot off more quickly.
- plant your inside foot when squaring to the basket for the shot.
- provide passers a target as a receiver.
- use shot fakes to get by the defense.
- lift the elbow, follow through, reach for the peach (basket).
- get power for the shot from the legs.
- practice shooting as if you were in a game.

DON'T . . .

- take giant steps. Don't pass up an open 12-footer to get a contested 8-footer.
- leave the off hand on the ball too long, because it could adversely affect the shot.
- fade on the shot.
- follow the flight of the ball—keep your eye on the target.
- dip or hitch. Catch the ball, get it to the shot area, and shoot.

Playing Without the Ball

Much of our practice time is devoted to instructing and reviewing offensive perimeter and post moves to get open. Players must know how to screen, how to use screens, and how to get open by reading the defense and using the v-cut.

A v-cut is a hard step or steps taken in the direction opposite from where a player wants to get open. Like the jab, the v-cut is used to get a defender off-balance or out of position and to thereby give the offensive player the advantage. So instruct your players to use the v-cut to set up a defender for a screen set. And tell players to also use the v-cut when trying to get open on backdoor cuts, basket cuts, or cuts to the perimeter.

Backdoor and Perimeter Cuts

A backdoor cut is most effective when an offensive player is being overplayed by the defense. Because the player does not have the ball, proper instruction and execution of the footwork involved is crucial to the success of this move.

1. Have the offensive player step with the inside foot (the foot closer to the baseline) into the defender to freeze him and reduce his quickness. The closer a player is to the defender, the better; the defender will have less time to react to the cut.
2. After taking this initial step, the offensive player then takes a hard step toward the perimeter or wing with his outside foot (the foot closer to midcourt).
3. If the defender does not cover this move toward the perimeter, the offensive player will be open for a pass. The player should turn and face the basket immediately after receiving the ball.
4. If the defender stays close on the perimeter move, then the offensive player should pivot and push off the outside foot, making the backdoor cut to the basket.

Reading the defense like this should allow offensive players to get open at virtually any point in the game. Again, it is important for the offensive player making the cut to close the gap between himself and the defender, or the defender will have time to react and deny the pass.

If the backdoor pass is prevented by the defense, then the offensive player can turn the backdoor cut into a v-cut that will help him get open. He initiates the backdoor cut and, when reading that it is no longer there, makes a v-cut and fades to the corner to get open. The defensive player will probably be so concerned with protecting the basket that the offensive player should be open to receive the ball in the corner or on the wing.

Screens

In teaching players how to set and use screens, I have found it helpful to emphasize that *both* the screener and the player using the screen are potential receivers. Players are more likely to be enthusiastic about setting the screen if they know they have as good a chance of getting the ball as the cutter coming off the screen. Carry this emphasis over into breakdown drills and practices as well.

Positioning for Screens

Stance and position are the elements that make up an effective screen. The screener should be in a strong, balanced stance with knees bent and feet shoulder-width apart. The arms should be slightly bent, but hanging along the sides; the hands should be protecting the crotch and midsection. It is not necessary to have the elbows any wider than the shoulders when setting a screen. Remember, the screener runs the risk of getting into foul trouble if he uses his arms to screen off defenders. The key to a good screen is proper positioning, not the width of the arms.

The screener should also avoid leaning while setting the pick. Leaning only reduces the strength and balance of the screener; it makes the screen less effective and often results in a foul against the screener. Instead, the player setting the screen should be taught to establish good position and to maintain a strong stance. It is then the cutter's responsibility to use the screen properly to get open.

Getting an Angle for Screens

To help the cutter use the screen effectively, the screener is responsible for setting the screen at an angle that will help the cutter get open. With only one exception,

screens should be set with the screener's body between the defensive player and the basket (see Figure 8.2a). This is true for all screens except the downscreen, in which a player moves "down" from the foul line extended and screens a defender. The cutter then comes off the screen, getting open by moving out from the baseline.

If the screener can be seen by the defender, he should set himself close enough to the defender that only a piece of paper could slide between them. If the defender is unable to see the screener, he must allow the defender enough room to take one step.

It is important for the screener to have two-thirds of his body toward the basket because if he sets the screen either too low or too high, the defense can get over or around the screen without any trouble (see Figure 8.2b).

Using the Screen

After the screen is set, the screener cannot move. It is now up to the cutter to get open.

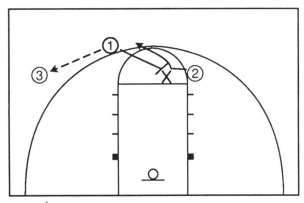

a

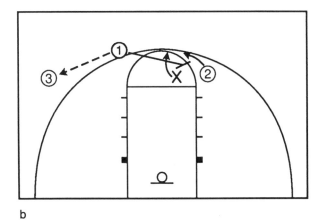

b

Figure 8.2 Proper (a) vs. improper (b) screening position.

The cutter must be taught to delay his cut until the screen is set. He must let the screen take place and then read the defense. If he moves too soon, the screen will be ineffective in helping him get open because the defense will be able to get around it. So emphasize to your players that they must be patient as cutters.

Players oftentimes want to play too fast. They will try to get open immediately and won't wait for the defense to react to the fakes and v-cuts. The cutter should take his defender away from the screen with a v-cut, and then rub him off in the screen by going shoulder-to-shoulder with the screener so the defender cannot get through (see Figure 8.3).

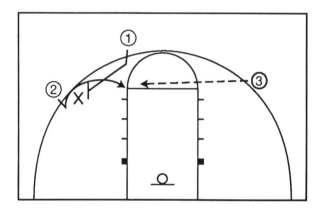

Figure 8.3 Proper use of screen.

If the defender anticipates the screen and tries to get over it, the cutter must read this and respond. Rather than coming back toward the perimeter on the v-cut, the player should head toward the hoop for the back-door pass (see Figure 8.4).

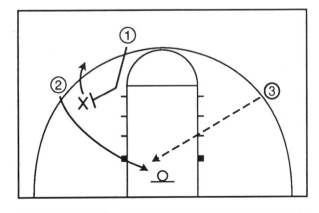

Figure 8.4 Reading defense: back cut.

If the defender tries to get over a down-screen, the cutter again should be able to read and react quickly. After the v-cut, the player might fade to the corner and receive a pass for the jumper (as shown in Figure 8.5).

One of the nice things about screens is that they can be effective even if they are not used properly. The offensive players force the defenders to make a choice. The important thing is that your offensive players are making the initial move, forcing the defense to respond, then reading that response and reacting to it with a countermove.

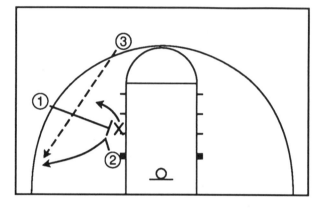

Figure 8.5 Reading defense: fade cut.

Screeners as Receivers

When the cutter comes off the screen, the screener should then roll open toward the ball to be a receiver. For example, let's say that the 4-player upscreens for 5. (An up-screen takes place when the screener comes "up" from the baseline to pick a defender. The cutter then gets open by coming off the pick toward the baseline.) The 5-player then posts up on the low block on the ball side, and 4 will be open for the jumper if he rolls back to the ball (see Figure 8.6). The defense is oftentimes more concerned with stopping the low post player, and, as a result, the screener in the high post (4) will be open for the shot.

You can even fake a pick to get a player open if you have used that player to set a screen earlier. On the perimeter, I call this a "change of pace." In Figure 8.7, 1 has passed to 2 and, because he has screened for 3 so often, his defender anticipates the

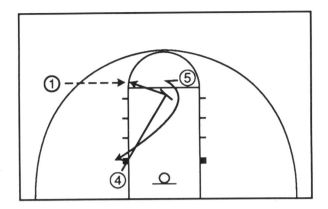

Figure 8.6   Upscreen: screener coming back to ball.

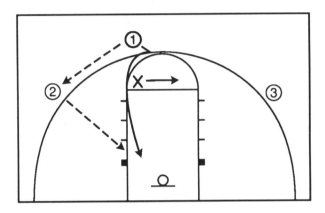

Figure 8.7   Change of pace: basket cut.

cuts between 2 and the helpless defender toward the basket for the pass and the layup.

This maneuver also works in the post area. We call it "duck." For example, in Figure 8.8, 4 has cross-screened for 5 so often that his defensive player anticipates it will happen again and moves over toward the screen. Player 4 begins the cross-screen to fool the defense, reads how the defense reacts, and then flashes back to the ball with his defensive player trailing in the lane.

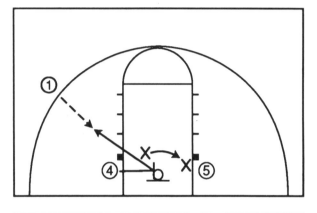

Figure 8.8   Duck.

screen and starts that way immediately after the pass to 2. Player 1 can read this and runs the change of pace. After he passes to 2, he can move toward 3's defender to set the screen; but instead of continuing, he v-cuts when he sees that the defender is anticipating the screen. He then

The same move would be effective even if 4 went all the way across and set the screen. He could then flash back to the ball before 5 was able to use the screen. This duck move works well against teams that switch in the post, because the player defending 4 will be looking to pick up 5. If 4 flashes back quickly to the ball, the player defending 5 will have no chance to switch and keep up.

Summary

The proper execution of basketball skills is essential for offensive success. Emphasize these fundamentals at all levels of your program:

- A team that handles (dribbles and passes) and shoots the ball well will obviously have a greater chance of being successful. Use drills to teach and improve.
- Individual skills can be broken down into two categories: playing with the ball and playing without the ball.
- Playing with the ball includes moves from a stationary position, and moves while dribbling, passing, shooting, and ballhandling.
- Playing without the ball includes screening and cutting to get open.

- Moves from a stationary position include the strong-side drive, crossover step, and jab step.
- Moves while dribbling ("moves on the move") include the stop-and-go, crossover dribble, reverse dribble, and fake reverse.
- The proper positioning and stance will insure an effective screen.
- Teach players using the screen to employ v-cuts, backdoor cuts, and perimeter cuts to get open.

Chapter 9

Developing a Running Game

The fast break is our first option in any offense at any time during the game. My teams have had great success running the primary break, which is created from steals, rebounds, blocked shots, made field goals, or made free throws.

Advantages of the Fast Break

I've emphasized the running style of play for three reasons:

- The break is the best way to create easy scoring opportunities and to control the tempo of the game.

- The break is the first and often most effective way of beating full or half-court pressure defenses.
- The break works well against a zone defense if your players push the ball up the floor and get a scoring opportunity before the zone has time to set up.

Fast Break Rules

Early in the season, convince players that they'll need to abide by two rules to make your break work.
The more you give it up, the more you get it back.

Emphasize to your players that the pass that leads directly to the score is no more important than the pass that sets up the pass that leads to the score. Players too often focus on making the assist pass that leads directly to the basket, often forcing the ball to teammates who are not open, which leads to turnovers and missed scoring opportunities.

Hit the open man.

If a teammate is ahead on the break, pass it to him. If he is closer to the basket and open, pass it to him. But as you emphasize the importance of passing, make sure your players know what a good pass is. They shouldn't try to overpass or pass to a player in trouble.

Fast Breaking After the Opponent Scores

Because the fast break is our primary offense, we run it as often as possible, including after an opponent scores. My rationale for doing this is simple. Even if our defense holds the opposing team to 40% shooting from the field, that, combined with made free throws, can mean 20 to 35 chances per game to fast break off of a made shot.

Obviously, the first thing your team will have to do after an opponent's score is to inbound the ball. Your first decision, then, involves selecting a player who will handle that chore. On made field goals, I have our 5-player (center) take the ball out for two reasons: (a) I learned from John Wooden that it is best to have a taller player inbound the ball because of his increased court vision, and (b) the center is often closest to the ball after it comes through the net, and he can get to it and inbound it quicker than most other players.

With the center inbounding, this is how we run our "Bingo" package after an opponent's score. Our 1-player (point guard) works to get open on the ball side as close to the inbounds man as necessary to provide a passing option, and the 4-player (power forward) posts up at the nearest foul line in case we need him to help relieve any full-court pressure. To get open, the 4-player heads to midcourt, then makes a hard v-cut to come back to the ball (see Figure 9.1).

Dos and Don'ts for the Fast Break

As with any offense, execution is the key to a successful fast break. Here are the most important points you must teach your players to Do and Don't when running the break:

DO . . .
- look up and see the whole floor.
- pass ahead to the open player (until someone has a good scoring opportunity).
- sprint the floor. (Run! Run! Run!)
- play under control.
- let the play make itself.
- read the numbers; go where you have an advantage.
- make the defense play you.
- get wide to fill the lanes.
- make the easy play.
- when bringing the ball down in the middle, stop at the foul line to make a play.
- use the chest pass on the break; the bounce pass is too hard to handle.
- if the back player (last trailer), delay at half court to cover the break defensively.
- be a good receiver.
- communicate!

DON'T . . .
- have your mind made up about what you want to do.
- overpass.
- jump to pass.
- pass to a player in trouble.
- pass a player into trouble.
- take giant steps. (Settle for the open 12-footer instead of a contested 8-footer.)

While this is happening, players 2 and 3 sprint the outside lanes closest to where they were when the opponent's basket was

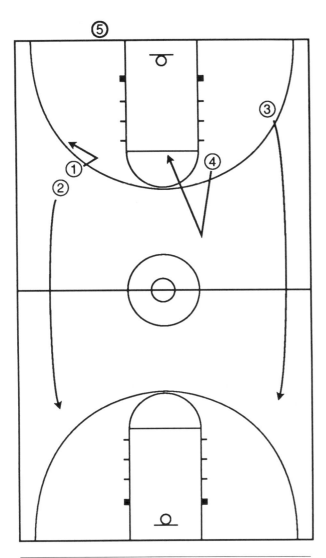

Figure 9.1   Bingo.

scored. If 2 and 3 find themselves on the same side of the floor when the ball goes through the hoop, whoever sprints to the closest lane first remains there while the other player crosses over to fill the opposite lane. After they take care of their rebounding duties I have players 2 and 3 sprint down the court immediately and at every opportunity, especially after made goals. This helps stretch the defense and makes it more difficult for them to set up quick full-court pressure.

Inbounding the ball, the 5-player first looks deep for the two players (3 and 2) sprinting up the court, and next for a short pass to 4 or 1. If, while reading the defense, 5 sees an advantage exists deep, then that is where the pass should go. If he does not

see an advantage, he should dump it off short. Remind your inbounder to stay out of the foul lane area behind the baseline so that he does not throw the ball against the back of the backboard when passing to a deep receiver. (I call this clearing the backboard.)

If 1 receives the ball far enough upcourt, he can push the ball up and create a 3-on-2 or 2-on-1 break. If the ball is thrown in to 4, 1 runs a diagonal cut down the court looking for the ball to try to create the quick 3-on-2 (see Figure 9.2). If the 3-on-2 situation is not available, 1 pushes the ball up floor and passes ahead to 2 or 3, if either one has gotten open. He need not pass ahead if neither 2 nor 3 will have an advantage over the defense after catching the ball.

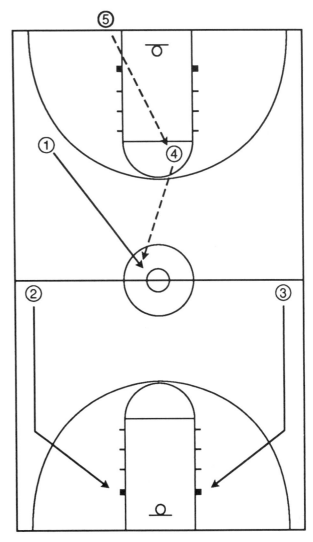

Figure 9.2   Bingo: guard in front.

Primary Fast Break

When executed properly, the primary fast break should create positive offensive situations that yield one of the following results:

- 1-on-1: layup or foul
- 2-on-1: layup or foul (two passes only)
- 3-on-2: layup or short jumper
- 4-on-2 or 5-on-2: layup or short jumper

When the defense has 3 or more players back to defend, players should go to the secondary break (see page 86).

1-on-1 Situation

This situation should always produce a high-percentage shot, whether it be a layup or a short jumper. When they are on a 1-on-1 breakaway, I encourage my players to attempt a shot for two reasons: (a) chances are it will be a good shot, and (b) it's human nature that offensive players generally change ends quicker than defensive players, which can result in a rebounding edge as offensive teammates are hustling down the floor in anticipation of a miss.

The best way to get a shot out of the 1-on-1 situation is to have the offensive player read the defender. If the offensive player feels he can beat the defender on the dribble, he should take it all the way to the basket and look for a driving layup.

If the defender does a good job against the dribble, then the offensive player should pull up for the short jump shot. (Certain time and score conditions may prompt you to tell your players to take only the layup if it's available. If it's not, you may want to have them pull back out and set up the half-court offense.)

2-on-1 Situation

One of the fundamentals you should teach your players about the fast break is that they *must get a shot off* when they have a numbers advantage. Ideally, the shot will be relatively uncontested and taken from close range. I tell my players that if they are in doubt about what to do in a 2-on-1 or 3-on-2 situation, shoot the ball (given the time and score situation). When a shot is taken we can either score, rebound the shot

if it misses, or at least prevent the defense from fast breaking as a result of our turnover. We must use a numbers advantage as quickly as possible because the remaining defenders are eventually going to get involved in the play.

In a 2-on-1 situation, the offensive players must fill the outside lanes and spread out wide enough to prevent the defender from playing them both at the same time. As the offensive players enter the scoring area (which I consider to be about one step outside the 3-point arc), one of them should take control of the ball. It is now the ballhandler's job to

1. make the defensive player guard either him or his teammate,
2. read the defensive player's choice, and
3. create an easy shot opportunity.

The ballhandler should always dribble with the inside hand. For example, a player on the right side of the court should dribble with the left hand. By using the inside hand, the ballhandler will not have to bring the ball across his body or the defender's body to make a pass. As a result, he can keep the ball away from the defense and also make the quick pass to his teammate.

To get the defense to commit, the ballhandler must look at the basket and be a scoring threat. If he is not a scoring threat, the defender can anticipate the pass and guard both players successfully.

Most importantly though, the ballhandler must stay under control and read the defense. More primary breaks are destroyed because of mental errors than physical errors. Too often, a player will decide what play he is going to make before reading the defense. Acting too soon, the ballhandler may jump to pass, have nothing, and be forced into a walk; or may charge or rush a shot; or may try to make a big play that looks good to the crowd but does not get the job done.

In a 2-on-1 break, the ballhandler should keep possession of the ball until the defender has decided to either guard the ballhandler or drop off and guard the other player. Once the defender commits, the offensive player should respond appropriately with either a dump pass to his teammate for a layup or a strong drive to the basket. If the ballhandler keeps these principles in mind, your team should get a good shot in every 2-on-1 situation.

3-on-2 Situation

Many of the same principles apply in the 3-on-2 break. Teach your players to maintain proper court spacing. If they spread the court and pass the ball effectively, the defense will not be able to adjust and guard all three players.

In the 3-on-2 situation, the middle player is the key, because he is the one who should have the ball when the offensive players enter the scoring area. The middle player should never penetrate farther than the foul line, unless the defense opens up and gives him the lane. Too much penetration by the middle player typically results in 3-second calls, charging fouls, and missed opportunities.

If the up player in the defense comes out too far to contest the break, the middle player should pass to one of the wings and create a 2-on-1 situation against the back player on defense (see Figure 9.3).

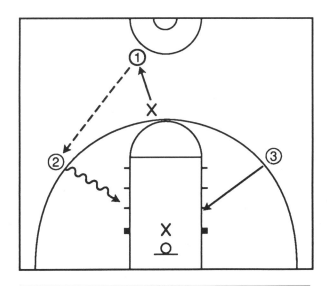

Figure 9.3   3-on-2: pass ahead.

If the defense stays back in a 3-on-2 break, the middle player should pass to the open wing, then step toward his pass. If 1 hits 2 on the wing, 3 must decide whether to cut behind the defense toward the basket or look to get open for the short jumper off the pass from 2. The diagonal pass from 2

to 3 is not automatic, and both the passer and the cutter should read the defense to see if it is available. The defense may have adjusted well, with the bottom player covering the first pass and the top player sinking into the hole to take away the pass from 2 to 3 (see Figure 9.4).

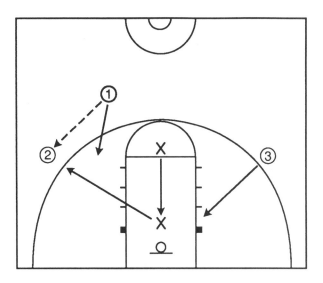

Figure 9.4   3-on-2: passer follows pass.

If the defense responds in this manner, the middle player will be open at the corner of the foul line for the jumper. This is an acceptable shot for two reasons. First, 1 is wide open at a reasonable shooting distance. Second, the offense has a distinct rebounding advantage. So even if the shot is missed, the offensive team should be able to get a second or even a third shot.

If 2 returns a pass to the middle player, he now has the option of attacking the back defender for a quick 2-on-1 with the 3 player. If the back defender commits to 1, then the ballhandler should dump a pass to 3 for a layup (see Figure 9.5).

4-on-2/5-on-2 Situations

This is a situation that teams rarely find themselves in. It is more common for the fourth and fifth players to become involved in the secondary break (described next). And in fact, players 4 and 5 behave exactly as they would in the secondary break.

The first three players down the floor operate as they would in a 3-on-2 situation. The fourth player down the court slices

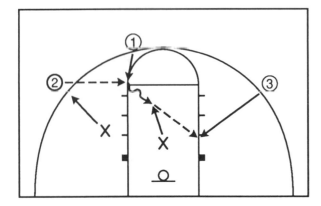

Figure 9.5 3-on-2: reversal.

through the lane to be a potential receiver or rebounder. The fifth player involved should hold up near midcourt to cover a possible break by the opposition in the event of a quick turnover.

These fast break scenarios are such an important part of the game that I recommend you try to spend 20 to 25 minutes each practice on fast break drills (see pages 86-93). It is through repetition that players will learn the various options available to them off the break.

The Secondary Break

If the primary break does not pan out, the secondary break begins. This will happen when the offense fails to execute the initial break options properly, or when the defense does a good job of getting enough players back in time to stop the first opportunity. The secondary break is triggered when either 2 or 3 takes the ball to the baseline after receiving the pass from 1 (who has followed the pass).

The 4-player should enter the scoring area as a trailer on the opposite side of the floor from 1. So, as the ball goes to the baseline, 4 makes a diagonal cut to the ball-side block for a feed from the wing (see Figure 9.6).

The 5-player delays in the backcourt to cover any quick break by the opponent that may result from a turnover or missed shot. He then fills the spot 4 vacates when 4 makes the diagonal cut.

Other options that can develop out of the secondary break include hitting 5 at the foul line for a jumper, reversing the ball to

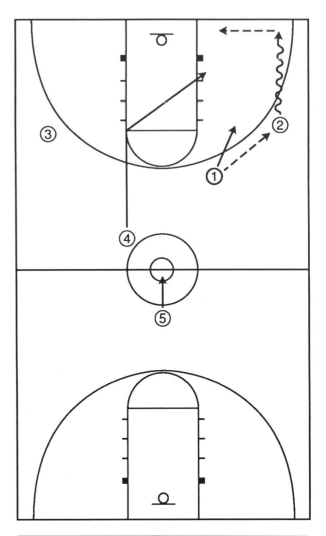

Figure 9.6 Secondary break: primary option.

3 as 5 slides down the lane to the low post, and 4 screening across the lane to help 5 get open.

Fast Break Drills

Fast break drills should improve your players' conditioning and reinforce proper fundamentals. After a season of performing these drills, your players should learn the good habits of sprinting the floor, looking up at all times, passing ahead, clearing the basket after scores, inbounding the ball quickly, being good receivers, and communicating on the break.

Fullcourt Layups

Have one of your players line up at half court with a ball, and place the remaining players along the right sideline. Instruct 1 to dribble to the foul line as if he is running the middle position on the fast break. When he reaches the foul line, he should jump stop and pass to 2, who has filled the right lane for the layup.

When 2 gets his own rebound (he only gets one shot), he must inbound the ball as after a made field goal. Player 1, who has moved across the court to become the outlet receiver, should then sprint the outside lane up the court. Player 2 will hit 1 with a baseball pass for the layup (see Figure 9.7).

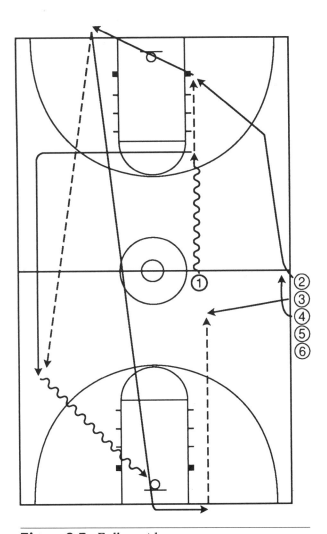

Figure 9.7 Fullcourt layups.

After making the pass, 2 should hustle down the court so that the ball never hits the floor. If 1 makes the layup, 2 takes the ball out of bounds, clears the backboard, and hits the new player (3) stepping out of line at midcourt. But if 1 misses the shot, 2 should rebound the miss, pivot, and outlet

the ball to the next player (3) stepping out of line. The process then starts over again with 3 and 4 assuming the roles of 1 and 2. The drill can be run on either the right or left side.

Three Lines Straight

Have your players get in three lines evenly spaced along the baseline. Every player in the middle line must have a ball. The first player in each line should run straight down the floor. These three players should stay in their lanes, passing the ball to each other as they move down court.

As they approach the scoring area, the middle player (1) should take control of the ball, dribble to one of the corners of the foul line, and hit 2 or 3 for a layup. As 2 and 3 approach the scoring area and reach the foul line extended, they should cut at about a 45-degree angle to the basket to receive the pass. As 1 makes the pass to the wing, he should step toward the pass, as on any fast break situation (see Figure 9.8).

After the made basket, the players must communicate and decide what lanes to fill on the return trip down the court. As they score their second layup, the next group of three players starts down the floor.

Three-Player Weave

This drill sets up the same as "Three Lines Straight," with the players lined up in three lines along the baseline and the player in the middle holding the ball. The difference in this drill is that each player runs behind the teammate that he passes to. In doing this, they will weave their way down the court. As the ball enters the scoring area, the player in the middle (at that point) takes control of the ball, jump stops at the foul line, and makes a scoring pass to one of the wide men sprinting toward the basket.

The players should sprint the floor, always looking to pass ahead. At the same time, they should stay wide and not crowd each other. It is very important that players *never* pass behind them to keep the drill going. If one player gets ahead of the others, he should drive to the basket for the layup. After the basket is made, the players communicate to each other about what lane they will fill, then return in the same fashion to the other basket.

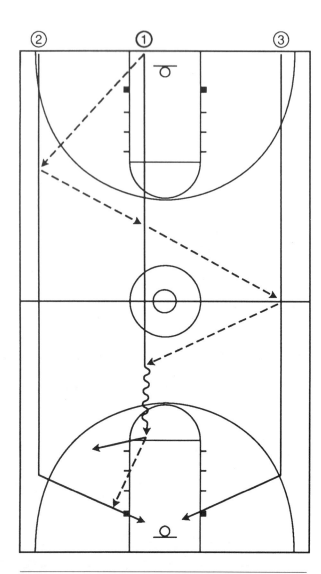

Figure 9.8   Three lines straight.

Five-Player Weave

This is a variation of the "Three-Player Weave" that gets more of your players involved. Put your players in five lines along the baseline. The player in the middle lane passes the ball to his closest teammate and then cuts behind two players. This process continues to the basket for a layup, followed by reorganization and sprinting-weaving-passing for a layup at the opposite end of the court.

Two-Players Full Court

Following is a series of fullcourt, two-player drills. Each of them has the same general organization, and will develop various fast break skills. They can be done simultaneously on opposite sides of the floor.

Have one of the two players positioned as a rebounder and the other as an outlet receiver. The rebounder throws the ball off the backboard, gets his own rebound, pivots, and throws the outlet pass to his partner, who is getting open on the ball-side wing. The rebounder must protect the ball while pivoting, keeping in mind where the defense might be playing.

The outlet receiver catches the ball and takes it to the middle of the floor. The rebounder fills the outside lane, staying wide and keeping good spacing between himself and the middle player.

Layup

The middle player takes the ball hard to the foul line with a high-speed dribble and jump stops. The sprinter, once in the scoring area, makes a 45-degree angle cut to the basket to receive the pass and score the layup (see Figure 9.9). The two players then reverse roles and return to the opposite end of the floor.

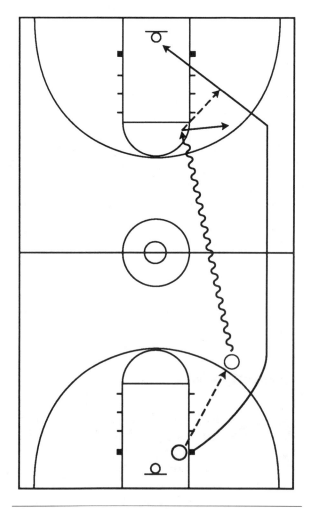

Figure 9.9   Two players full court: layup.

Jump Shot

In this drill, the middle player hits the sprint player for a short jumper from the wing off the fast break. Emphasize to your players how important it is for the shooter to be under control when preparing to shoot. The shooter should get his feet squared up to the basket and directly underneath the shoulders, and he should take short, quick steps to catch the ball in a balanced position for his shot. After the shot, the players reverse roles and return to the opposite end.

Another variation of this is to have the outlet men dribble to the middle of the floor and shoot a jumper from the foul line. In this drill, it is important for the sprint player to enter the scoring area under control, ready for the rebound. If the player sprints out of control, he runs the risk of burying himself under the basket and of being out of rebounding position. The shooter must also enter the scoring area under control with head up, good balance, and proper footwork when he shoots the ball.

V-Cut for Jumper

The outlet player receives the pass from the rebounder and pushes the ball down court to the foul line. The middle player hits the sprint player on the wing as he enters the scoring area (see Figure 9.10). The sprint player then squares up to the basket and fakes the shot. While this is happening, the middle player makes a v-cut away from the ball and comes back toward the ball for the short jumper. When coming back to the ball, the player should have his hands up and his inside foot planted so that he can get the shot off as quickly as possible. The two players then reverse roles and return to the other end.

Fade

Players must use their imagination for this drill to be truly effective. As the sprint player approaches the scoring area, he makes a hard cut to the basket to prepare for the pass from his partner. Now, however, the sprint player must imagine that the defender is back and has recovered to prevent the pass. The wing player then reads the defense and, instead of cutting through the lane, makes a quick v-cut and fades to the corner for the jumper off the pass from the middle player.

Chase

The rebounder hits the outlet receiver, who then uses a high-speed dribble to get to the

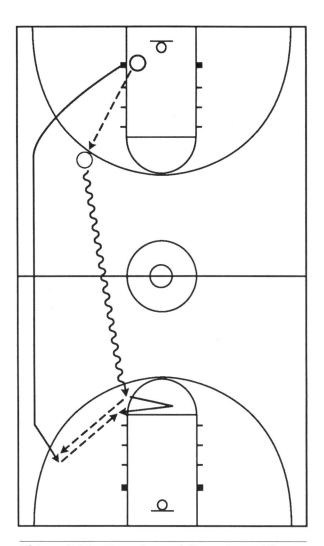

Figure 9.10 Two players full court: v-cut for jumper.

other end of the court for a layup. As the dribbler pushes the ball ahead, the rebounder attempts to chase him down from behind and either to tip the ball, block the shot (without fouling), or create enough noise to distract the player into missing the shot.

3-on-2/2-on-1

As shown in Figure 9.11a, this drill begins with three offensive players (1,2,3) at one basket and two defense players (X4,X5) at midcourt. The drill starts when one of the offensive players rebounds a missed shot and outlets the ball. The three offensive players then fill the right, left, and middle lanes. At this time the two defensive players sprint back to defend their basket, communicating to each other as to who will stop the ball and who will take the hole to protect the basket.

The defender protecting the basket (X5) picks up the wing who receives the first pass. The ball defender (X4), who initially stopped the ball's penetration, drops to cover the basket. The back defender (X5), who went out to the wing on the first pass, must go out under control to contain the ball. The ball defender (X4), who had dropped to the hole, must split the other two offensive players. If the ball is returned to the middle player, then the defensive players recover their original positions.

When the offensive players score or a turnover occurs, the two defensive players become the offensive players and the drill enters the 2-on-1 phase. The middle player in the initial 3-on-2 situation (now X1) sprints to cover his basket defensively against the two new offensive players (4,5). The other two players (X2,X3) step out of bounds to become the defensive players in the next 3-on-2 situation (see Figure 9.11b).

If the middle player was the shooter in the 3-on-2, have your lowest numbered player on offense sprint to defend the basket. This allows the shooter to concentrate on the shot and not worry about being responsible for covering the break. Emphasize to the defensive player in the 2-on-1 situation that he must recover in time so as not to give up a layup.

On a score or turnover in the 2-on-1 situa-

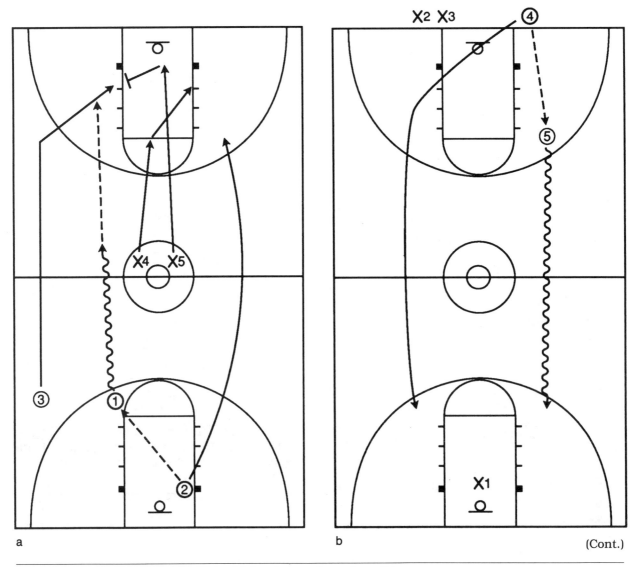

a   b   (Cont.)

Figure 9.11   3-on-2/2-on-1: initial set (a) and secondary phase (b).

tion, the defensive player (X1) switches back to offense (1), outlets to one of two new players (6,7) coming onto the court from the starting baseline, then fills the unoccupied lane for the 3-on-2 at the other end (see Figure 9.11c). To keep the drill going, you need to keep two offensive lines at one end and two defenders at the other.

Recognition

This drill starts with a five-player offensive team at one basket, ready to run the break. The coach stands along a sideline at the other end of the court with three or more players standing on the sideline who will play defense when called upon.

Have a manager shoot the ball to get the

drill started. As the offensive team starts up court, send a certain number of players from the sideline to play defense against them (see Figure 9.12). The offensive players are responsible for recognizing the defense and playing accordingly, scoring on either the primary or secondary break.

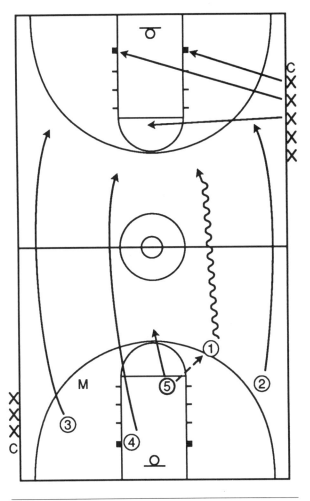

Figure 9.12 Recognition.

You can vary the number of defensive players and give them special instructions to see if the offense can read the defense and recognize what is available. For example, you might tell the defense to play tight on the perimeter players to see if the offensive team can find the open post player. Or you might tell the defense to sag into the lane to see if the offense can find the player for the open jumper. And in some instances, you might tell one player to jump the outlet pass to make sure the offense is not becoming casual with the ball when they begin the break.

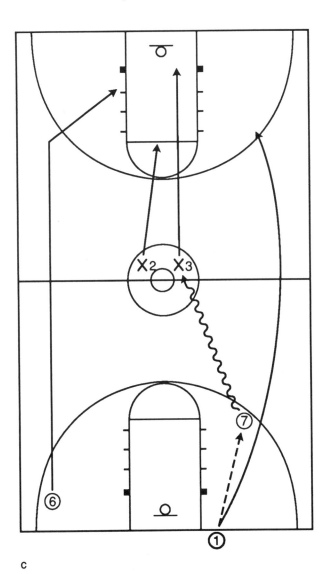

c

Figure 9.11 (continued)   3-on-2 after 2-on-1 (c).

Whether they score or commit a turnover, the same five players stay on offense and return in the same fashion to the other basket.

4-on-4 Transition

Start with four defensive players spread along the foul line, one at each corner of the foul line and one on each wing. Have four offensive players line up along the baseline opposite the four defenders. The drill begins when you throw the ball to one of the offensive players and call the name of a defensive player. The player whose name you call must run, touch the baseline, and then sprint to help the other three defensive players, who are retreating and defending the opposite basket (see Figure 9.13).

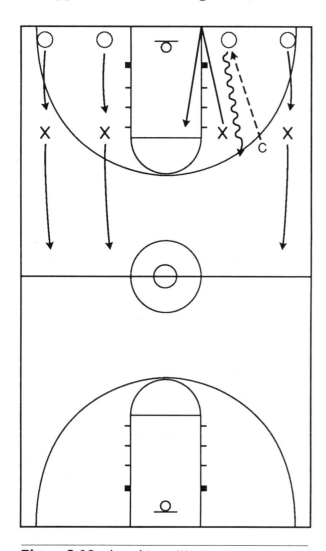

Figure 9.13   4-on-4 transition.

The offensive players run the primary and secondary break (if necessary) while the defensive players communicate and help each other until the fourth defensive player recovers. (The offense is typically forced into the secondary break because the defense should have enough players back by then to shut down the primary break.)

This drill can be done with any number of players, from 2-on-2 through 5-on-5. The drill ends when the offensive team scores, turns the ball over, or the defense rebounds a miss.

Change

I recommend this drill if your team is not changing from offense to defense quickly enough, or if they are not challenging the opponent's fast break. Start with 5-on-5 in the halfcourt area. On your whistle, the offensive team gives up possession of the ball and sprints back to defend its basket. The defensive players switch to offense and break for the score. Give the new offensive team an opportunity to score off the break or out of your halfcourt offense before resetting.

If your team still has difficulty changing ends, stop the drill and have them do some sprint work. As I've said, I don't use sprints as a form of punishment, but as conditioning. If the players are not changing ends well, it must be because they are not in shape and need to work on sprints. Sprint work will also help develop the mental toughness that allows players to continue to play their game even if fatigue sets in.

Hip Drill

Have your players form one line on the right wing. Each player attacks the basket using a high-speed dribble, as if he is about to score a layup off the break. As the player drives, you have two options. You can yell, "Hip!", which is a signal to the player to stop quickly and pull up for the jumper. Or you can say nothing and allow him to score on the layup.

The purpose of this drill is to simulate a defensive player stepping in front of the dribbler in an effort to take the charge. This drill should condition your players to play under control while preparing for—and even anticipating—the unexpected.

I also have our teams run this drill when our players are trying to create too much, instead of just getting good shots. This drill helps keep the players from playing too fast and helps them stay under control when driving to the basket.

Recovery

Position a coach or manager at each end of the court, and five offensive players at one end of the court. Those players will rebound a shot (taken by the coach/manager at that end) and run the break. Tell your players before the drill begins whether to score out of the primary break or out of the secondary break. On some occasions, you may even have them enter into your halfcourt offense.

After the coach/manager has taken the shot to begin the drill, your offensive team rebounds, runs the break designated by you, and scores. As the offensive team is scoring, the coach/manager at that end of the court throws a ball down the court to the other coach/manager (who took the initial shot). The players who just ran your break must then sprint back on defense, trying to beat the ball down the floor and prevent an easy layup.

This drill will emphasize to your team the importance of changing ends of the floor, and it will improve their quickness in doing so. Plus, your point player (whoever that is when the shot is taken) will learn to cover the break instead of watching the play.

Chapter 10

Developing a Halfcourt Offense

As I've stated, I prefer to run the fast break as the primary offense, and we try to score off the fast break as often as possible. However, some teams, on some occasions, force us to set up the halfcourt offense. When that happens, we must be prepared with a designed offense that will be effective against either a man-to-man or zone defense.

Man-to-Man Offense

At DeMatha, we run a motion offense designed to take advantage of our players' individual offensive fundamentals and their ability to work as a unit to get good shots. The movement in our offense is based on the fundamental basketball concepts of reading the defense, setting and using screens, cutting, and identifying and taking advantage of 2-on-2 or 3-on-3 situations as they present themselves.

The most effective way to teach players the offense is to break it down to perimeter and post movement. Focus on constant repetition of individual and position offensive fundamentals, eventually working your way up to 5-on-5 play. Building up to 5-on-5 helps the players learn the responsibilities of each position first, before integrating those responsibilities with those of the remaining positions. This building process

95

promotes greater understanding of the overall offense as well as of each player's role in that offense.

In a motion offense, the screener is just as important as the player coming off the screen; the cutter who does not receive the pass is as important as the cutter who does; the pass that leads to the assist is as important as the assist; and the passer is as important as the scorer because they are working together toward the same goal—a good shot.

This does not mean that every player has the same role. Rather, it means that when your team has the ball, each and every player on the floor can do something to help get a good shot, whether it's setting a screen, maintaining balance in the post, reversing the ball, or catching the ball and facing the basket. If a player cannot consistently hit the 15-foot jumper, then it is not in his or the team's best interest to work to get him a shot from that range. One of the strengths of the motion offense is that it allows you to adjust to your personnel and provides the flexibility for different players with different skills to contribute to the offense at appropriate times during a game.

Breakdown Drills

Before getting into the specifics of the man-to-man offense, I want to share with you the breakdown drills I use to teach my players the motion offense. Because the offense allows for individual moves and a great deal of two-player and three-player basketball, you should develop players' skills for these situations. Break the offense down so that players learn how to work as individuals and as part of a smaller unit, before learning how to work as a five-player team.

I use a number of post and perimeter drills to teach my players to read the defense, to learn motion principles (such as spacing and balance), and to anticipate situations of which they can take advantage.

I believe it is best to have the perimeter players become familiar with the proper movement in their 3-on-3 situations, and the post players with the proper movement in their 2-on-2 situations, before combining the two groups for a five-player offense.

When the five-player team is first brought together, I have them run drills with no de-

---

Motion Offense Fundamentals

- Keep good spacing, using the 3-point arc to help.
- Read the defense.
- Remember that screeners are often good receivers.
- Pass and move; don't stand still.
- Reverse the ball—take advantage of shifts in defense.
- Feed the post from below the foul line extended.
- Don't play fast—let the play make itself.
- Be greedy receivers—come to the ball.
- Use v-cuts to get open.
- Catch, turn, and face the basket—be a threat.
- Communicate on backdoor cuts and screens.
- Dribble with a purpose: to attack the basket, to get out of trouble, to improve a passing angle, or to advance the ball upcourt.
- Pass away from the defense.
- Move with a purpose.
- Be prepared to set screens and receive screens—read your teammates.
- Be patient as screener, cutter, and passer.
- When passing, wait for screens to be completed—let the possibilities develop.

---

fense, so the offensive players can learn the movement, balance, and spacing that is needed to successfully execute the offense. Then I have the players work against a defense that is playing half-speed, which helps build the offense's confidence and familiarizes the players with how the defense reacts to their movement. Finally, I let them go full-speed against a live defense, using the movements they have learned and repeated in the drills.

Two-Player Perimeter Drills: Shallow Cut Series

Getting the ball to the wing is a key to starting our motion offense. This can be done through the dribble or the pass. A shallow cut is one way to accomplish this using the dribble. In a shallow cut, a player dribbles from one offensive position to another, and the player in the position now occupied by the dribbler rotates to fill the spot vacated by the dribbler.

For example, a point guard may dribble from the point to the right wing; the right wing then rotates to fill the spot at the point. Sometimes a shallow cut is necessary to get the ball to the wing when a perimeter player is being overplayed, or to relieve pressure on the point guard's dribble by getting him to the wing where he has more options.

1. Player 1 dribbles over and shallows 2 off the right wing. Player 2 relocates to the top of the key, using the 3-point arc to help with balance and spacing. Player 1 shoots the jumper from the wing (see Figure 10.1).

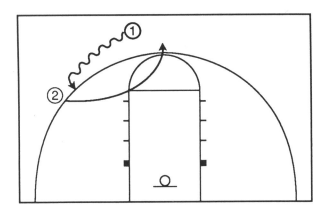

Figure 10.1   Shallow cut.

2. Player 1 again dribbles over to the right wing. The 2-player relocates to the top, and steps up for the return pass from 1 and the shot (see Figure 10.2).

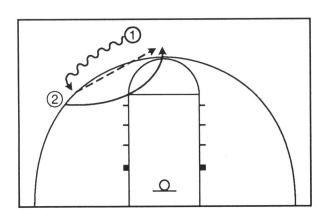

Figure 10.2   Shallow cut: return pass.

3. Player 1 dribbles over to the right wing; 2 relocates to the top for the pass from 1. Player 2 comes to meet the pass, catches it, faces, fakes the shot, then drives into the elbow and draws 1's defender. Player 1 steps up for the shot after receiving the pass from 2 (see Figure 10.3).

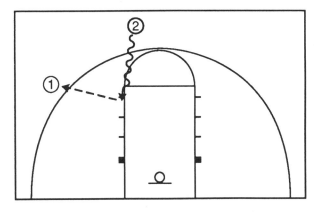

Figure 10.3   Shallow cut: drive and pitch.

4. Player 2 dribbles to the top, and 1 relocates to the wing, receives the return pass from 2, and takes the shot (see Figure 10.4).

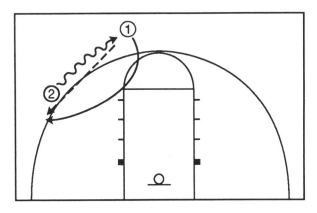

Figure 10.4   Shallow from wing.

5. Player 1 dribbles at 2, as if he is going to shallow him out. Player 2 begins to relocate, but instead v-cuts and fades to the corner for the pass from 1 and the jumper (see Figure 10.5).

6. Player 1 dribbles at 2 who, instead of shallowing to the top, continues through the lane to the opposite

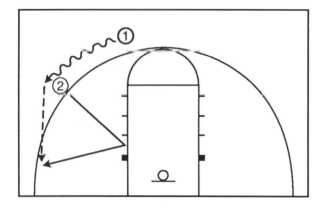

Figure 10.5   Fade.

wing. Player 1 skip passes (throws a cross-court pass) over the defense to 2, who steps up for the jumper (see Figure 10.6).

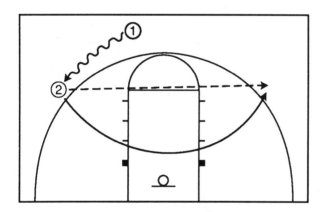

Figure 10.6   Circle and skip pass.

7. Player 1 passes to 2 and then v-cuts away. He can then either cut to the basket for a layup or replace himself at the top for the jumper (see Figure 10.7).

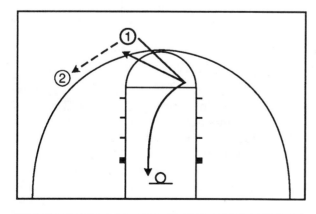

Figure 10.7   V-cut for shot.

8. Player 1 shallows 2 off the wing and then reverses the ball to 2 at the top (see Figure 10.8a). Player 2 dribbles toward the opposite wing while 1 fakes a cut to the basket (to put the defense on its heels) then v-cuts back to the ball for the jumper (see Figure 10.8b).

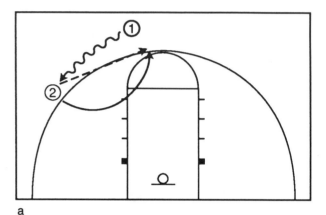

a

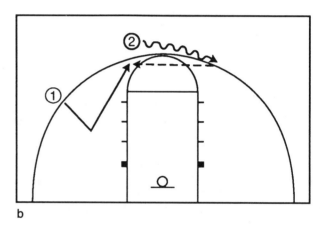

b

Figure 10.8   V-cut from wing.

9. Player 2 starts at the block, receives an imaginary downscreen, v-cuts, and gets open on the wing. Player 1 passes to 2 who squares and shoots (see Figure 10.9).
10. Player 1 shallows 2 off the wing and feeds the post with a bounce pass to the target hand presented by the coach. After the pass to the post, 1 and 2 relocate and look to step up for the jumper (see Figure 10.10). The coach passes to either one, with the other fading back to cover the break.

Three-Player Perimeter Drills

The next step in building to a 5-on-5 offense is to add your third perimeter player to the

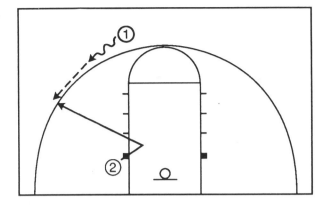

Figure 10.9   V-cut to wing.

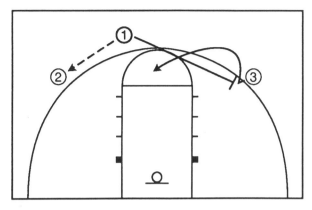

Figure 10.11   Screen away.

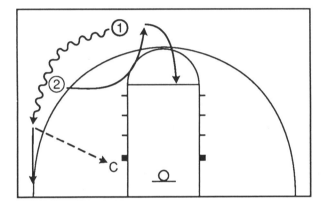

Figure 10.10   Relocation.

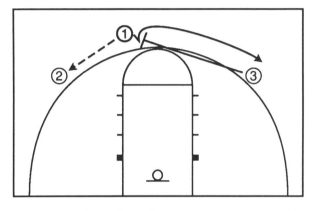

Figure 10.12   Backscreen.

perimeter drills. The addition of the third player adds the final dimension to the perimeter portion of the offense. Once these drills are successfully executed, the perimeter players should have a good understanding of their roles both individually and collectively in the offense.

1. Player 1 passes to 2 and then screens away for 3. Player 3 can make one of three cuts off the screen: (a) v-cut for the jumper from the top (as shown in Figure 10.11), (b) v-cut and go backdoor, or (c) v-cut and fade to the corner. Player 2 passes to 3 for the score.
2. Player 1 passes to 2 and then receives a backscreen from 3. Player 1 v-cuts and uses the screen to get open on the opposite wing (as shown in Figure 10.12). Player 2 has two options: (a) skip pass over the top to 1 for the jumper, or (b) pass to 3, who opens back up to the ball as a receiver.

3. Player 1 passes to 2 and receives the backscreen from 3. Player 1 begins to use the screen but cuts to the basket instead, as shown in Figure 10.13. Player 2 can make one of two plays: (a) hit 1 on the cut, or (b) hit 3, who opens up to the ball after the screen.

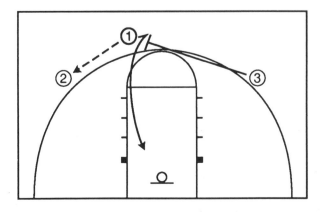

Figure 10.13   Basket cut.

4. Player 1 passes to 2 and receives a backscreen from 3. Player 2 reverses the ball to 3, now at the point, who passes to 1, now on the left wing. Player 3 then receives a backscreen from 2 and the skip pass from 1 for the shot on the right wing (see Figure 10.14). Use this drill if your players get in the habit of setting only one perimeter screen per possession.

5. Player 1 shallows 2 off the wing. Player 2 receives a backscreen from 3 as he relocates to the top, and uses the screen to get open on the opposite wing. Player 3 opens up back to the ball (see Figure 10.15). Player 1

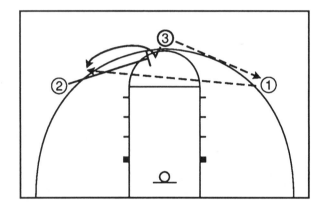

Figure 10.14 Reverse, backscreen, and skip.

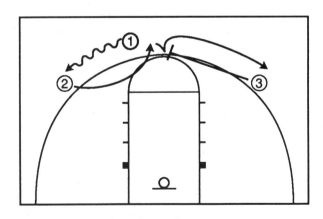

Figure 10.15 Shallow to backscreen.

can (a) skip pass to 2, or (b) hit 3 shaping up to the ball.

6. Player 1 passes to 2 and receives the backscreen from 3, using it to get open on the far wing. Player 3 opens up to the ball (see Figure 10.16a). Player 2 swings the ball to 3, who uses a shot fake to get by the de-

fender. Player 3 penetrates and passes back to 2, who is stepping up for the shot (see Figure 10.16b).

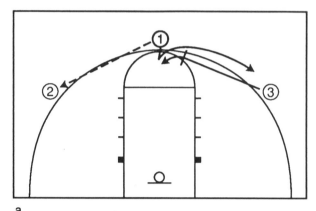

a

b

Figure 10.16 Backscreen, penetrate, and feed.

7. Player 1 shallows out 3 who then receives a backscreen from 2 (see Figure 10.17a). Player 2 opens up after setting the screen and receives the pass from 1. Player 2 starts toward 3, who makes a hard cut to the basket and then fades to the corner for the pass from 2 and the jumper (see Figure 10.17b).

Progressing From Two- and Three-Player Perimeter Drills

After working 2-on-0 and 3-on-0, you can introduce defensive players into the drills and play 2-on-2 and 3-on-3. At times, you may want to limit the number of dribbles the offensive players can take, or place a minimum on the number of passes that they must make before a shot is attempted (other than a layup). This will help the of-

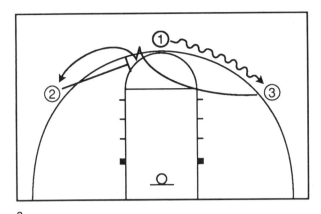

a

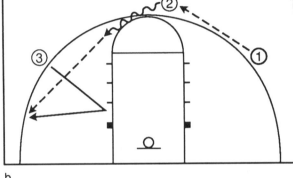

b

Figure 10.17   Drive and fade.

fense play under control and at a speed that will make the players read the defense and move with a purpose. Remember, your toughest task will be slowing them down so they do not miss scoring opportunities.

Post Player Development

Post play in the motion offense usually involves two players. On occasion, I will have the team go to four perimeter players with one post to help open up the middle and to create more room for the individuals to operate offensively.

Balance and spacing are as important in the post as they are on the perimeter. When we play with two post players, I like to maintain balance by having one player in the high post and one in the low post, with each on different sides of the lane. This gives the post players plenty of room and stretches the defense, which will help the two as they work together to get open.

Post Drills

These are the drills we use to get our two post players to work together as a unit. Note

that a coach (C) serves as the perimeter passer in each of these drills.

1. Player 4 starts in the high post and downscreens diagonally for 5, who v-cuts and flashes to the high post for the pass from the perimeter. Player 4 opens back up to the ball and tries to seal his defender for the feed from 5 (see Figure 10.18).

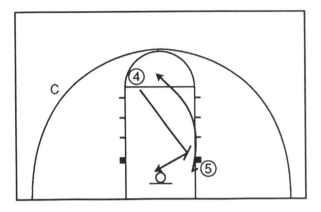

Figure 10.18   Downscreen: cut high.

2. Player 4 screens diagonally for 5, who v-cuts high and flashes into the low post. Player 4 opens up to the ball and slides high in order to maintain balance in the post. Player 4 may flash to catch the ball at the foul line for the jumper. The coach passes to either one for the shot (see Figure 10.19).

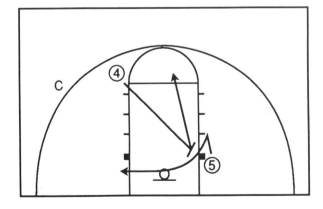

Figure 10.19   Downscreen: cut low.

3. Player 4 screens diagonally for 5, who v-cuts and flashes high. Player 4 runs "duck" because the defensive

post men switched, and he rolls back to the ball in the low post (see Figure 10.20). If the pass is not made into the post, they maintain balance and spacing, continuing to screen to get open.

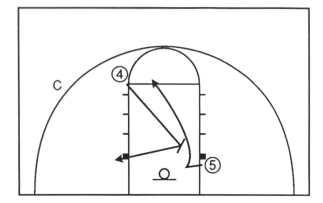

Figure 10.20   Screener back to ball.

4. Player 4 begins to screen for 5 but immediately flashes back to the ball because the defense is anticipating the screen. Player 5 flashes to the high post looking for the jumper (see Figure 10.21).

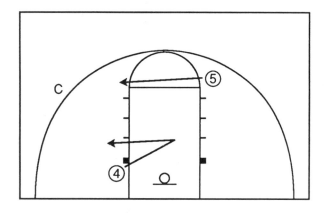

Figure 10.21   Fake screen.

5. Player 5 starts high and slides down to the low post. Player 4 maintains balance by starting low and flashing high (see Figure 10.22). The coach passes to either, or waits for a screen to take place.
6. Player 5 backscreens 4 in the high post (as in Figure 10.23a), then opens up to the pass from the perim-

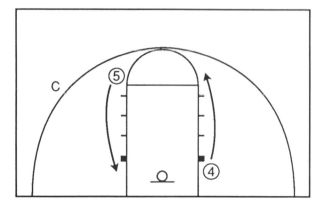

Figure 10.22   Balance the post.

eter for the foul line jumper. Player 4 hooks in and seals his defender for the feed from 5 (see Figure 10.23b).

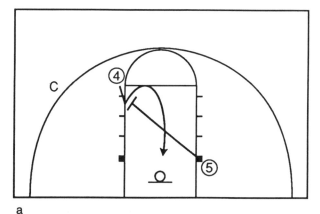

a

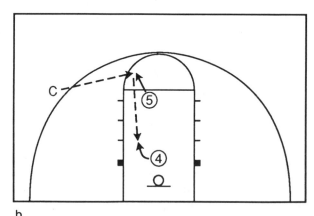

b

Figure 10.23   Upscreen (a) and feed (b).

Note: Each of these post drills can also be initiated with an upscreen as well as a downscreen. Remind the cutters and the screeners that they must go to either the high post or the low post to maintain balance. If they flash into the midpost area, it reduces the offensive options that the two post players have.

For example, in Figure 10.20, if 4 screens for 5, and 5 cuts to the midpost, 4 cannot come back to the ball because there is no room for him to occupy either the high or low post without getting in 5's way.

Progressing from Post Drills

Run the post options with only offensive players first, and then add two defensive players. Your next step after working the perimeter and post players separately is to have one unguarded perimeter player involved in the post drills, and one unguarded post player in the perimeter drills. This exposes both positions to what the other one is doing, which allows greater understanding of the roles in the offense and will help the players to function better when you combine all five players.

The final step before going live 5-on-5 is to run a five-player offense with no defense, concentrating on the basics emphasized in the breakdown drills and the principles listed earlier in the chapter. Tell the players to take their time as they adjust to playing with one another and get a feel for how to read the defense and their teammates' offensive movements. Patience and repetition are the keys to learning and executing any motion offense.

The "5 Game" Motion Offense

The 5 Game is our main motion offense, and it is primarily a way of providing some initial structure. This structure will help your players develop good habits such as spacing, balance, and timing. It also gives the players a basic set to return to if they begin to play without regard to the principles that you emphasize in the motion offense.

The standard 5 Game involves three perimeter and two post players, but many variations and options are available to players in this offense. What you should emphasize to your players is that each option and variation they employ must include the basic elements of a motion offense—cutting and screening.

5 Game in Motion

Start your motion offense in a 1-2-2 set, with wing players wide and high on the perimeter, and one post player occupying each block. The point player should pick a side and stay out of the middle of the floor so the defenders guarding the wing men cannot steal the entry pass.

Begin the offense by having your point player pass to one of the wings. After 1 passes, he can cut through the middle and look for the ball on the way to the basket, or he can screen away for 3, who will then replace 1 at the top.

When the ball gets to the wing, the post player on the ball side (4) screens away for the opposite player (5), as shown in Figure 10.24. Player 5 waits for the screen, makes a v-cut to get his defender moving in one direction, and uses the screen effectively to get open coming across the lane.

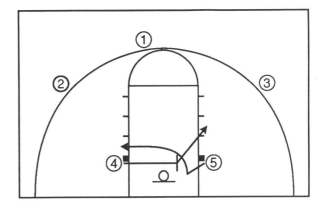

Figure 10.24   Cross-screen.

Do not allow 5 to simply flash across the lane when he sees the wing catch the ball. Not only will he probably be covered, but he will take 4 out of the play by preventing him from screening and then possibly rolling open to the ball as a receiver.

If the defense switches in the post, have your players run "duck." The screener comes back to the ball while keeping the new defender on his back. Player 5 stays on the weak side. Again, this is effective only if 4 and 5 are working together.

If the wing player passes to the post player, the wing should either exchange with the player at the top of the key or relocate to an open spot on the perimeter as his defensive player digs in the post. By reading his defender's movement in the post, he can get open for the jumper. Teach him to key on the direction his defender's back is facing—that's the direction he wants to go to get the jumper.

For example, if his defender's back is to the baseline, your wing player (2) should move to the baseline for his open jumper. This makes it difficult for the defender to recover and defend the jump shot, because he must swing open to the ball instead of just taking an advance step to cover 2.

If the wing passes the ball back to the point, have him screen down for the post player (see Figure 10.25), or have the post player set a backscreen for the wing player. If the wing player (2) screens down for the post player, have 2 open back up to the ball after the screen. By reading where his defender is in relation to the screen and using the screen effectively, your post player (5) should be able to get open.

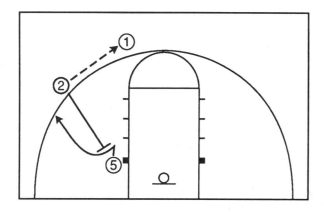

Figure 10.25   Downscreen from wing.

If the post player's (5) defender fights over 2's downscreen, have 5 fade to the corner and create space between him and the defender for the shot. If the defender plays behind the post player on the screen, have 5 peel around the screen for the feed from the top and the layup (see Figure 10.26). If the wing (2) does downscreen after he passes the ball to the top, and the ball is reversed, 2 becomes the post receiver on the ball side while the post player heads to the wing (see Figure 10.27).

It is this type of movement that makes the 5 Game motion offense so difficult to defend. It will allow you to take advantage of the particular skills your players have (e.g., posting up perimeter players or having post players on the perimeter), and it will put your players in positions to exploit

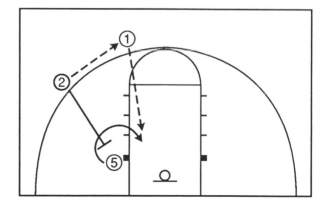

Figure 10.26   Peel cut.

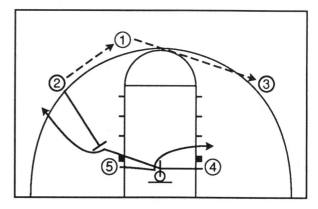

Figure 10.27   5 game movement.

the defense in game situations. The movement has guidelines, but it is unpredictable and allows enough freedom that the defense cannot expect the same pattern each time.

5 Game Guidelines

Have your players follow these basic principles when running the motion offense, but emphasize to them the necessity of reading the defense before each and every movement:

- *As the point player*, pass to one wing and exchange with the other by using the screen or the basket cut. Or, the point can use the dribble (shallow cut) to exchange with a wing.
- *As a wing player*, downscreen on any pass back to the point.
- *As a post player*, after a count of one, screen for the opposite post anytime a pass is made to the wing on your side.

Remind your players that being ready to receive a screen is just as important as being ready to screen. They owe it to their teammates to move effectively when one of them tries to help another get open.

"Specials" out of the 5 Game

While the basic movement in the 5 Game is triggered by players reading the defense, I do implement designed plays that are choreographed to give the defense different looks and to take advantage of adjustments the defense may make. These designed plays can add to your offense's effectiveness. I call these options "Specials" out of the 5 Game.

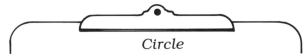

Circle

"Circle" is a play that takes advantage of teams whose defensive post players switch. Player 1 uses the dribble to enter the ball to the wing. As he does so, 4 flashes high to the elbow looking for the ball, and 3 circles through to screen for 5 (see Figure 10.28). If the defense is switching, an immediate mismatch is created between 5 and 3's defensive players. The same can be done on the other side with 2 screening for 4.

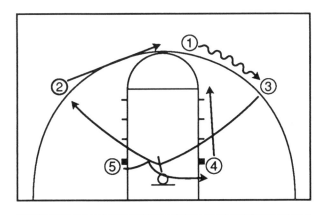

Figure 10.28 Circle.

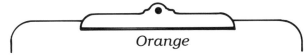

Orange

"Orange" is another special out of the 5 Game. Player 3 begins the play by screening for 5 and then shaping up to the ball. Player 5 becomes a perimeter player and

receives the pass from 1. If 3 cannot get the post feed from 5, he moves across the lane to the opposite block, as 4 moves up the lane slightly to make room for him (see Figure 10.29a). Meanwhile, 2 walks his defender down to a position where he (2) can use the double screen set by 3 and 4. As he comes off the double screen, 2 then looks for the pass from 5 (see Figure 10.29b).

If 5 does not pass to 2 coming off the double, he hits 1, who has made a v-cut and

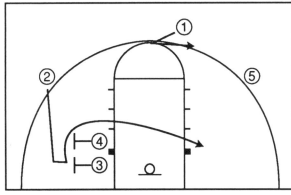

a

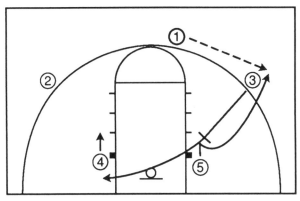

b

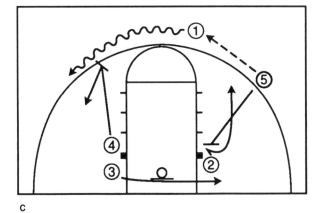

c

Figure 10.29 Orange.

returned to the point. Player 5 then sets a down screen for 2 at the block, helping him to get open for the shot. At the same time, 3 moves back across the lane and establishes position on the low side of 5 to allow 4 and 1 to work a two-player game on the right side if 2 is not open. Player 4 flashes up the lane and sets a screen at the top of the circle for 1, who looks for the drive or the quick jumper off the screen. After 1 uses the screen, 4 rolls in the direction of the ball, looking to seal his defender for the feed from 1 (see Figure 10.29c). If 1 shoots the ball, you have two players (3 and 5) rebounding from the weak side and 2 covering the break defensively.

Zone Offense

You can use various formations to attack a zone defense. The one you select must be effective against the alignment of the zone you are facing. You should attack an even-front (two players) zone with an odd front

(one player), and vice versa. This will allow your offensive perimeter players to get into the gaps of the defense where they can create offensive opportunities for themselves and their teammates.

The offensive sets (shown in Figures 10.30 a-d) will give players the freedom to move. And they will help your players stay organized and properly spread out to attack each of these types of zones.

Although the sets themselves are important to insure balance, spacing, and organization, even more important are the principles you teach your players to use when attacking any zone defense. As with the motion offense, you must teach your players several fundamental skills that pertain specifically to playing against zone defenses.

Not all of the zone defenses that you face will be exactly alike; however, the principles of playing a zone and playing against a zone are universal. So a fundamentally sound offense should work well against a zone defense.

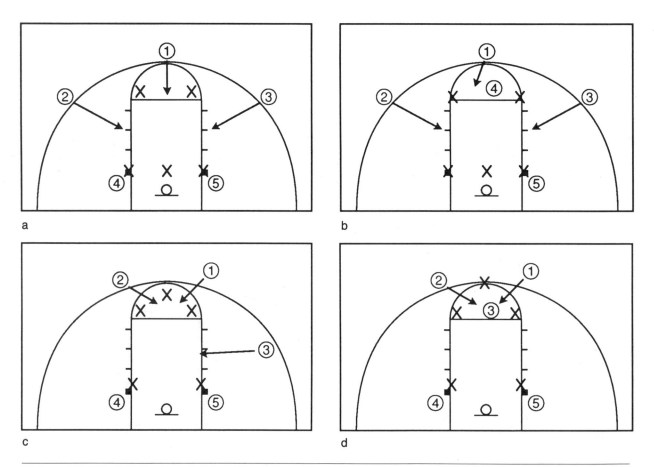

Figure 10.30   1-2-2 set (a), 1-3-1 set (b), 2-3 set (c), and 2-1-2 set (d).

Zone Offense Fundamentals

- Fast break; attack before they can set the defense.
- Attack the zone; don't play passively.
- Take good shots.
- Play with patience and poise. The zone wants you to shoot quickly.
- Gap and split the zone. Make two defenders play one offensive player.
- Keep good post timing and movement.
- Find open areas and step up for the jumper.
- Screen the defenders in the zone.
- Keep good rebounding position. Hit the offensive boards.
- Drive the zone. Use the dribble to freeze the defense, create 2-on-1 opportunities, or improve passing angles.
- Make the defense work by reversing the ball.
- Make someone in the zone play you (particularly perimeter players).
- Use the skip pass.
- Look to the basket. Be offensive minded.
- Use pass fakes and shot fakes to move the defense.
- Dribble away from an area, and then fill the area with another player (vacuum principle).
- Take the defender as far as you can, stretching the defense to create gaps and help with reversal.
- Communicate. Call a teammate's name if you want to screen.
- Use shallow cuts to move the ball and the zone.
- Play out of sets (see Figures 10.30a-d).
- Balance the floor.
- Keep good spacing. Perimeter players should use the 3-point arc.

Drift: The Zone Offense

I call our basic zone offense "Drift" because it's designed to get the players to drift into the open spaces and seams in the zone they are playing against. I like this offense against a zone for two reasons: (a) it gives us two post players, which helps us attack the zone from the inside; and (b) it assigns basic movements, but at the same time allows for a great deal of freedom for players

to apply basic zone offense principles (such as stepping into an opening).

Start Drift in a two-guard front, and have 3 always come to the ball-side wing. As 1 passes to 2, 3 moves through the lane behind the zone. Player 2 swings the ball to 3, then drifts to the open area on the wing opposite 3 (see Figure 10.31a). Player 4, who is in the low post on the ball side, stays for a 2-second count, then backs out after 3 has received the ball on the wing and looked into the post. Player 5 then slides down into the medium post, and the offense is now in a 1-2-2 set, shown in Figure 10.31b.

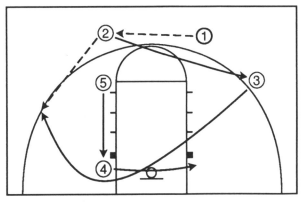

a

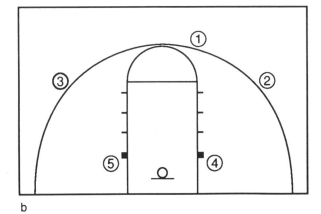

b

Figure 10.31 Drift.

When the ball is reversed (from 3 to 1 to 2), the post on the ball side (4) stays for the two count, then backs out to the other side. The opposite post (5) moves across the lane high toward the ball (see Figure 10.32) flashing into the gap from behind the defense, while keeping his feet active and looking for the pass from the wing.

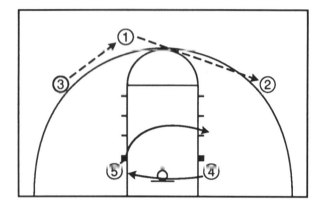

Figure 10.32   Drift movement off reversal.

Making the Zone Move

Sell your players on the fact that they must move the zone in order to get a good shot. One of the most effective ways to move the zone is by using the skip pass, the old cross-court pass that goes across the zone. To receive the skip pass, the perimeter players must (a) find a gap and not hide behind a defender or get buried along the baseline, and (b) stay behind the 3-point arc to create 3-point opportunities and to stretch the defense to open up the post players.

Another way to move the zone is using the dribble. After 1 catches the ball on the reversal from 3, he attacks the outside shoulder of the opposite guard in the zone and creates a shot for himself or for 2 (see Figure 10.33). If the bottom player in the zone comes out to play 2 on the wing, 5 steps up the lane for the feed from 1. Player 5 could also screen (using the same screening techniques as in a man-to-man offense) the bottom player in the zone to help 2 get open for the jumper.

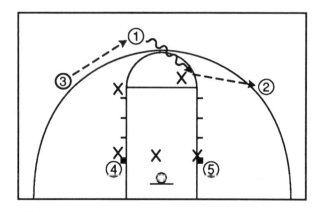

Figure 10.33   Dribble penetration.

From the original two-guard alignment 1 can pass to 3, while 4 and 5 x-cut, and 2 drifts to the wing opposite 3 as in Figure 10.34a. Player 5 then backs out, 4 slides into the low post, and you are back into the 1-2-2 drift set (see Figure 10.34b).

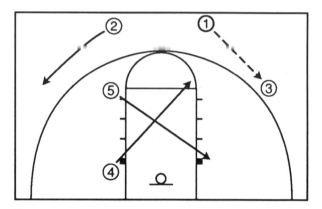

a

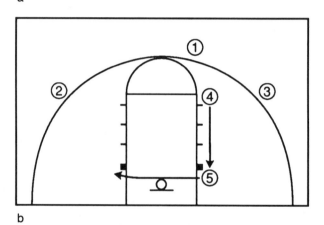

b

Figure 10.34   X-cut entry.

Your players can also reverse the post movement and have the low post come to the ball from behind the zone. The advantage of having your players flash to the ball from behind is that they can read and seal off the defender before the defender is even aware of their presence. Additionally, attacking from behind allows the post player to reverse pivot and gain an inside rebounding position if he is denied the cut and a shot is taken.

Remind the players flashing to the open post that they are passers as well as shooters. For example, with the defense drawn in to play the post, 5 can pitch the ball back out to a perimeter player stepping up for the jumper. Oftentimes, player 5's best option is to pass the ball to a weak-side perimeter player stepping up into a gap for the shot (see Figure 10.35).

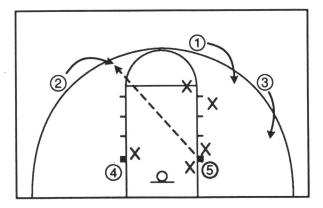

Figure 10.35 Skip pass.

Drift Offense Options

One set offense is usually not sufficient to crack a defense. This is why it is important to have options to run out of your basic offense. The primary use of these options is to give the defense a different look and force it to adjust. Options can also be used to disguise plays and thereby confuse the defense. For example, you can give the defense the same look as one play when you are actually executing another.

Shallow Cut

Player 1 dribbles to 2 on the wing, and 2 shallow cuts up to the top to replace 1. As he cuts, player 2 could also screen the top guard in the zone to give 1 more room on the wing. As the ball moves to the wing, 4 backs out, and 5 slides into the medium post (see Figure 10.36).

Baseline Stepout

Player 4 steps out to the medium baseline on the ball side. Player 5 then slides from the high post to the low post and looks for the ball. Player 3 finds the open area on the opposite wing and reads the high post defense to see if he (3) can flash into the open gap (see Figure 10.37).

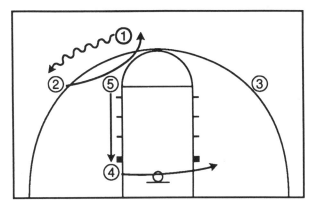

Figure 10.36 Drift: shallow entry.

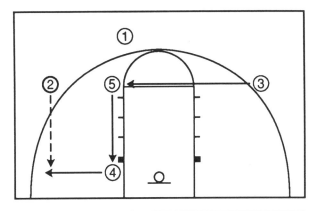

Figure 10.37 Drift: baseline stepout.

Release

Player 5 releases and steps off the high post to be a receiver on the perimeter for 2. He (5) can then look inside for 4 stepping in and sealing the low post defender; or he can look

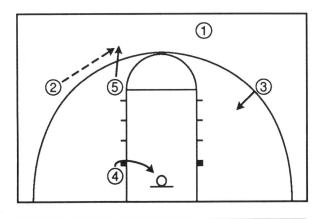

Figure 10.38 Drift: release.

to the weak side for 3, who should be finding the gap on the weak side (see Figure 10.38). If the pass goes to 3, 4 flashes low to the ball side from behind the defense, and 5 reenters the post. Player 4 then backs out of the post, and 5 flashes in to create the regular drift movement.

Circle

The perimeter movement in "Circle" is as effective against a zone as it is against a man-to-man defense. Player 1 dribbles at either wing player and circles him through to the opposite wing. The weak-side wing then replaces the point (see Figure 10.39). This has been very successful for us in getting shots for the right players.

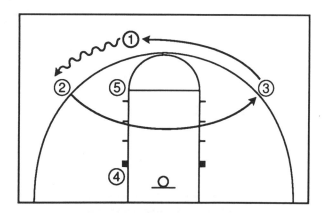

Figure 10.39   Drift: circle.

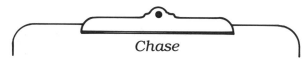

Chase

Player 1 dribbles at the wing player as if he is going to circle him through to the other side. When 2 gets behind the zone, he v-cuts back out to the corner, as shown in Figure 10.40. Player 1 ball fakes to 3 to convince the zone that 2 is moving through the lane.

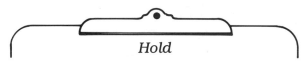

Hold

After 1 enters into the drift movement with a pass to 2, 2 passes back to 1 who is looking

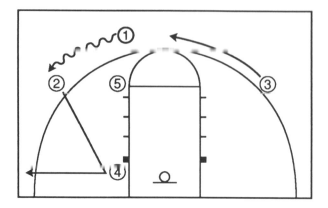

Figure 10.40   Drift: chase.

for the gap in the top of the zone. Player 2 moves through the lane underneath and behind the opposite low post to the far corner, while 4 sets a screen on the low defender to help 2 get open coming off the baseline. Player 1 passes to 3, who looks for 2 coming off the screen (see Figure 10.41). Timing is very important.

If 2 is not open, 3 can hit 4 stepping up the lane if the zone shifts and denies the pass. Player 3 should also look for 5 flashing to the middle for the short jumper.

If 3 cannot hit either receiver, he throws back to 1. Player 2 then moves back to the other side behind the zone; and everyone is back into the drift set.

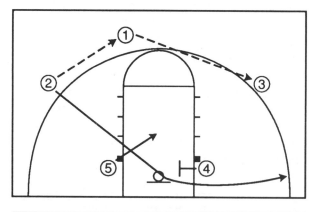

Figure 10.41   Drift: hold.

Double Screen

This option starts with 4 and 5 stacked on the right block, and 3 positioned on the left block. Player 1 dribbles right, and 2 shallow cuts to the top. Player 3 uses the double screen by 4 and 5 to get open in the right corner. As the ball goes to 3, 4 peels off 5 and looks for the pass (see Figure 10.42). After screening, 5 opens up to the ball and looks for the post feed.

If nothing is available, 3 reverses to 1 and runs the baseline, using 4 and 5 to help him get open on the opposite side.

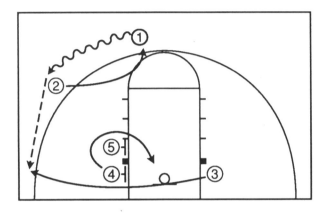

Figure 10.42   Drift: double-screen entry.

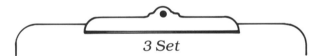

3 Set

Player 1 dribbles to the right wing as 2 breaks to fill the gap at the top vacated by 1. Player 4 can help 2 or 1 get open by screening the top defender in the zone. Player 5 sets a screen on the low defender to get 3 open on the perimeter and then opens up to the ball (see Figure 10.43).

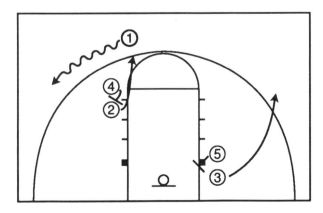

Figure 10.43   3 Set entry.

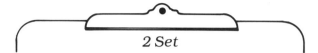

2 Set

Player 1 picks a side, allowing the perimeter player in the stack on the ball side to make the middle cut and become the top player in the zone offense. Players 4 and 5 look to screen the bottom players in the post to help free the perimeter players (see Figure 10.44). After screening, 4 and 5 should look to seal and step up the lane for the post feed.

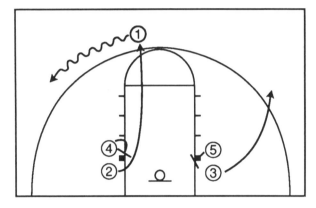

Figure 10.44   2 Set entry.

Note: The 3 and 2 Sets are particularly useful in attacking a zone defense because they force the defense to adjust to the set and thereby change the defensive alignment. If the defense does not adjust, some players will be left unguarded for easy scoring opportunities. Playing out of these sets also creates overload situations for your team and creates confusion for the zone. Finally, the 3 and 2 Sets allow your post players to attack the zone from behind, flashing into open gaps in the lane and screening the zone to help produce shots for your perimeter players.

Drift vs. Odd Man Front

Drift can be used to attack a 1-2-2 zone by making one adjustment to your perimeter players. Player 1 picks a side, pushing the wing toward the corner. The opposite wing (3) then "tilts" the offense to create a two-guard front. He stays behind 1 to create a good passing angle so that the defense can't steal the ball through the passing lane (see Figure 10.45). By moving the zone and overloading the wing, you have essentially changed the defense to a 2-2-1 zone.

Now have your players follow the fundamental zone principles to attack the defense. On the reversal, 3 dribbles hard to the corner, 1 follows, and 2 tilts to stay behind the ball. Post movement continues as in Drift, but you can have the opposite post flash to give you the overload.

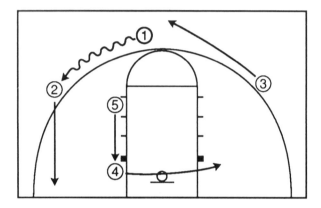

Figure 10.45   Drift tilt.

Zone Drills

I prefer to have my team use the same principles out of different sets rather than run a different offense for each zone we face. To do this, my players must know the zone principles I have outlined in the previous several pages. After you teach the principles of the zone offense, the best way to work on them is to have players apply them in zone situations. Again, I suggest breaking things down into post, perimeter, and team play.

Post Drill Station

The first area we break down is the proper movement of the post players against a zone. Proper post movement is crucial because a zone defense often clutters the post area. I work our post players against two basic zone sets.

1. *Two posts vs. back of a 2-3 or 2-1-2 zone*
   Starting from the positions illustrated in Figure 10.46, the offensive players work on screening for each other, flashing to open areas (prefera-

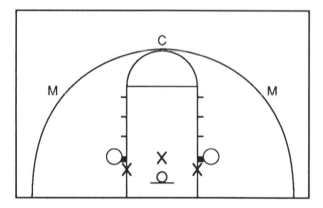

Figure 10.46   Post zone station: two on blocks.

bly in the lane), stepping out on the baseline and facing the basket, and sealing defenders. They should look to work as a two-player team.

2. *Three baseline players vs. back of a 3-2 or 1-2-2 zone*
   Set up along the baseline (see Figure 10.47), post players work on same principles as in previous drill.

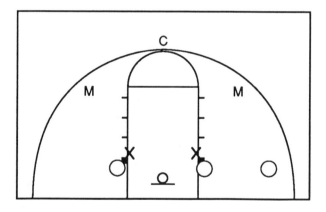

Figure 10.47   Post zone station: three on baseline.

Perimeter Drill Station

In their drills, perimeter players should focus on using the dribble to penetrate; splitting the gaps between defenders and looking for the short jump shot; trying to absorb two defenders, and then passing to a teammate in an open area; throwing the skip pass across the zone; and screening the perimeter defenders in the zone.

1. *Two perimeter players vs. top of a 3-2 or 1-2-2 zone*

Offensive players work on driving gaps, stepping up for the shot (off guard), tilting (overloading the zone), shot fakes, and pass fakes. Managers in corners simulate baseline pass (see Figure 10.48).

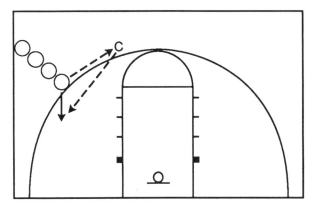

Figure 10.50 Perimeter zone station: return for shot.

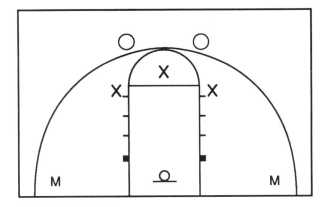

Figure 10.48 Perimeter zone station: two-guard front.

2. *Three perimeter players vs. top of a 2-3 or 2-1-2 zone*
From the positions indicated in Figure 10.49, offensive players work on skip passing, driving the gaps, and looking for the stepup jumpers.

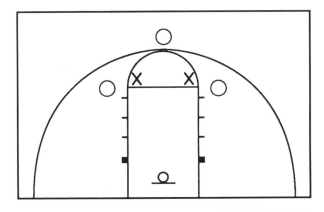

Figure 10.49 Perimeter zone station: one-guard front.

3. *Individual zone jump shot work*
Move players around to different spots on the court. The player starts with the ball, throws to a coach or teammate, and then steps up for the return pass for the shot (see Figure 10.50).

4. *Zone penetration and dish-off work*
Offensive player drives at the outside shoulder of the defender and passes to the wing for the shot, as shown in Figure 10.51.

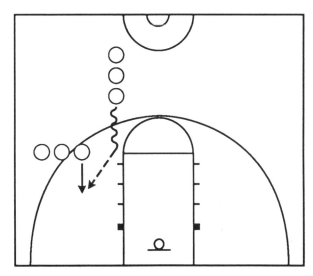

Figure 10.51 Perimeter zone station: drive and pitch.

5. *Perimeter screening work*
Wing player screens the guard in the zone, allowing for penetration and a shot by the point (see Figure 10.52).

6. *Proper footwork for jump shots*
Have the perimeter players shape up out of the 2 set and 3 set, practicing the correct footwork for getting their shots off. You can work both sides of the court at the same time, as shown in Figure 10.53.

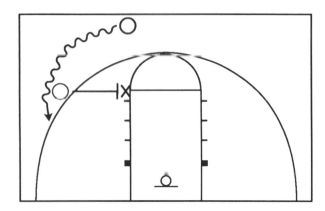

Figure 10.52   Perimeter zone station: screen and shoot.

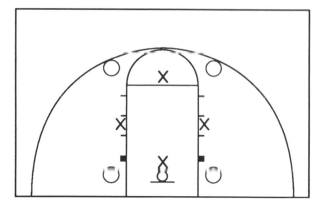

Figure 10.54   Box vs. Diamond.

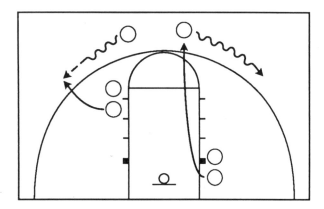

Figure 10.53   Perimeter zone station: 2 and 3 sets.

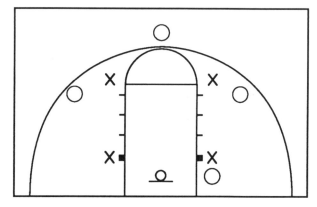

Figure 10.55   Diamond vs. Box.

Team Drill Station

Once players learn and execute the zone offense principles in post and perimeter drills, move on to team drills.

1. *Motion breakdown drills for both post and perimeter players*
   Work on shallow, circle, chase, and skip pass. (See pages 103-106 on 5 Game motion offense.)
2. *Box offense vs. Diamond defense—4-on-4*
   Work on all zone principles from the set illustrated in Figure 10.54.
3. *Diamond offense vs. Box defense—4-on-4*
   Emphasize getting into the seams and other zone principles from set shown in Figure 10.55.
4. *Four offensive players vs. 2-3 zone*
   Advantage is given to the defense so the offense is forced to work extra hard. Good ball and player movement is required.

Improving Offensive Teamwork

Whether you are running a man-to-man or zone offense, teamwork is the key to success. And much of the responsibility for developing offensive teamwork falls on the coach. We've got to sell our players on the importance of playing together. We've got to convince the players that the team will accomplish far more if no one is concerned with who gets the credit. To do this, we must sell the players on the fact that if the team does well, everybody goes uptown together. But if only a few individuals do well, the team goes nowhere.

For the Good of the Team

The world is full of teams that had great individual stars, but still were not great teams. Some of the greatest players to ever play basketball have never worn championship rings or been a part of a championship team at any level. For that reason, many excellent players have gone unnoticed.

If you think about it, the success of a team in a certain year will be remembered long after the amazing exploits of one individual. You always hear people talking about the great Yankee teams, the great Green Bay Packers teams, the great Boston Celtic teams, and we hope the great DeMatha teams. These teams had great players, but what is important is that these great players put the success of the team ahead of their individual achievements.

Your players can also reach this level of teamwork if you effectively convince them that the team is their foremost concern. Develop in the players an eagerness (not just a willingness) to put the team first and themselves second. Selfishness is part of human nature, and the coach must try to suppress each player's innate selfishness *to an extent* for the good of the team.

I tell our players there is nothing wrong with being a greedy rebounder or greedy defensive player. I want to see that type of greed. But there are certain areas where greed can be damaging to a team. The obvious example is the player who wants to take all the shots, or the player who wants to build up his assists and is unwilling to give up the ball unless it leads directly to a shot.

I want the kind of player who is willing to pass up a shot for a better one by his teammate, to make the pass that will lead to the assist pass. Through constant selling and emphasis, you can get the players on your team to demonstrate this type of unselfishness—the kind that leads to championships!

Beyond the X's and O's

So many times at clinics coaches come up to me and ask for the secret offense, the magic defense, or the trick out-of-bounds play. I tell them I don't think there is any such thing; rather, I advise them to work on developing their players' teamwork and their execution of offensive and defensive fundamentals. These things are far more important than any brilliant coaching tactic.

The tactical side of the game is important, but it is beyond the X's and O's that champions are developed. It is by having the one-on-one meeting with a player,

by recognizing problems in advance and heading them off, by convincing your players that the team comes first, by holding team meetings, by finding motivational poems that stress teamwork and character, by monitoring academics, by working hard to help players get college scholarships, by emphasizing off-season workouts, and by doing all the little things that a special relationship is built between the players and you—their coach.

Vic Bubas, the former coach at Duke University, told me that when the Atlantic Coach Conference Tournament approached, he used to get as positive as he could to get the players in a confident, positive frame of mind. He would tell his players, "Gee, you're looking good. I've never seen you stronger. You're rebounding well." That his players believed in him is evident in the fine record Vic established in ACC tourney play. If you show confidence in your players, you'll be amazed at how much the players' self-confidence increases and what kind of payoff it can bring.

 SOMETHING TO CHEW ON

In 1978, DeMatha went undefeated and won the National Championship. In our closest game of that season, Paul DeVito went to the foul line for us and had to make two big shots. Paul loved to chew gum; so when he approached the foul line and glanced over at me, I pulled a stick of gum out of my pocket, held it up, and smiled. He smiled back—and sank both of the free throws.

Four games later and in front of 12,000 people watching the City Championship, Paul was right back again at the foul line facing two crucial free throws. He looked over at me again and pulled the gum out of his mouth, as if to ask me, "Do you have any more?" I signaled back to him that I had two pieces in my pocket. He laughed, stepped up to the foul line, and nailed both shots.

 TAKING THE PRESSURE OFF

An experience that attests to the importance of coaching beyond the X's and O's happened in a game nearly 20 years ago. We were playing Long Island Lutheran on the road in front of a packed house; the fans were screaming for our heads. One of our seniors that year was Ray Hite, who would later play at North Carolina.

The team was down by two with time running out, when Ray drove to the bucket and got fouled just as the buzzer sounded. That left Ray with a 1-and-1, and no time left on the clock.

The opposing coach called time-out in an attempt to freeze Ray. As the team quietly sat down, I said to them, "We have to start getting ready for over-time. We've never lost an over-time game, so we should be in good shape."

I then turned to Ray and said, "If you make these two free throws, I'll give you a carryover permission (meaning it's good from year to year)." He burst out laughing. Ray walked out to the free throw line, swished the first one, turned to me and winked, and then proceeded to swish the second one as well. Afterwards he came back to the bench to make sure the manager marked down that Ray Hite had a carryover permission.

With one comment I took some of the pressure off of him. I didn't say, "If you don't make these two free throws, the game is over." Instead, I was able to change his whole reason for shooting the free throws and alleviate some of the pressure, allowing him to step up to the free throw line as relaxed as possible.

Later in the overtime period, a chunky 9th-grader named Adrian Dantley scored 9 points, and we went on to win the game.

These stories illustrate how important it is for the coach to instill in the team the proper attitude. All the tactical strategy in the world will not work if the players on the team do not work with and for each other. It is the coach who can develop this attitude among his players—an attitude that will result in a family atmosphere and, ultimately, translate into success on the basketball court.

Chapter 11

Special Situations

I've talked about the fast break and about running a halfcourt offense against man-to-man and zone defenses. One or all of these three strategies will make up the bulk of your offensive attack throughout any given game. The remainder of your offense will consist of how you handle special situations, such as the last few minutes and out-of-bounds plays.

Time and Score

How a team performs during the closing minutes of games will have much to do with its success. Anytime your team is in the last 3 minutes of a game, have your players follow these rules to control the situation:

- Maintain constant mental concentration and poise. Good players get it done under pressure.

- Stay in your offensive pattern and continue to move and work for a good shot (movement is vital to stir the defense).
- Read the defensive player on every pass, anticipating a gamble by the defense.
- Go inside more than normal for the high-percentage shots.
- Get the ball on the foul line by keeping constant basket pressure on the defense. Foul shots are money in the bank.
- Be active on the offensive boards. Second and third shots are most critical at this point.
- Save three time-outs for the very end of the game.

These rules work only if your players are in excellent physical condition, and if you have spent time working on these various situations in practice.

Keeping a Lead

If your team is ahead in the last 3 minutes of the game, have your players look for either layups or foul shots. Even though it may seem best to simply spread it out and run out the clock, you should never completely take away the thought of scoring on offense. I have seen too many games that were lost when the offensive team tried to freeze the ball and, in effect, played to lose, not to win. In those situations, the offense played so cautiously that the defense actually had the advantage. Always have your players attack the defense and look to score. In the final 3 minutes, though, players should patiently look for only the very high-percentage shots that will result in an easy basket or getting fouled.

Playing Defense With the Lead

If you are on defense and ahead by 3 or more points during the closing seconds, force your opponents to drive by running at the dribblers and thus not allowing any 3-point attempts. Under these conditions you *want* your players to get beaten on the dribble, because this will force the offensive players inside the 3-point arc. At the very least, it will force the offense into making more passes to get the shot off. If you are successful in forcing the offense to drive with the ball, you must then instruct your perimeter players to not rotate off their men to stop the penetration. Otherwise, the players they are guarding will be able to spot up around the arc for the 3-point shot.

You can also disrupt the offense's structure and timing in the last seconds by pressing or double-teaming to create turnovers or rushed shots. For example, your players could run at and double-team their best outside shooter while rotating to pick off the passes in the perimeter area, leaving the post players open for only a 2-point shot.

(For complete information regarding defensive skills and strategies, see chapters 12 through 14.)

Coming From Behind

If you are behind in the closing seconds and have the ball, the strategy is much the same as if you were ahead. Your team should look for a layup or perhaps a 6-footer, but it is best to draw a foul in this situation. By going to the line, your team can set up defensively, save valuable time, and score while doing so!

If you are down by more than 2 points, the defense will be extended to prevent the 3-point shot. In this situation, you must read the time and score situation to determine whether you want to take the 2-point basket or attempt the 3-point shot. If you are behind by 4 or 5 points, you will still need two possessions to tie or win the game, so it may be advisable to get 2 points if they can be scored quickly. Other factors in your decision will include

- the amount of time left in the game,
- the number of time-outs you have remaining,
- the personal foul situation,
- how well the opponent is shooting from the foul line,
- who is shooting well for you, and
- whether you are making a run at them defensively.

I caution you against going to the 3-point shot too early. I have seen teams shoot their way out of a game because they forced difficult 3-point shots in an attempt to get all of the points back at once. You won't get all of the points back at once, so you'll need some help from your defense.

Defending When Behind

Your defense will have to do a great deal more for you than will your offense in this situation. The offensive team will likely spread out and move away from the basket, which means your defense is more likely to get layups off of steals. If your team is down, your players will need to play hard-nosed defense and allow the opponent only one scoring opportunity per possession. Inside of 30 seconds, another good catch-up tactic is to foul opposing players with poor shooting percentages from the free throw line. Obviously, the best way to handle the closing minutes of a game is to take control of the game early in the fourth quarter.

Last-Second Plays

I have three time and score plays that my teams use quite often in the closing moments of a game. I call the plays Victory, UCLA, and 4-C. They are effective against either a man-to-man or zone defense.

All factors being equal, I recommend choosing the play that your team executes best and feels the most comfortable with. Other factors, such as the opponent's defensive alignment, should also be considered. On occasion I will call a play, see the defense we're facing, call another time-out, and change to another play.

Victory

"Victory" begins in a 1-4 alignment with 5, 4, 3, and 2 located along the baseline, and 1 (or another designated player) taking his player 1-on-1 from the top of the key. As 1 penetrates, he should be ready to either take the shot or to dump off when the other defensive players help out. There are two options you can run out of this set to create shots for your players.

Option 1: As 1 looks to penetrate, have your post players screen for the guards to get them open going to the corners. If one of them is open, 1 then hits that player with a pass (see Figure 11.1), and he squares up and shoots. After 4 and 5 have screened, they should open back up to the wing to see if they can receive the post feed from the guard in the corner or catch the pass off of 1's penetration.

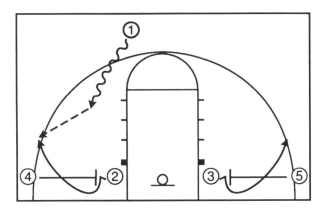

Figure 11.1   Victory: option 1.

Option 2: Player 1 dribbles right, and 5 pops out to create a two-man front. As 5 goes to the guard position, 2 and 4 set a double screen on the ball-side block, and 3 uses

the double screen to get open in the right corner. Player 1 should look to feed 3 for the shot (see Figure 11.2). As 3 comes off the screen, 4 can roll and be a post-up player; 2 can back out to the opposite wing and look for the skip pass from 1 in case the defense shifts entirely to the right.

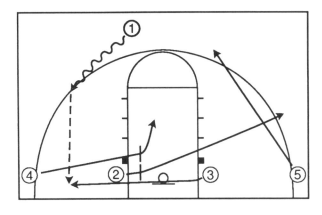

Figure 11.2   Victory: option 2.

UCLA

The second play is called "UCLA." I put it in our playbook after seeing it executed with such great success by John Wooden's UCLA teams.

It begins with a two-man front, with 1 driving hard at 2, and 2 shallow cutting to replace 1. As this is happening, 3 flashes to the hash mark to be a receiver, and 4 flashes into the high post from behind, clearing the left side of the floor. Player 1 hits 4, who then looks for 2 sneaking on the back door (see Figure 11.3). If 2 is not open, he fades to the corner and 1 and 3 balance the floor.

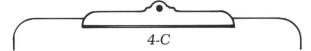

4-C

This play, "4-C," allows for plenty of movement by the players and keeps them working to be receivers and looking to score. The initial alignment is like a 2-3, with a two-man front, a high post, and two wing players.

Whenever a player in one of the guard positions passes to the wing, have him cut to

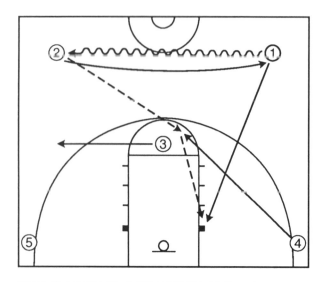

Figure 11.3   UCLA.

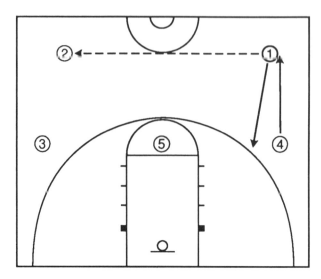

Figure 11.5   4-C: exchange.

the basket. As this happens, the off-guard replaces him, and the off-wing fills the guard spot (see Figure 11.4). If you keep the offense high (out above the foul line), it will eliminate help-side defense and create back-door opportunities for the wings when the guards have the ball.

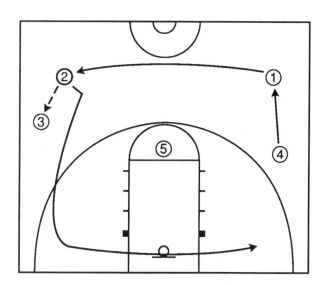

Figure 11.4   4-C: guard through.

On a guard-to-guard pass, the guard who passed the ball exchanges with the wing on his side (see Figure 11.5). This occupies the off-side help and can create more backdoor opportunities for the players on the other side of the floor. Again, remind your off-ball players to never stop moving and your ball-handlers to constantly look for cutters.

If there is any difficulty because a player has picked up his dribble and is under pressure, the high-post player must release, find the open area, and be a receiver. If either wing picked up his dribble and is in any trouble, then the ball-side guard screens for the high post to make him a receiver (see Figure 11.6). The screener (2) then shapes up to the ball to be a receiver after the screen.

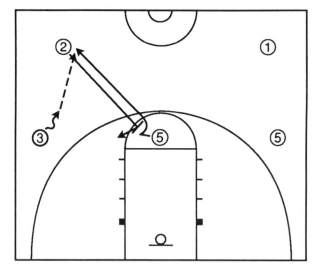

Figure 11.6   4-C: screen post.

Now 5 is a guard and 2 is in the high post. This may be a situation you want to create, if you have a mismatch you can take advantage of late in the game. If 5 is in the middle, he is your safety valve if a receiver is needed.

He can also create the back door for himself by coming out high and reading the defense if he is overplayed. Movement such as this is critical to an offense in time and score situations.

Crunch Time: The Last 10 Seconds

When a team scores a field goal and goes ahead of us with less than 10 but more than 3 seconds to go, my preference is not to call a time-out, but to quickly pass the ball inbounds and attempt to score with our quick break. If properly prepared, your team should be capable of getting a shot off from 12 feet and out within 3 seconds, or a layup in 4 seconds. That being the case, I would rather surprise our opponents before they can set up the defense.

Many games are lost because the team that scores relaxes for just a second to celebrate their "win," only to have a well-drilled team strike back quickly for the real win. Surprise is an essential element here, but control is just as important. Our quick break must be well-organized if it is to be effectively executed.

If the other team scores, and the clock runs down to 3 seconds or less, I always want a time-out while the ball is in the net. If you are unable to create a quick dead-ball situation here, the running clock might kill any opportunity at a shot before your team even inbounds the ball. In this situation, you need a fullcourt play that gives you the opportunity to score with very little time left.

Ladder

This fullcourt play can be used from either the baseline or the sideline. The inbounder should be your best long-distance passer (usually the 1-player). It is imperative that the inbounder know whether he can run the baseline, or whether he must remain at a designated spot.

When the inbounder slaps the ball, 4 backscreens for 5, who reads the defense and makes his cut. Player 4 then flashes to the ball. After a one count (following the ball slap), 3 sets a backscreen for 2, who reads the defense and makes his cut. Player

3, after screening, looks for the open area in which to flash (see Figure 11.7).

Tell your inbounder to look for the deep pass first because the deep screen will take place first. In addition, your receivers should break open at different times so your inbounder will have other options to go to should the first receiver be covered.

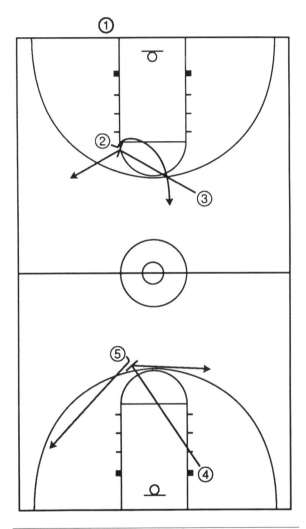

Figure 11.7 Ladder.

If this play is run from the sideline with the same screens (as it can be), your players would open up in different areas of the court, depending on where the ball was taken out of bounds.

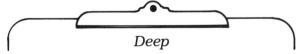

Deep

In this fullcourt play, 2 takes the ball out, and 1 and 3 position themselves at each elbow of the foul line. Players 4 and 5 are outside the 3-point arc and very close to the hash mark. On the ball slap, 4 and 5 begin down court and then come back (v-cut) to set screens. Player 4 screens for 1, and 5 screens for 3. Players 1 and 3 use the screens and sprint wide, looking for the deep pass over the top of the defense. Both 4 and 5 come back to the ball to be receivers after having set the screens, as shown in Figure 11.8.

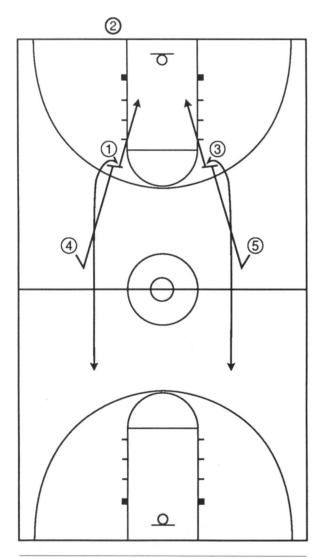

Figure 11.8 Deep.

Again, tell your inbounder to look deep first, with the short pass as the second option. Depending on the situation, you may need a deep pass for the score, or you may just need the short pass for the possession of the ball. If there is trouble, 1 and 3 can

sprint back to the ball to be receivers. The sprint men must look over their inside shoulders so they can see the entire floor, stay balanced, and keep themselves from running out of bounds. You can also invert player positions so that your best ballhandlers are in the 4 and 5 slots, coming back to the ball for the short pass.

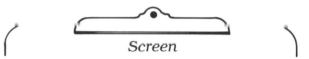

Screen

If you have very little time left on the clock, "Screen" is one more option you can employ to get a shot off. This play is possible only after an opponent has scored and your inbounder is allowed to run the baseline.

Player 1 sets a screen on the player defending the inbounds pass and looks to take the charge. When the screen is set, 3 runs the baseline. Player 4 looks to be a receiver in an open area, while 5 sets a screen for 2 under the basket at the opposite end of the floor. Player 2 moves to get open in the corner, and 5 cuts back to the ball after the screen. The inbounder (3) should throw long to an open area for the last shot, as shown in Figure 11.9.

Out-of-Bounds Plays

I am presenting here many of the out-of-bounds plays that our team has used over the years. I tell my players that our number one priority with these plays is to gain possession of the ball, **not** to create a shot opportunity.

I never have all of these plays in our playbook during any one season. Instead, I select the ones that I feel that year's personnel will be able to execute most effectively. I like to have a primary out-of-bounds play to use against a man-to-man defense, and a primary one to use against a zone. Once my team executes the primary plays well, I then add two secondary out-of-bounds plays (one each for man-to-man and zone defenses).

Because each play has several options, proper execution should insure that at least one of those options will be open. Therefore, you really only need one or two plays that your team executes well against man-to-

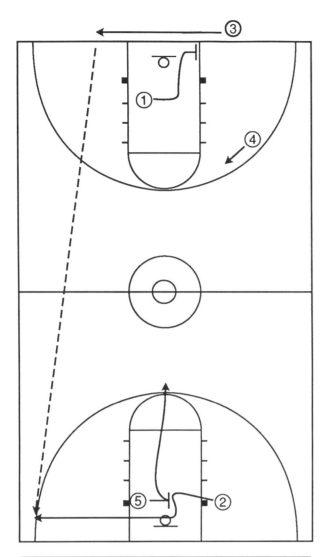

Figure 11.9 Screen.

man or zone defenses. It is better to be able to execute a few plays very well, than to run a dozen or so plays in which the execution leaves something to be desired. Never give your players more than they can handle.

In game situations, I frequently let the inbounder call the play that he feels is appropriate. I trust players' instincts when it comes to having the feel of the game. They are the ones that have been playing against the opponent's defenses, and they often have a good idea of what is and isn't working. Therefore, I believe players are capable of calling good plays.

There are times, though, when I want to call the play. I communicate the plays using a combination of words and hand signals. I call the formation verbally, and follow that with a hand signal indicating

the option number I want them to use. For example, I will yell out "Box!", which tells my players to line up in the Box formation; then I will signal the number 1 with my hand, telling them to run the first option of Box.

The inbounder is often the key to all of these plays. He should have steady balance and a good, firm grip on the ball that enables him to throw a crisp pass. Additionally, taller players often make the best inbounders because they can see over the defense and have a better chance of spotting an open receiver.

Out-of-Bounds Plays vs. Man-to-Man Defense

Against man-to-man defenses, I like to use the Box formation. A team can run many plays out of this formation, once again using the principles of screening and cutting. All of these plays can be used when inbounding under the basket or along the sideline against a man-to-man defense. (Some inbounds plays, as described on pages 128-132, can be run only from the sideline.)

It is important that the players wait for the inbounder to hit the ball on any inbounds play. Why? Because the defense may leave someone unguarded near the basket. If so, the inbounder should forget about slapping the ball and pass it immediately to the open player. Once the ball is inbounded, the passer should almost always enter the opposite side of the court from where the receiver caught the ball.

You can stagger the formation in your out-of-bounds plays to give your players more room to get open under the basket. The spacing of the Box formation should be determined by you and your players as you read the defense. You can run the Box spread very wide, or you can run it in tight. In our Box formations, the players in the lane are frequently in line with the basket, and the outside players are about two steps off the lane.

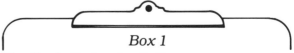

Box 1

On the ball slap by 2, 5 screens across for 4, who uses a v-cut to get open. After a 1-second count (to stagger the times at which the receivers get open), 1 screens for 3. Both screeners come back to the ball to be receivers (see Figure 11.10).

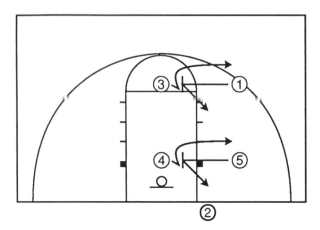

Figure 11.10 Box 1.

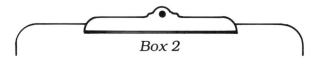

On the hit, 5 upscreens for 1, and, after a one count, 4 upscreens for 3. Again, both screeners come back to the ball. It is important to have your screeners come back to the ball to give your inbounder as many receivers to throw to as possible (see Figure 11.11).

Your cutters must wait for the screens and read the defense to get open. And again, the inbounder enters opposite and gets to the point to cover the break in case of a turnover or a quick shot.

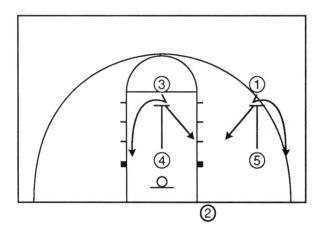

Figure 11.11 Box 2.

On this option, the Box shifts over a few feet so that the two posts are on the blocks and two perimeter players are on the opposite ends of the free throw line. On the hit, 5 cuts to the ball-side corner, and 4 slides across the lane looking for the ball. Player 3 screens for 1, who uses the screen and cuts to the opposite block. Player 4 is trying to get open in the area around the ball-side block, and 3 releases to the top to look for the lob over the defense as well as to cover the break defensively (see Figure 11.12).

The ideal pass is to 1 for the layup. However, if 2 sees someone else is open before 1, he should pass the ball to that player. (Remember, the purpose of the play is to gain possession, not get a shot.) Once again, after 2 passes the ball in, he enters the court opposite the pass.

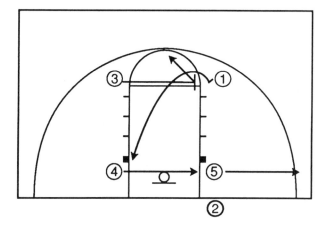

Figure 11.12 Box Out.

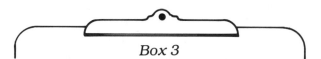

On the hit, 5 upscreens for 1, who moves to the corner as 5 comes back to the ball. Player 3 cuts to the ball side but stays outside the 3-point arc, which helps to create a passing lane from 1. After 1 receives the inbounds pass, 4 sets a screen for the inbounder (2), who looks for the ball off of the reversal on the opposite wing from where he inbounded the ball. After setting the screen for the inbounder, 4 shapes up to the wing for the possible post feed from 2 (see Figure 11.13).

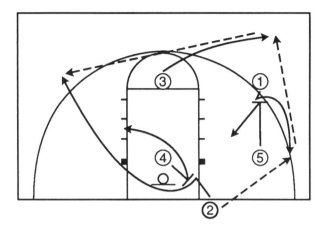

Figure 11.13 Box 3.

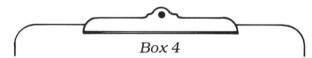

On the hit, 5 upscreens for 1, who reads the defense and uses a v-cut to get open in the corner. After 5 screens, he receives a screen from 4, who started in the lane. Player 5 gets open near the opposite block, and 4 gets open near the ball-side block as he comes back to the ball (see Figure 11.14). Player 3 releases to the perimeter as a safety receiver, or he pops to the corner to stretch the defense along the baseline and to give 4 and 5 more

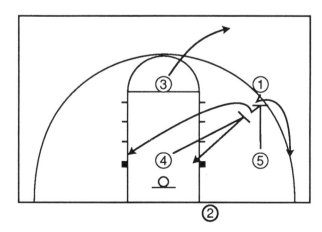

Figure 11.14 Box 4.

room to get open in the paint. Player 2 passes in and enters opposite.

Timing is critical in this play, particularly for the 4 player; he must not start across the lane until 5 has completed his screen for 1.

This play revolves around the offensive players' ability to read the defense and take advantage of one of several options. The offense, on the hit, reads the defense. The first option is to have 5 upscreen for 4 and then come back to the ball, as shown in Figure 11.15. If 3 has a quick cut to the ball, he can make that cut while the screen is taking place. He may be able to slide in as his defensive player helps with the inside screen. Player 1 works on his own to get open. Player 1 is responsible for covering the fast break unless he receives the ball. In that case, break coverage falls to 3.

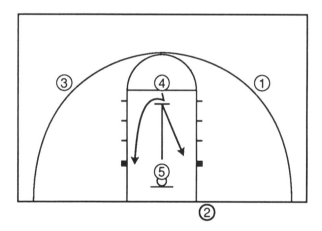

Figure 11.15 Special.

Out of this set, any movement in which the offense reacts to the defense can be effective in getting a player open. For example, 5 could screen for 4 and then receive a screen from 1 that would have 5 coming to the ball-side block to get open.

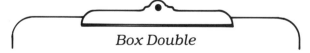

Starting from the same positions as for Box Out, 1 pops to the corner to receive the pass from 2. Players 5 and 4 slide to the middle of the lane and set a double screen for 3, who rubs off the screen looking for the ball from 1 (see Figure 11.16).

If 1 is overplayed and not open for the inbounds pass, then 3 should look for the lob pass from 2. After setting the screen, 4 and 5 must be ready to break out of the double and find open areas to become potential receivers. They may have to flash hard to the ball to help get it in bounds, or they could split into a high/low post. If 4 or 5's defender helps on 3 coming off the screen, then that unguarded post player should flash to the ball and seal any defenders for the feed from 1 or 2.

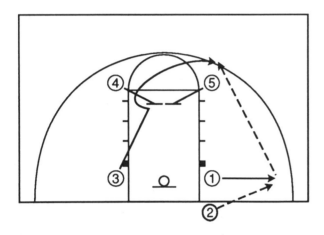

Figure 11.16   Box Double.

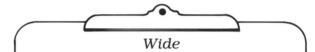

Box Option

Run Box 2, but do not have either screener come back to the ball. Instead, after 1 receives the ball from 2 in the corner, 2 steps inbounds to see if he can get the immediate post feed from 1 (see Figure 11.17).

If the pass is not there, 2 screens across for 3, who comes hard across the lane looking for the ball from 1. Keep in mind that you can make changes to put specific players in specific roles to take advantage of their abilities (such as posting up 2 in this play).

Out-of-Bounds Plays vs. Zone Defense

When inbounding against a zone, have your players keep all of the principles of

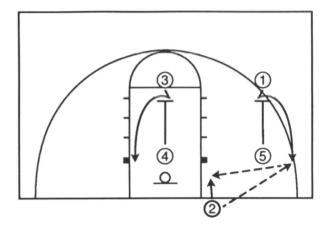

Figure 11.17   Box Option.

playing against a zone in mind. Remind them to look for gaps, and to flash to be receivers. As with the man-to-man plays, these can also be run from anywhere on the court when you are facing a zone defense.

Wide

Player 5 seals one of the low players in the zone, and 2 dives into an available open area from behind the zone. Player 2 can also start higher on the wing and fade to the corner behind the zone. If 4 has problems getting the ball in, have 3 screen the outside defender of the zone, and have 5 pop out to the corner (see Figure 11.18). Player 3 shapes up under the basket, looking for the feed from 5.

Another play, which we call "Wide Option," uses the same formation but stacks 3 and 5 on the ball side. On the ball slap, 3 uses 5 to get open.

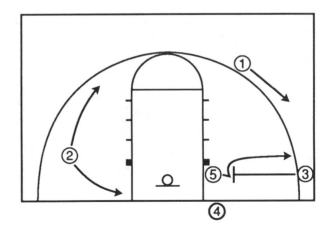

Figure 11.18   Wide.

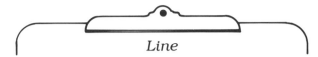

Line

On the hit, 2 breaks to the corner and then fades to the top. Player 4 steps into the lane as if he is going to receive the lob from 1. Instead, 4 screens the middle defender of the zone, 5 slides in behind 4 and times the lob from 1 (see Figure 11.19).

Player 4 can even jump for the ball, but he must realize that the pass is intended for 5. Player 3 should look for open areas outside the lane.

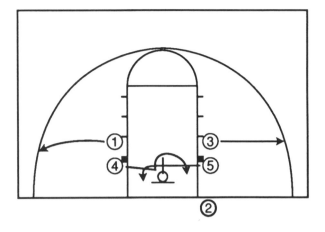

Figure 11.20 Stack.

ceiver over the top of the zone. Players 5, 3, and 1 all have the same movement as in the original Stack (see Figure 11.21).

This option gives you a player (4) at the point to cover the break if there is a turnover or a quick shot. Player 4 also serves as a receiver on the perimeter in case the zone decides to trap in the corners.

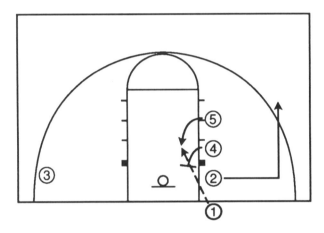

Figure 11.19 Line.

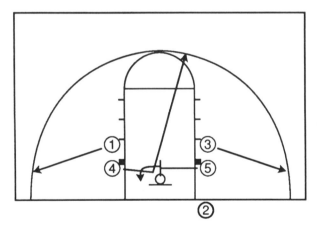

Figure 11.21 Stack: Color Option.

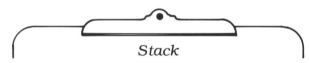

Stack

On the hit, the ball-side post (5) screens the middle defender in the zone, which allows the opposite post player (4) to come across the lane looking for the ball. Player 3 breaks to the ball-side corner, and 1 breaks to the opposite corner (see Figure 11.20).

This gives you a 1-4 set, which spreads the zone along the baseline. This alignment makes it difficult for the defense to take away every option.

Stack: Color Option

We trigger this option by calling for "Stack," and then yelling any color after that. On the ball slap, the ball-side post (5) sets the same screen as in regular Stack, but now 4 uses it to go high and be a re-

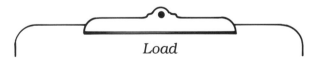

Load

On the hit, 4 clears away from the ball across the lane, and 3 breaks to the corner. Player 2 screens the top player in the zone so 1 can cut to the wing, then 2 clears to the top of the zone (see Figure 11.22).

This play gives you plenty of options to gain safe possession of the ball, which is the number one priority in any out-of-bounds play. After 5 inbounds the ball to 3, 5 can

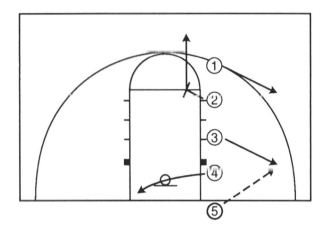

Figure 11.22　Load.

get into quick post-up position in the area vacated by 4. If the ball is passed to 3 or 2, 4 can flash to the ball-side high post and create an immediate overload. If the defense attempts to trap the corner, you have three receivers, with 4 and 5 in scoring position.

Maryland

Begin in a 1-4 alignment. On the hit, 5 screens the ball-side guard in the zone or the low defender on the ball side of the zone. Player 1 uses the screen to find the gap in the zone. Player 4 then screens the top defender in the zone away from the ball, and 3 uses it to get open at the point or down on the baseline. Players 4 and 5, after the screen, flash into the open gaps looking for the ball (see Figure 11.23). Player 2 passes in and enters opposite.

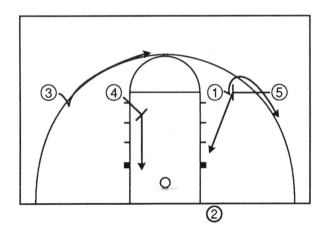

Figure 11.23　Maryland.

The purpose of this play is to stretch the zone and create gaps into which your players can flash. With a quick reversal, you could get 2 the jump shot as he comes inbounds from behind the zone.

Sideline Out-of-Bounds Plays

All of the plays just described can be run from the sideline as well as under the basket. There are, however, certain plays that are effective only when inbounding from the sidelines. Universal inbounding principles, such as having a tall, firmly balanced inbounder and looking first for safe possession of the ball, still apply.

Box 3: Sideline

This is a different play than the Box 3 run from under the basket. On the hit, 3 screens for 1 and then comes back to the ball to be a receiver. Player 5 backscreens for 4, who goes to the opposite wing. Player 5 then continues to the open area in the corner, as shown in Figure 11.24.

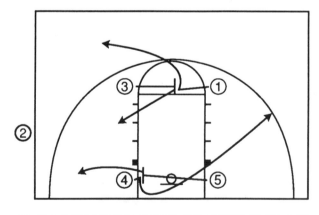

Figure 11.24　Box 3: Sideline.

Player 2 may be able to throw over the top of the defense to 4 for the jumper. If he is not able to do so, you still have three strong receivers coming to the ball. You could have 2 hit 1, and have 1 look for 4 coming off of 5's screen. Player 5 could then shape up on the ball-side block for the feed from 4 instead of continuing through to the corner.

Box 4: Sideline

This is also a different play than the Box 4 run from under the basket. On the hit, 3 screens for 1 and comes back to the ball. Player 5 uses 4's screen and clears through to the corner. You again have three receivers coming to the ball. Unlike the Box 3 option, 4 attempts to seal off his defender for the lob from 2, rather than cutting to the opposite wing. This pass should not be forced, however; the priority is safe possession of the ball.

Box Read

From the same initial alignment as Box 3 and Box 4, have your offensive players read the defense to get open. Player 3 or 4 could flash straight to the ball, or they could screen for each other. This option can be used against zone or man-to-man defenses to guarantee safe possession of the ball.

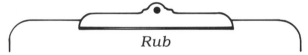

Rub

On the hit, 2 backscreens for 5. At the same time, 3 sets a screen for 4, then flashes back to the ball. After rubbing off 3's screen, 4 proceeds to the foul line, where he sets a screen for 5. Player 1 looks for the lob to 5 going to the basket, or looks to hit 2 or 3 coming to the ball. Player 4 flashes to the open area after setting the screen for 5 so that he (4) also can be a receiver (see Figure 11.25).

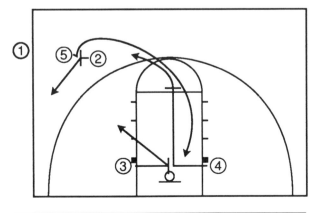

Figure 11.25   Rub.

Rub Tight

Start in a Box Set, and adjust your personnel to take advantage of their specific abilities. On the hit, 4 begins to screen for 5, and 2 backscreens for 3. Both screeners come back to the ball after setting their screens. Player 5 floats up to the foul line after the screen from 4, and then sets a second screen for 3 (see Figure 11.26). Player 1 looks to lob the ball to 3 or to pass the ball into any of the other players flashing to the ball.

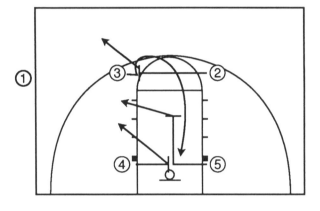

Figure 11.26   Rub Tight.

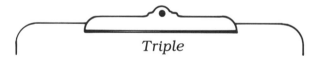

Triple

You can run this play anywhere along the sideline. On the hit, 2 screens for 3, who gets open in the back court. After setting the screen for 3, 2 then receives a screen from 4 and gets open going toward the basket. Player 4 comes back to the ball to be a receiver (see Figure 11.27). Player 5 starts on the opposite block and is ready to flash to the ball as a receiver if he is needed. The triple stack should be positioned well off the sideline to allow the players plenty of room to get open and flash back to the ball.

Wide Box

On the hit, 2 screens for 1 and holds. Player 4 flashes to the ball, and 5 breaks to the sideline looking for the ball. The inbounder

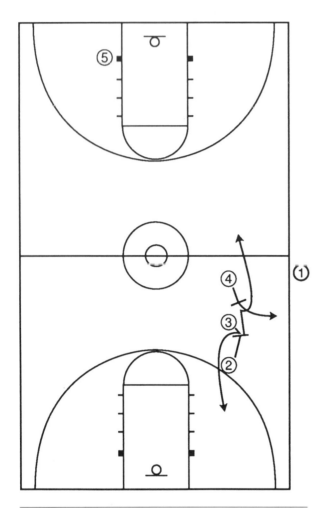

Figure 11.27   Triple.

(3) can pass to 1, 4, or 5 for safe possession of the ball. If the pass goes to 4, he looks for 2 sneaking backdoor, as shown in Figure 11.28. This option is often available because 5 has cleared the weak side to become a potential receiver. The back door

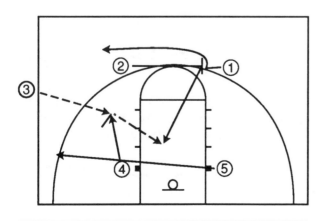

Figure 11.28   Wide Box.

can work by inbounding the ball to 1, who passes to 4 flashing high, who then hits 2 for the layup.

Line: Sideline

Like Triple, you can use this play anywhere along the sideline. Player 2 calls "Line" and follows it with either the number "1" or "3." The number called specifies who will be the screener and who will be the cutter. For example, if "1" is called, 1 (on the hit) sets the screen for 3 and then comes back to the ball. 5 sets a backscreen for 4, who cuts to the basket looking for the deep pass. 5 shapes up to the ball after the screen, leaving three receivers moving toward the sideline (see Figure 11.29). Player 4 keeps any centerfielder busy and prevents double teams off the inbounds pass since they must concern themselves with protecting the basket.

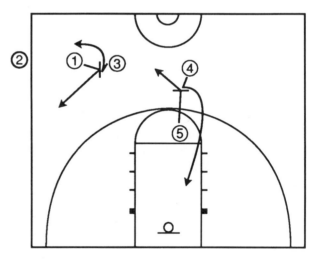

Figure 11.29   Line "1."

8 Play

I like to use this play in time and score situations. I call it the "8 Play" because it takes about 8 seconds to run through each of the three options. On the hit, 4 diagonally screens for 5, who comes out as high as he needs to in order to catch the ball. Player 1 works on his own to get open, and 3 flashes hard to the ball. Everything starts when the ball gets to 5. Player 2 inbounds to 5 and then runs a hard backdoor cut with the help of a screen from 3, as shown in Figure 11.30a. The first scoring option is for 5 to hit 2 on the back door.

If that option is not available, 3 circles around 5 looking for the handoff and playing two-player basketball with 5. This screen and roll is the second scoring option. If 5 cannot get the ball to 3, the entire right side of the floor is cleared out for 5 to take his defender 1-on-1.

If there is no opportunity for the two-player game, 3 takes the handoff and penetrates to the opposite side of the floor. Player 3 looks for 2 coming off a double screen set by 4 and 1, who slid to the opposite block when 5 received the pass (see Figure 11.30b). The shot by 2 off the double screen is your third scoring option. If there is nothing available, enter into your half-court offense.

8 Play: Zone Options

The 8 Play can also be effective from the sideline against a zone in time and score situations. The primary difference is that you are likely to end up with a jump shot rather than an inside shot.

On the hit, 1 flashes across the top of the key to receive the pass from 2. After the pass, 2 cuts through the zone to the opposite side. Player 4 sets a screen on the low defender in the zone to help free 2 for the shot. The first option is to have 1 dribble, penetrate, and pass to 2 coming off the baseline screen (see Figure 11.31a).

If nothing is available, 2 steps up to the wing so that 3 can cut through the zone into the corner. As 3 cuts through, 5 trails him into the post area and then flashes high to the ball side, giving you an overload. The second option is to hit 3 for the jumper from

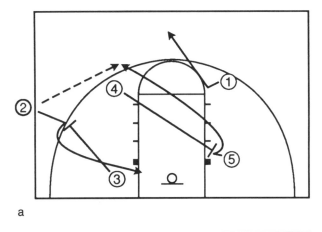

a

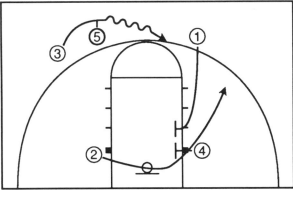

b

Figure 11.30 8 Play: option 1 (a) and option 3 (b).

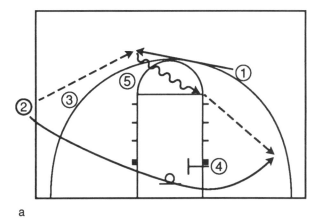

a

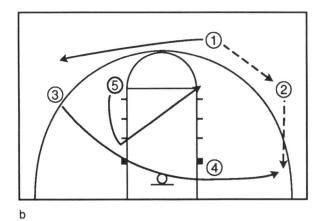

b

Figure 11.31 8 Play: zone option 1 (a) and zone option 2 (b).

the corner on the ball side (see Figure 11.31b).

After 1 swings the ball to 2, 1 floats to the open area on the opposite side of the court and looks for the skip pass. So if the second option is not available, 2 can pass to 1 for the jump shot, or 1 can feed 4 or 5 as they follow the ball after the skip pass.

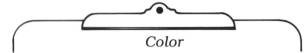

Color

On the hit, 5 screens for 3, and 1 screens for 2. Player 4 hits 2 and makes a hard cut to the basket, looking for the backdoor pass (see Figure 11.32a). If 4 does not receive the pass, he positions himself on the ball-side block.

If the first option is not open, 2 reverses the ball to 1, who dribbles to penetrate the left wing. Player 5 sets the cross-screen for 4, who looks for the feed from 1. If 4 makes a curl cut, 1 may hit 5 as the defense recovers to defend 4 (see Figure 11.32b). Player 1 may also reverse the ball back to 2 to start the offense.

Color: Quick

There is also a play in our Color series that I call Quick Option for situations in which only 1 or 2 seconds remain in the period. In this case, 4 can hit 5 on the curl in, after 5 has set the screen for 3 (see Figure 11.33).

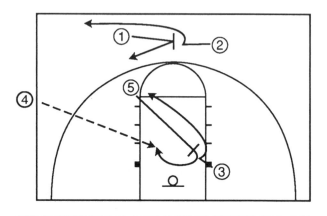

Figure 11.33   Color: quick option.

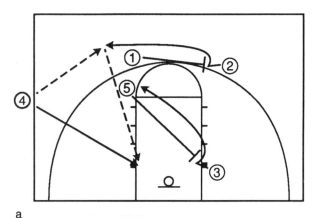

a

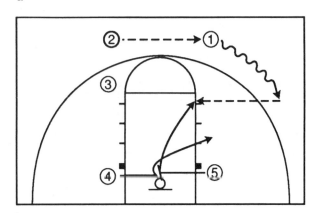

b

Figure 11.32   Color: option 1 (a) and option 2 (b).

Part IV

Coaching Defense

Chapter 12

Basic Defensive Skills and Strategies

In previous chapters I mentioned that I emphasize defense and rebounding to my players. Here's why: Over time, the teams with the best records are the teams that defend and rebound the best. Consequently, I feel that *every* player must be able to play good defense, no matter what the position.

In professional baseball's American League, each team is allowed to use a designated hitter—a player whose only job is to provide offensive punch and help the team score runs. That player does not have to play defense. But no such position exists in basketball. Every player on the court must be able to play smart defense and be willing

to give the all-out effort that often separates an average defensive player from a great defensive player.

For coaches who may not be blessed with an abundance of talent in a given year, defense can be a great neutralizer. A team of average talent can become a better-than-average team if it creates turnovers, forces the opposition's offense to work for everything it gets, and does not allow easy shots. But that won't happen unless every member of your team knows and executes proper defensive techniques and tactics.

As a coach, you should work with your players and motivate them to develop the desire to be great defensive players. This is where you will earn your paycheck. You'll have to counteract the fact that in all sports offense gets the most glamour. And the only way to do that is to provide more attention and praise to the great defensive players on the team and constantly emphasize the benefits of a good team defense.

Position Skills

All players must be willing to work at defense and to develop good footwork, which should minimize the number of times they are out of position. Ideally, you look for quickness in all of your players. However, defenders must be able to match up against the size and skills of the players they are guarding. Here's a look at the most common attributes and responsibilities of each defensive position.

Point Guard

Oftentimes, the point guard (1) is the quickest player on your team and is therefore assigned to guard the quickest player on the opposing team. The 1-player is frequently one of the more knowledgeable players on the team and is often asked to be the team's leader on defense as well as offense. His feel for the game should enable him to take the proper defensive angles to slow down a fast break or prevent penetration.

When playing pressure defense, the point player is often the one who forces the opposing ballhandler into the trap the defense is trying to set up. He will also call the defensive signals, relaying messages and instructions from the bench to his teammates on the floor. In short, he is an extension of the coach on the court.

Shooting Guard

The 2-player (off-guard) is often assigned to the opposing team's best outside shooter. Therefore, he must be a good perimeter defensive player. By this I mean that 2 must be mobile enough to follow his player around as he tries to free himself, and 2 must be determined enough to work through or around picks the opposing offense sets to get the ball into their shooter's hands.

The off-guard should also be more of a rebounder than the point guard for two reasons: (a) the player he's defending will often be playing closer to the basket; and (b) the player he's defending will shoot more often, thus the 2-player will have more block-out responsibilities, which should lead to more rebounding opportunities.

Small Forward

If the off-guard is not checking the other team's best shooter, that responsibility will most likely fall to the small forward (3). He, too, must be a good, mobile perimeter defensive player with enough quickness to stay with good outside shooters.

Occasionally, you are blessed with a small forward who can defend both the perimeter and post effectively. It is not unusual for us to have a 3 who is a perimeter player at the offensive end of the court, but who is assigned to a post player on defense. Because the small forward is often juggling between post and perimeter, he must be intelligent enough to make the necessary adjustments. Also, because of his frequent post duties, the small forward should be a good defensive rebounder.

Power Forward

The power forward (4) is usually one of your bigger and more physical players. This is true on defense as well as offense. The 4-player should be able to play tough post defense on the opposing team's inside players. But, because he may also be forced to guard a forward who likes to play outside, 4 should have the versatility to go out to the perimeter and play good defense. And, at times, he may be forced to switch to a guard if the other team executes a pick successfully.

As for inside play, 4 must be able to prevent easy inside buckets by sliding off his own man and stopping opposing players who have penetrated the lane. Finally, he must be an excellent rebounder who can crash the defensive boards whenever a shot goes up, then get the ball out to a guard to start the fast break.

Center

The 5-player should be your best inside defensive player and, along with the power forward, be one of your top two defensive rebounders. The center must be strong and physical to prevent his player from getting a good inside position that could lead to an easy basket. He must be strong enough to block out effectively for rebounding purposes. The center should also be able to provide help defense to any perimeter players who have penetrated the lane; he should be a good enough shot blocker to give the offensive players something to think about when they take the ball inside. Like the power forward, your center should also be a good outlet passer who can start the break after pulling down a defensive rebound.

Types of Defenses

A coach can use countless varieties of defenses. But I recommend choosing the defense that best fits your team's abilities as your *primary* defense. Then identify two or three secondary defenses that will allow you to adjust to the many different situations that will arise during games.

Man-to-Man

The most conventional defense used in basketball is the straight man-to-man defense in which each defender positions himself between the offensive player to whom he is assigned and the basket (see Figure 12.1). In this defense, the weak-side players are sinking and jamming the middle to prevent defensive penetration with the ball, and to make the offense take lower-percentage outside shots.

Strengths of a Man-to-Man

This basic defense is most effective against teams that do not have good outside shooters. It also gets the job done against teams that don't have the patience to run sound offenses and work for the open shot. Against teams that are patient, this defense can force them into longer possessions and therefore take some time off the clock. This

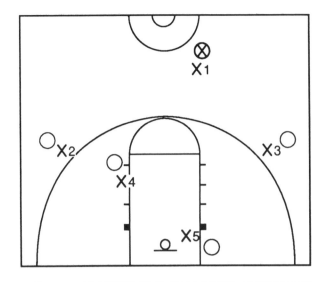

Figure 12.1   Basic man-to-man.

may be an advantage if your team has the lead, or a disadvantage if you are trailing.

Weaknesses of a Man-to-Man

The biggest weakness of this defense is that it does not create many turnovers. Also, this defense does not force the offense to make many adjustments; it does not dictate anything to the offense, other than stopping up the middle. It allows the opposition to run their offense, which is the main reason I do not like this defense. I also feel the game has changed and rendered this basic defense somewhat obsolete; players today are shooting the basketball too well to allow outside shots, and the addition of the 3-point line has made those shots more costly to give up.

Pressure Man-to-Man

A defense I prefer instead of the straight man-to-man is the halfcourt pressure man-to-man, which has been made famous by teams like North Carolina, Duke, and Indiana. I have been using this defense at DeMatha since the 1950s, and my team uses some form of it more than 90% of the time.

The only time I will take us out of the pressure man-to-man is when we

- want to use up the clock,
- face a team that plays poorly against a zone, or
- try to give the offense a different look.

From this defense, you can keep the offense off-balance just by varying the intensity of the pressure in the man-to-man. You can turn the pressure up by playing the defense full court, or you can turn it down by picking up the offense at three-quarter court or half court.

Sometimes I'll call for a traditional sagging man-to-man on defense one time, then the next time pick right back up with the pressure man-to-man. I also use an entry defense in which our players let the offense bring the ball up court and successfully complete the first pass before turning on the pressure. You never want to give the offense the same look every time down the floor. Stick with what's working well, but keep the opposition guessing.

The pressure man-to-man defense is similar to the regular man-to-man, the biggest difference being that we place extreme pressure on the ball and contest every single pass. Players position themselves between their opponent and the ball, but only when the player they are guarding is one pass away—receiving distance—from the ball. If the player they are guarding is more than one pass away, they should be clogging the middle (see Figure 12.2).

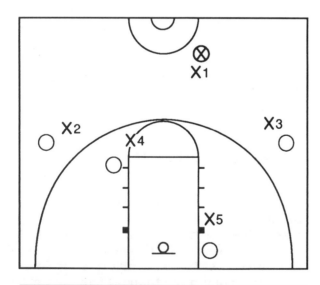

Figure 12.2   Pressure man-to-man.

Strengths of a Pressure Man-to-Man

What I like about this defense is the pressure element. It is designed to create turnovers and to drive teams almost completely out of their offense, forcing them to free-lance. It is a defense that is on the attack at all times, always looking to create opportunities rather than react to what the offense is running.

Great pressure defense teams do not have to spend much time working against the opponent's offense in practice; the pressure will force the opponent out of that offense anyway. Great pressure can break most offenses and force teams into individual play.

The pressure man-to-man is extremely effective against teams that

- have suspect ballhandling,
- prefer to run a conservative offense and don't like to fast break,
- aren't as talented and quick as your team, and
- are not organized and disciplined offensively.

Weaknesses of a Pressure Man-to-Man

One of the risks with running a high-intensity pressure is that you are occasionally going to give up some easy shots, and even layups. Teams with excellent ballhandlers can present problems for this defense, especially if those ballhandlers are taller than your defenders and have a good view of passing lanes.

However, I believe the turnovers that result from this defense should outweigh the number of easy baskets you may give up in return. I generally figure possession of the ball is worth about 1 point. So if you give away one layup but get three turnovers, you are still ahead of the game.

Another risk is that you stretch your defense over a wider area of the floor. If you are not careful, this can result in a rebounding disadvantage. And if your team is not in good condition, this defense will quickly tire your players. On the other hand, if the defense is farther away from the basket, so is the offense. This helps neutralize any offensive rebounding advantage.

Man-to-Man Defense Variations

Out of this pressure man-to-man defense, you can add variations. You can trap, play a switching man-to-man, or employ the run-and-jump. The run-and-jump is like a switching man-to-man, in which the defender nearest the ball runs toward the offensive player with the ball. The player guarding the ball then jumps over to the player left open by the defender. Unlike in the conventional switching man-to-man, the defenders switch before the offensive players can screen or criss-cross. You can try this with a few individuals or with the entire team; you can extend this defense three-quarter court or full court by using all of the same basic principles.

You can also extend the straight man-to-man full court. Again, this probably will not result in any turnovers. But the advantage here is that it can slow the other team down, which can be helpful when trying to use up the clock or when playing a fast-breaking team.

Zone Defenses

Another type of team defense assigns all five defenders a particular area or zone to defend (see Figure 12.3) rather than a particular offensive player. This defensive strategy can be implemented through various player alignments, the most popular being the 2-1-2, 2-3, 1-2-2, 1-3-1, and 3-2.

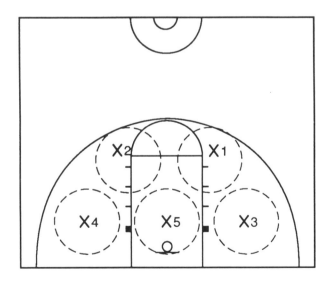

Figure 12.3 2-3 zone defense.

Strengths of a Zone

The biggest advantage to a zone defense is that it puts your defensive players exactly where you want them, regardless of where the offense puts its players. The offense does not dictate the floor position of the defenders. For example, a zone can insure that your big men will always be near the bucket, even if the opposition's big men decide to go outside. In this particular case, the zone team would have the rebounding advantage with its big men always in position. And once the rebound is controlled, the zone alignment provides quick outlets for the fast break.

Zone defenses are often effective against teams with good inside players or poor outside shooters, because most of the shots over the zone will come from the outside. Zones are also good for slowing teams down and taking time off the clock because the offense may have to take more time to get a good shot. Consequently, a zone can work quite well against a relatively impatient team that likes to make one or two quick passes and then shoot the basketball.

Some teams just do not like to play against a zone defense. In fact, the reason I first installed a zone at DeMatha was because several teams in our league hated to go against it. So I made sure those teams saw a zone. After all, one of the objectives of coaching is to force the other team to do things they do not work on in practice.

Zones lend themselves very well to trapping. Some of the best defenses today are halfcourt zone traps (see Figure 12.4). Zone traps, or any of the other zones, can also be stretched from quarter-court to full court with the principles remaining intact.

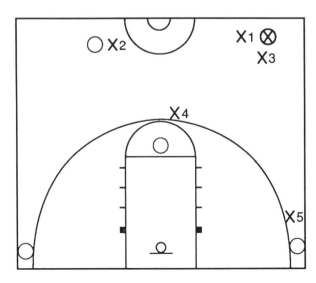

Figure 12.4 Halfcourt zone trap.

Weaknesses of a Zone

Zone defenses are susceptible against good outside shooting teams. The quickest way to bring a team out of a zone is to start hitting bombs right over it. The 3-point line has stretched zones out even farther because no team can afford to give up uncontested 3-pointers if the other team can make those shots.

Even if the outside shots are missed, there is another potential problem. Although zones put defensive players in excellent rebounding position, there are no exact block-out responsibilities because the players are defending an area and not a player. This can leave a pathway for a slicing offensive player to slip through and grab an offensive rebound.

A somewhat less tangible weakness of a zone is that it does not present the individual challenge presented by a man-to-man. For example, a great man-to-man defender approaches every game thinking to himself, "I'm going to shut my player down tonight." But the defender's feeling of individual responsibility is not as strong when an offensive player scores against a zone. He can think, "He didn't score against me. I wasn't guarding him."

Also, if your team does not change ends of the floor very well, a zone can be vulnerable to a fast break. When playing a zone, it is important that the defenders hustle back and set the zone up before the opposition's offense goes to work. If the offense gets there first or even at the same time, the zone is in trouble and will probably face a numbers disadvantage until a shot goes up or a foul is called.

Combination Defenses

Although 99% of all defenses are man-to-man or zone, there is a third category to consider: combination defenses. Because of their unorthodox principles, such defenses are often referred to as "junk" defenses.

One of the most popular combination defenses is the Box-and-One, shown in Figure 12.5. In this defense, four of the players play a 2-2 zone (box) around the lane while the fifth player plays man-to-man on the opposition's best player.

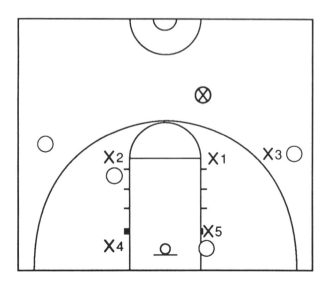

Figure 12.5 Box-and-One defense.

The Diamond-and-Two has three players playing a zone in a triangular shape, with the other two defenders assigned to the opponent's best offensive players. And another combination defense, the 1-3-1 Chaser, has the point player chasing the ball all over the floor while the other players remain in their zones.

Strengths of Combination Defenses

The biggest advantage to a junk defense is that it may catch the other team unprepared. You may be able to disrupt their offense by showing them something that they have not seen or worked on in practice. Also, if a junk defense has been successful against that team before, you may take them out of the game mentally because they've had previous trouble with that particular defense. For example, the other team's best player may hate to play against the Box-and-One. Advance scouting should give you this kind of information.

Weaknesses of Combination Defenses

The main weakness of junk defenses is lack of preparation. Chances are a junk defense is not going to be your primary defense; therefore, you may not get to spend much time perfecting it. If your players feel slightly unprepared with the junk defense, they will be less confident, which takes away the mental edge the junk defense is supposed to provide. A well-prepared and patient offensive team may be able to work against the unfamiliar defense and still come away with a good shot.

My teams have faced many junk defenses over the years. One year, Gonzaga High School played a Box-and-One against our player John Gwynn. John scored 48 points against them, and we never saw another junk defense that season. (John, incidentally, went on to a great career at the University of Connecticut.)

Summary

How well your *team* plays defensively will determine its success. Great teams are always good defensive teams. This chapter included the following points to help you be a better coach of defensive techniques and tactics:

- All players should be able to play defense.
- The defensive point guard is usually your quickest player, is assigned to the opponent's quickest player, and is usually the floor leader on defense.
- The off-guard on defense is oftentimes assigned to the other team's best outside shooter.
- The small forward ideally can play both perimeter and post defense, and can potentially be assigned to the other team's best outside shooter.
- The power forward should be a big, strong, inside defensive player who is a good rebounder.
- The center should be a strong defensive player in the post and also be a ferocious rebounder.
- The conventional man-to-man defense effectively clogs the middle and forces outside shots, but it reacts to the offense instead of forcing the offense to react to it.
- The pressure man-to-man defense aims to force the opposing team out of its offense by applying continual pressure on the player with the ball and on anyone who is one pass away from the ball.
- You can implement variations out of man-to-man defenses such as a switching man-to-man or the run-and-jump.
- Zone defenses allow you to place defensive players in areas of your choosing, but these defenses are vulnerable to patient teams with good outside shooters.
- Block-out responsibilities are sometimes confusing in a zone.
- Some defenses are a combination of zone and man-to-man. These "junk defenses" can be useful in select situations, but are not usually effective as primary defenses.

Chapter 13

Teaching Defensive Skills

The best way to teach team defense to players is through a step-by-step process. Begin by concentrating on individual techniques. A team defense will be only as good as the individual defensive skills of the players on the team. That's why you should have your players constantly work on their individual defensive fundamentals.

Footwork

The most basic defensive fundamental is the proper stance, and this is where you should begin your instruction. Teach your players to slightly stagger their feet, with one foot slightly ahead of the other (like a boxer's stance). Their feet should be at least shoulder-width apart, and their weight equally distributed on both feet (which will help them maintain their balance during the game). The knees should be bent, with the thighs at about a 45-degree angle to the floor.

It is imperative that you teach your players to stay low while in the defensive stance. This will make them quicker, stronger, and more explosive. A player's back should be fairly straight, and his head should be up and directly over the shoulders. This will also help with balance, which is the key to a good defensive stance. Anything that takes away from a player's balance detracts from his defensive ability

Finally, players should keep their hands in front of their body with their palms up. This gives the dribbler something to worry about. Players should *not* attempt to reach in and steal the ball because doing so destroys their balance and, thereby, their ability to contain the ball.

Steps

Once your players have the proper stance, you should next teach them the steps necessary to contain and pressure the ballhandler. These are the basic steps they will need to perform their defensive duties:

- Retreat Step
- Advance Step
- Swing Step

Retreat Step

The first defensive footwork skill I teach is the retreat step. This move is essential for defending a player who makes a right or left move toward the basket.

The player should begin in the proper defensive stance with one foot slightly in front of the other. The retreat step is then executed by having the player push off his front foot, take a step backward with the rear foot, and then slide the front foot back to reestablish position and balance. A defender must stay low while taking the retreat step, and should never bring the feet any closer together than shoulder-width. While retreating, the player should not do anything to destroy his balance, such as bringing his feet together, rising out of his stance, or hopping instead of sliding the feet.

Advance Step

The advance step can make your players actors instead of reactors on defense. If properly taught, this move will allow your players to control and dictate what the offense does. The offensive players will be too concerned about reacting to the defense to initiate any moves against your defensive player.

After receiving the ball, a good offensive player will get in the triple-threat position with the opportunity to drive, shoot, or pass. I want my players to eliminate as many offensive possibilities as they can by forcing the offensive player to immediately put the ball on the floor. This is the object of the advance step.

The advance step is, simply, the opposite of the retreat step. It is performed by pushing off the back foot while stepping forward with the front foot, then sliding the back foot forward. Again, players should keep their feet shoulder-width apart to maintain good balance.

When taking the advance step, a player must also be prepared to immediately execute the retreat step to stay between the dribbler and the basket. Both the retreat step and advance step are based on two simple movements: step and then slide.

By taking the advance step, the defensive player will force the offensive player to dribble the ball. Depending on how he decides to play him, the defender could then force the offensive player into a number of other situations. For example, he could take a retreat step. The offensive player, having used his dribble on the initial advance step, will probably be forced to shoot with the defender staying off of him and giving the shot; or the defender could decide to keep the pressure on the offensive player and force him to drive. In both instances, the defensive player is initiating and the offensive player is reacting to him.

Emphasize to your players that you want them to use defensive footwork to control, rather than just stay with, their player. You want them to force the opponent's offense to play a certain way—a way that makes it less effective. Proper execution of the advance and retreat steps increases your players' chances of shutting down the opposition.

Swing Step

Most offensive players are instructed to drive in the direction of the defensive player's front foot. The swing step is a defensive maneuver to counter this attack and also counter an offensive player's change of direction. This move will help defenders avoid getting beat by an offensive player slicing to the basket.

The swing step is executed by having your players pivot on their back foot while swinging their opposite elbow and front foot in the direction taken by the offensive player. From this action, the defensive player regains offense-defense-basket position and continues to stay ahead of the offensive player. Teach your players to stay low while executing the swing step. If they come up and out of their stance, they will be slower to react and more likely to be beaten by the offensive player.

Don't Get Beat

I have one rule for the player guarding the ball: *Don't get beat.* Although I emphasize ball containment, defenders must apply "intelligent" pressure on the ball. By that I mean players should not defend offensive players so loosely that they can pass or shoot as they please, nor so tightly that they cannot prevent drives to the hoop.

However, if one of your players gets beaten on defense, he is by no means out of the play. Tell him to get out of his defensive stance, pick out a point on the floor that he can get to before the offensive player, and run to that spot. Otherwise, if the player stays in his defensive stance, he will never recover. The offensive player will use his body to close the gap and keep the defensive player on his back. But if the defender has run to the point ahead of the offensive player and then gotten into the defensive stance, he can regain control of the situation. So an on-ball defensive player who has been beaten should first get in front of the dribbler, then reestablish position and stance to contain him, and finally force the ballhandler in a particular direction by using the proper footwork.

Footwork Drills

Defense is played with the mind, heart, and feet. The mind tells you what to do, the heart gives you the desire to do it, and the feet put you in the proper position to execute it. The most important physical skill in good defense is footwork. Therefore, it is important that you have a series of drills designed to familiarize players with the

Teaching Reminders on Individual Defense

These are the main points to emphasize to your players about individual defense:

- Stay low.
- Stay balanced, with your feet staggered, shoulder-width apart.
- Move your feet in a step and slide sequence.
- Pressure and contain the ball.
- Dictate and control the moves of the ballhandler. The left foot forward forces the dribbler left; right foot forward forces the dribbler right.
- Keep your chest open to the offensive player.
- Keep your head up.

proper footwork to develop quickness of foot.

Slide Drill

Purpose. I begin every year with this drill to review with my players the importance of defensive footwork and to eliminate any bad habits they may have picked up over the summer.

Organization. The coach stands under the basket, facing the team, which is spread out across the floor in several lines. Each player begins with the left foot forward.

Procedure. After getting them in their defensive stance, give them one of three instructions: advance, retreat, or swing. Upon hearing your instruction, the players are to execute either one advance step, one retreat step, or one swing step. After they have completed one step, the players stay in their defensive stance and await the next instruction.

Coaching Points. After players have become skillful at these steps, you or one of your coaches should take a ball and dribble slowly down the court. Carefully observe your players to see if they react to your dribble with the proper defensive step. Remind them that on any offensive attack step, such as the jab step, they should take a retreat step, so as not to give the offensive player an opening. Also remind them to keep their chest open with the ball and to stay low as they advance, retreat, and swing. As you dribble down court, change directions to work the players on their swing step, and use the pull-back dribble to work on their advance step.

Directional Drill

Purpose.   To develop the ability to change direction quickly, this drill forces your players to rapidly execute a series of defensive steps.

Organization.   Line your players up as you did in the Slide Drill and have them assume the defensive stance.

Procedure.   The drill begins on your whistle. You face the players and point either left, right, front, or back. Your players must then keep moving in the direction you point until you point in a different direction. If you point at them, they retreat; if you point over your shoulder, they advance; if you point left or right, they slide laterally in that direction. (Remind players that they should point their lead foot to avoid ankle injuries should they have to stop quickly.)

Coaching Points.   Once again, the players should stay low, keep their feet shoulder-width apart, and keep their heads up to see your instructions.

Hey Drill

Purpose.   This is one of my favorite drills, and one that the team also enjoys. It combines into one drill all of the basic steps of defensive footwork. Players get to work on the advance step, retreat step, and swing step, while having some fun.

Organization.   Stand on the baseline under the basket and have your players facing you in three lines across the floor. They then assume the defensive stance, each player with the same foot forward.

Procedure.   When you blow your whistle, the team responds quickly by executing an advance step while simultaneously yelling, "Hey!" to get in the habit of challenging the shooter. They follow the advance step with a retreat step, a swing step, and then two retreat steps.

When they have completed these five steps, they are still in a good defensive stance and the opposite foot is now their front foot. They are prepared to begin the process again on your whistle. Repeat until the team has traveled the length of the floor.

Coaching Points.   Again, observe players to see that they are properly executing each step. Remind players to keep their heads up, stay low, maintain balance, and point their toes in the direction they are headed.

Quickness Drills

Basketball is fast becoming a game of quickness (no pun intended). Although being a good defensive player depends greatly on other factors as well (hard work, desire, and determination), becoming quicker can only make your players better defensive players. Contrary to what some may think, quickness can be improved. Here are a number of drills that will enhance your players' quickness.

Machine Gun Drill

Organization.   You can do this with an individual or with the whole team, as in the Slide Drill. The players assume a good defensive stance.

Procedure.   After the sound of your whistle, the players move their legs up and down as rapidly as possible. The sound of each foot alternately tapping the floor is similar to the rapid fire of a machine gun.

Coaching Points.   Tell your players to get their knees up high for maximum benefit from this drill. See how many times your player's right foot can hit the floor in 15 seconds, then double the figure to get the total number of times both feet hit the floor. Use these numbers to chart improved quickness. Repeat as needed.

Directional Machine Gun Drill

Organization.   See Machine Gun Drill.

Procedure.   The players start doing the machine gun drill. You then point either left or right; the player follows your signal, turns in that direction, and turns back to you as quickly as he can. Remember that the player should continuously do the machine gun throughout the drill.

Line Jumps

Organization.   Have your players pick out one of the lines on the floor and stand next to it.

Procedure.   Making sure they keep their feet together, see how many times players can jump back and forth over the line in 15 seconds.

Lane Slides

Organization. Position players on one side of the lane in a defensive stance. You can run this drill simultaneously at both ends of the court with as many players as you prefer.

Procedure. As the name indicates, players in this drill slide from one side of the lane to the other while in a defensive stance. When their lead foot touches the line on the opposite side of the lane, they stop and start back across.

Triangle Drill

Organization. Line up three players on the foul line, facing the basket with their left foot forward. With an assistant helping, you can do this drill simultaneously at both ends of the court. I have found that using more than three players at each station generally crowds the players involved.

Procedure. On your whistle, have the players take two retreat steps, a swing step, two lateral steps to the left, then two advance steps back to the foul line extended. Their right foot should now be the lead foot. Repeat three times. After the third time, the players should turn and sprint to the far foul line to repeat the drill there. Have another group of three fill their spots on the original end.

Cross

Organization. Put your players in one single-file line under the basket along the baseline.

Procedure. On your whistle, have the players advance step and slide to half court, staying in a defensive stance with their right foot forward. Once they touch the midcourt line, they take one slide to the right and retreat step to the foul line. They then swing open and slide to the sideline on their right, keeping their lead (right) foot pointed in the direction they're headed. After they touch the sideline, they take a retreat step, then they slide laterally across the court to the other sideline (see Figure 13.1). After they have completed the circuit, they turn and jog back to the baseline.

Coaching Points. Keep your players well spaced in this drill. As one player reaches the foul line, the next player can begin sliding forward. Anywhere from 6 to 10 players can be involved in the drill at one time.

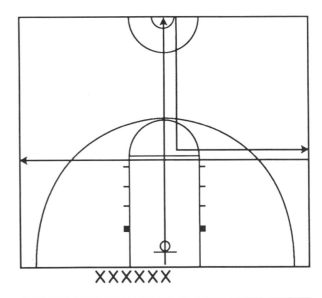

Figure 13.1 Cross drill.

They must talk and communicate to each other to avoid running into one another at the crossing point. Communication is an important part of any successful team defense, and this drill helps you to emphasize this to your players.

Fullcourt 1-on-1

Purpose. This is the most effective drill to develop your player's individual defensive skills.

Organization. Position all of your players behind the baseline and have them divide themselves into pairs. Each pair will get one ball.

Procedure. One player stands behind the baseline, turns and faces the defender, and attacks out of the triple-threat position. The defensive player's objective is to pressure and contain the dribbler, keeping his hands active in case of a free ball, and not allowing the dribbler to advance the ball up court without trying to dictate the pace of the dribble. Have the defensive player turn the dribbler, forcing him to change directions as many times as possible on the trip up court. You want the trip to be as long and hard as possible for the dribbler—one he won't likely forget the next time his team has the ball.

The next pair does not begin until the previous group passes the opposite foul line. When the entire team has reached the opposite baseline, the players switch roles (offense to defense and vice versa) and repeat the drill in the other direction.

Coaching Points. Do not allow the same players to face each other every day. Variety makes for stiffer competition and it gives each player an opportunity to play against varying levels of quickness.

Also, when running this drill, you should emphasize the following points to the players:

- Be one arm's-length away from the offensive player.
- Stay ahead of the ball (dictate and dominate).
- Constantly put pressure on with the hands (without losing balance), and keep the feet moving by sliding.
- Play the ball from the floor up, with palms up and fingers jabbing at the ball.

- Turn the dribbler by sliding in front of his intended path.
- Do not cross your feet or bring them together; you'll lose your balance.
- Do not turn your head or your back to the ball.
- Turn the dribbler, forcing him to change or reverse his direction (a basic rule in our trapping defense).
- If you get beat, pick out a point ahead of the offensive player, run to that point, then pick up the dribbler.

In teaching this drill, you are beginning to build your halfcourt and fullcourt team defenses. It all starts here, because every player must be able to contain the opposing offensive player if your team defenses are to be effective.

Chapter 14

Teaching Team Defense

Once your players have grasped the individual defensive principles and skills described in chapters 12 and 13, you'll need to show them how to apply them as part of a five-player unit. Find a convenient method of identifying your defenses to make clear to every player what exactly you have in mind.

Defense by the Numbers

I have found that a numerical system suits our purposes best. I apply a double-digit number to identify the particular halfcourt defenses. If the code begins with a 2, it iden-

tifies a man-to-man defense; a 3 identifies a trapping zone defense; and a 4 identifies a straight zone defensive series. For example, this is how we number our man-to-man defenses:

22-Regular = Standard Man-to-Man
22-Tough = Pressure Man-to-Man
23 = Regular Trap
25 = Blitz Trap
26 = Blitz Switch

In addition, to identify where I want my players to pick up the offensive team, I divide the court into four areas (see Figure 14.1). If I call for the defense to be in the 4

Opponent's basket

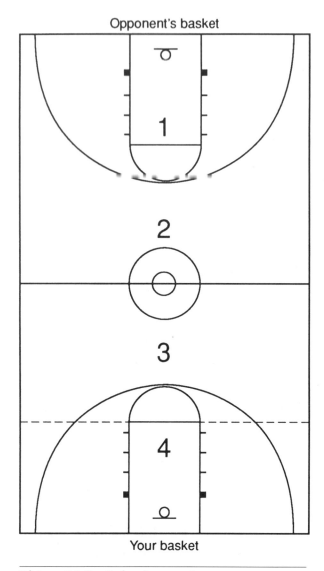

Your basket

Figure 14.1 Defensive court areas.

area, they pick up full court; in the 3 area, they pick up at three-quarters court; in the 2 area, they pick up at half court; and in the 1 area, they pick up at the top of 3-point arc. And so, a 22-Regular in the 2 area would mean a man-to-man defense that picks up the offense at half court.

Defensive X's and O's

Our primary defense is called 22-Tough. This is a pressure man-to-man deny defense with help-side rotation. It is aimed at making the opponent's offensive players work to get the ball and, ideally, go without the ball because we are overplaying the passing lanes. Good defensive players force

their opponents to work very hard for everything they get.

One objective of the 22-Tough defense is to invite the backdoor pass. Such a pass often appears to be a viable option to the offense because the defenders position themselves in the passing lanes and off their player. However, with proper weak-side positioning, the defense should be able to pick off most backdoor passes. So the 22-Tough, by preventing passes to players who are cutting to the basket, places even more pressure on the offensive players to get open on the perimeter.

If you want to extend this overplay full court, you can call for 22-Tough in the 4 area. The same pressure man-to-man principles apply, except that the players now deny passes all over the court.

In 22-Regular, defenders play man-to-man but position themselves between the offensive players and the basket instead of between offensive players and the ball, as is done in 22-Tough. The 22-Regular allows offensive players to catch the ball, but the defenders should never get beaten by the dribble or the backdoor cut. The basic rule of this defense is for the defenders to keep everything in front of them.

25 is our Blitz Trap, and 26 is our Blitz Switch. When playing against a team that plays out of a 1-4 set, you may wish to use an "Entry" defense, which allows the offense to complete the first penetrating pass. These defenses and others will be covered in more depth later in this chapter.

I find this defensive coding system is very effective because it can cover not only everything you might use defensively, but also everything you are likely to encounter in games throughout the season.

Defensive Principles

Our defense is built on many basic principles. You should emphasize these principles to your players as you teach them how to perform as a defensive unit:

- Be in excellent physical condition.
- Concentrate!
- Talk to each other on defense.
- Be ready to play; don't need to get ready to play.

- Pressure the ball. This will cut the ball-handler's vision in half.
- Stop penetrating passes.
- Dig (sag) to help if the ball enters the post.
- Help and recover.
- Stop the offense from reversing the ball.
- Force the ball outside.
- Move when the ball moves.
- Play aggressively and with enthusiasm.
- Don't allow the offense to play in straight lines.
- Stop moves to the basket.
- See the ball and the offensive player.

Rotation Rules

Inevitably, when playing pressure man-to-man, your players will have to rotate defensive positions to cover the opposition. Against any type of offensive set, the rules remain the same. First, the high post *never* gets involved in the rotation. Second, the low post, off-forward, and off-guard rotate one offensive player closer to the ball. If the ball is thrown into the post, have the defensive players that are one pass away collapse and dig in, then retreat to their correct positions once the ball is back on the perimeter.

Defensive Positioning

Being in the proper position and knowing the responsibilities associated with that position are crucial to good team defense. If a player is in the correct position, he has an excellent chance of making the right play. If a player is even a half step out of position, he may end up committing a foul or getting beat.

For our pressure man-to-man defense to be successful, each defensive player on the court must know and be able to execute various responsibilities. These responsibilities are constantly changing, depending on the offensive player being guarded and his position in relation to the ball's position.

Defending on the Ball

Have the player guarding the ball put intelligent pressure on the ballhandler in an effort to stop the dribble. The defender should attempt to make the player put the ball on the floor, and then force him to pick it right back up for a "dribble used."

Defending From One Pass Away

The defender whose offensive player is one pass away from the ball should be positioned between that player and the ball. The defender should also be slightly off of the offensive player. From this position, the defender decreases the offensive player's quickness and gives himself more time to recover and contest the backdoor cut. The defender's chest should face the offensive player, and his back foot should be positioned so that it cuts the offensive player in half. The defender's front foot, outside arm, and hand should be in the passing lane.

Denied the ball this way, the offensive player is forced to go backdoor, where the help-side defense is positioned. It also allows the defense to continue to dictate and control the tempo of the game. But to do so, your players must always see both the ball and their player while they are in the overplay position.

This type of defense makes it difficult for offensive players to get open. For example, an offensive player can take two to three full steps toward the basket before his defender is required to take one step to contest the pass. Therefore, this overplay position makes it more difficult for the offensive player to use the v-cut to get open. And the defender does not have to react to every single step the offensive player makes.

Defending From Two Passes Away

The defender whose offensive player is two passes away from the ball should have one foot in the foul lane. He should position himself to see both his player and the ball. This puts the defender in position to either stop the penetration on the ball side of the court or to react to the lob pass to his player.

Defending From Three Passes Away

When a defender is guarding an offensive player who is three passes away from the ball, the defender should position himself in the lane. From this location, the defender is in the best possible spot to stop the ball-side drive.

Basic Rules of Man-to-Man Pressure Defense

- Do not let the offensive players catch the ball. If they should catch the ball, put aggressive but intelligent pressure on the ball. Get the dribbler to pick up his dribble and close up on him.
- Completely overplay the first receiver. Get off the player and toward the ball with one hand in the passing lane.
- When the offensive player is not an immediate receiver (two or more passes away), the defender should be well off his player and in position to help or deny the flash.

Defensive Team Drills

The Horseshoe Drill

Purpose. To teach your players their basic responsibilities in the 22-Tough defense.

Organization. Designate two offensive guards, two defensive guards, two offensive wings, and two defensive wings. In the early stages of practice, your players will get a better picture of the defensive rotation if you do not include the post players. Make all of your players participate in the drill to become familiar with the rotation, because even your post players may be forced to guard a wing in some situations. Position your offensive players as shown in Figure 14.2, with the two guards and two forwards above the foul line.

Procedure. Initially, have the offensive players remain stationary as the defensive players adjust to where the ball is on the court. This allows your players to learn how to play position and help-side defense, and it makes it possible for you to teach as the drill is being run. Because this is a teaching drill, your defensive players should allow the passes to be completed to the offensive players.

Tell the offensive team to pass the ball around the perimeter until they hear the whistle, at which time whoever has possession of the ball holds on to it. The defense is allowed to continue to move after the whistle to gain proper defensive position. Now, you can examine the defense to make certain that each defensive player has adjusted his position with respect to the location of the ball. On your command, the offensive team once again moves the ball, and the process is repeated.

After you are certain that each player on the team knows the position he should be in with respect to the ball, it is then time to show how the defense rotates when a back-door cut is attempted. On your command, the wing should drive to the basket.

The defender guarding the ball (X3) allows the wing to drive. The help-side forward (X4) sprints across the lane to stop the drive, as shown in Figure 14.3. Then X4 yells as loudly as he can as he approaches the dribbler. This yell serves two purposes: (a) it distracts the dribbler, which may cause him to pick up his dribble or even commit a turnover; and (b) it alerts the other defenders that the rotation is on.

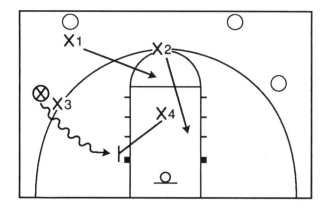

Figure 14.2   Horseshoe drill: initial positioning.   **Figure 14.3**   Horseshoe drill: drive by wing.

X4 should stop the offensive player outside the lane. If the dribbler is allowed into the lane, too many problems are created for the defense. To keep the drill going, the offensive player should not shoot unless he has an uncontested layup. If he is stopped along the baseline, the ball is reversed.

When X4 challenges the drive, X2 rotates down the lane to seal off X4's offensive player—the weak-side wing. X1 moves toward the foul line to protect against an open player in this dangerous scoring area.

If the offensive player shoots, the block-out assignments correspond with the position of the players after rotation. X4 blocks out the shooter; X2 blocks out the weak-side wing; X1 blocks out the nearest guard. After correcting any errors, reset and begin passing the ball around the perimeter once again.

Rotation from the guard position is slightly different. If X1's man drives to the outside, X3 must stop the dribbler (see Figure 14.4). If X3 cannot get there in time to stop the drive, then X4 must come across the lane to stop the ballhandler, and X2 then seals off the wing area.

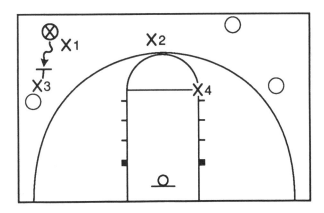

Figure 14.4   Horseshoe drill: drive by guard.

If the dribbler takes an inside route, X2 should stop him before he penetrates the scoring area. If X2 cannot get there in time to stop the drive, he should seal off the ball-side wing area, and X4 should stop the dribbler.

Horseshoe With the Post

Purpose.   To teach players to rotate and defend against a low post.

Organization.   As the season progresses, run the Horseshoe Drill with either a high-post or low-post player. If the post is high, the player guarding him is not involved in the rotation and is one pass away no matter where the ball is on the court. If there is a low-post player, there is a slight change in defensive assignments, but the principles remain the same.

Procedure.   On the drive, the player defending the low post (X5) rotates to pick up the dribbler. X4 rotates down to cover the offensive low post. The off-guard, X2, seals off the off-wing, and X1 slides toward the foul line and stays alert for the pass (see Figure 14.5).

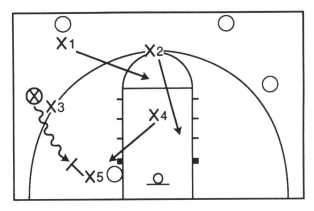

Figure 14.5   Horseshoe with the post.

Horseshoe With a One-Man Front

If the offense shows you a one-man front, the rotation rules on page 151 apply, whether the offensive players are stationary or driving to the basket. Again, X5 rotates to stop the drive; X3 picks up the low-

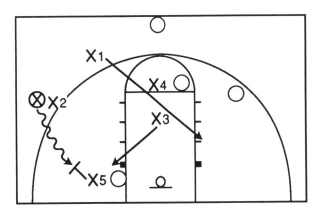

Figure 14.6   Horseshoe with a one-man front.

post offensive player; and the defensive point player must rotate and pick up the weak-side wing. The high post, following the rule, is not involved in the rotation (see Figure 14.6).

Fogler Drill

Purpose. To confront players with every defensive situation they could face in a game: guarding the ball, guarding the cutter, guarding the player one pass away from the ball, and guarding the player two or more passes away from the ball.

Organization. Begin with two guards and two forwards as you did in the Horseshoe Drill.

Procedure. In this drill, the offensive and defensive players will be active. X2's player starts with the ball, with the defensive players defending as shown in Figure 14.7. Because this drill is used to teach defensive positioning and responsibilities, the defense allows the offense to complete their passes, and the offensive players do not break from the established pattern. Let's follow one defensive player through the rotation of the drill.

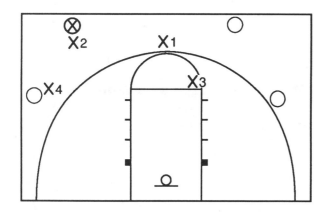

Figure 14.7   Fogler drill: initial alignment.

When the ball is passed to the wing, X2's role changes from guarding the ball to guarding the player one pass away from the ball. X2 must take an advance step into the passing lane to deny the return pass.

After passing the ball, X2's player cuts to the basket, attempting to get between X2 and the ball. X2 must deny him this position, and this is why it is *so* important that X2 slides in the direction of any pass his player makes. As the passer cuts toward

the basket, the player who received the pass holds the ball until you tell him to reverse the ball. The offensive players rotate as the cutter moves through the lane and now positions himself where the off-wing originally started. When the offense shifts, X2 stops in the lane, because his player is now more than two passes away from the ball (see Figure 14.8). He now becomes the help-side defense.

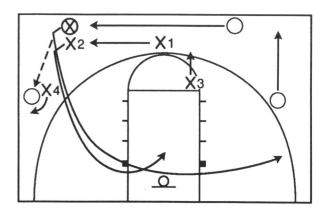

Figure 14.8   Fogler drill: on-ball to help-side defense.

On your command, the offense now reverses the ball, leaving X2 two passes away. X2 should take a step or two up the lane to get into the passing lane once the ball is reversed to the off-guard. This position on the court allows him to deny his player the ball, if he were to flash across the lane to the ball. If the ballhandler passes to the off-guard, X2 is one pass away and should be up in the passing lane denying his player the ball (see Figure 14.9).

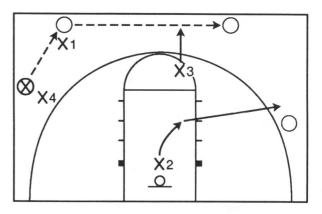

Figure 14.9   Fogler drill: denying wing pass on reversal.

Offensively, on any guard to guard pass, the passer and the wing on his side exchange with each other (see Figure 14.10a). This helps to work the help-side defensive player on adjusting from one pass away to two passes away. It also gets defenders in the habit of talking to each other.

X3's player then passes to the wing, making all the defenders adjust and placing X2 on the ball. On the pass to the wing, X3 slides in the direction of the pass, denying the passer the basket cut; X4 steps into the passing lane and denies his player the pass. X1 steps up to the lane to deny the off-guard reversal pass, and X3 replaces X1 as the weak-side defender in the lane (see Figure 14.10b). (Compare to Figure 14.8.) The drill continues as before, until players are back at their original positions.

Coaching Point. Remind your players that they must see both the ball and their player on defense, especially as those play-ers adjust from being one pass away to two or three passes away from the ball.

Breakdown Drills

All of your players must be able to play each of the defensive positions in the Horseshoe and Fogler drills if they are to contribute to your team defensively. These two drills require the use of all of the necessary defensive skills. When I want individuals on the team to improve in a particular defensive skill, I have them perform one of the following breakdown drills.

Guard Overplay

Purpose. To build the skills and confidence of players to deny the ball from the players they are guarding.

Organization. The offensive player starts at the wing position, anticipating a pass from the coach nearest him in the guard position. X1 assumes the defensive overplay position.

Procedure. Begin the drill by having X1's player work to get open and X1 contesting the ball by staying between his player and the ball. Player 1 works to receive the ball on the wing or farther back near midcourt. Attempt to throw the ball to the offensive player. If the defender is overplaying correctly, he should intercept the ball with no problem.

When you call the offensive player's name, he will make a hard backdoor cut to the basket. X1 denies the backdoor pass by pushing off the front foot, turning his head so that he can continue to see both the ball and his player, and closing the gap between himself and his man's path to the basket. He keeps his arm up to deflect the pass and to create a psychological barrier to the passer.

As the offensive player approaches the lane, X1 will open toward the ball and front his man sliding across the free throw lane. The cutter moves to the opposite wing, looking for a pass from you as you dribble the ball to this side of the court. X1 remains in the deny or overplay position on this side of the court, but this time he has his opposite hand in the passing lane and the corresponding foot forward. He should still be looking straight ahead, splitting the distance between his player and the ball so he can see them both (see Figure 14.11).

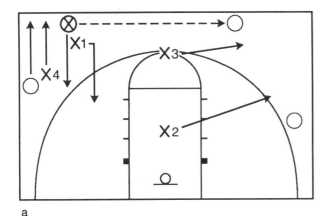

a

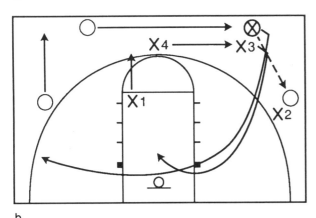

b

Figure 14.10 Fogler drill: passer and wing exchange (a) and on-ball to help-side defense (b).

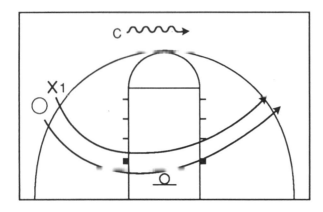

Figure 14.11 Guard overplay guarding the cutter.

Coaching Points. Intentionally allow the defense to be successful in intercepting or deflecting your pass to the offensive receiver. This helps build the confidence of the defensive player and makes him believe he can force his player to go without the ball.

One problem you will encounter is that as X1 closes to deny his player the ball on the wing, he will get too close to the offensive player. Doing this makes the offensive player quicker, and will create problems for the defender. He should continue to be one arm's length away.

Teach your players to ignore the offensive player's first step to the basket. If they are continually reacting to the first step, the offensive player can take a quick step back and receive the ball on the perimeter. Also, your players must not open up to the ball too soon or too late. They should open up as soon as the offensive player is in the lane, or as soon as he sees the pass being attempted.

Constantly remind your players that in game situations there will be pressure on the ball and a player on the weak side that will make the backdoor extremely difficult to complete. The rule of 22-Tough defense is to not let the player have the ball. He must be made to play without it. No player has ever scored without the basketball.

Halfcourt 1-on-1

Purpose. To execute all of the defensive steps and principles while guarding a player in game conditions.

Organization. Designate one offensive player and one defensive player. You run

this drill at both ends of the floor, with half of the team at each basket.

Procedure. Instruct the offensive player to slice the defenders to the basket. Have the defender force him to either the baseline or the middle of the court, and tell him to cut off the offensive player's drive before he gets to the basket. Play until the offensive player scores, or the defensive player has rebounded (or otherwise gained possession of the ball).

2-on-2: Perimeter

Purpose. To apply, under game-like conditions, perimeter man-to-man defensive principles and footwork (particularly defending the ball and defending one pass away).

Organization. Begin with two offensive guards and two defensive guards. Have them play in a live situation using the entire halfcourt area.

Procedure. Have the defenders play 22-Tough, and tell them to keep all of their defensive principles in mind.

2-on-2: Post

Purpose. To apply, under game-like conditions, post man-to-man defensive principles and footwork.

Organization. Begin with two offensive players in the post, corresponding defensive players, and a coach on each wing who will look to feed the post players as they get open.

Procedure. Have the defenders work to deny the post player the ball from the baseline side (while the ball is inside the free throw line extended) and to be active defenders in the help side. The coaches can drive to the basket whenever they want, at which time the post defenders must help and recover to stop the ball (see Figure 14.12).

Post Defense

Purpose. Post defenders are constantly changing their position in relation to the ball. This drill teaches post defenders how to continually move to maintain proper position between the ball and the man.

Organization. Begin with a post offensive player, a post defensive player, a coach, and two managers. The post defender should be positioned behind the offensive player. The

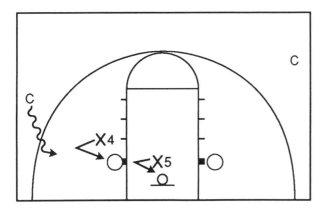

Figure 14.12   2-on-2: post.

coach is at the point, the managers on the wings.

Procedure.   The defensive player must react to your pass to either wing and gain defensive position on the post (see Figure 14.13). Begin the drill by having the offensive player play at half speed to allow the defender to get the footwork down. When the defender is confident with the footwork, you can then play it live.

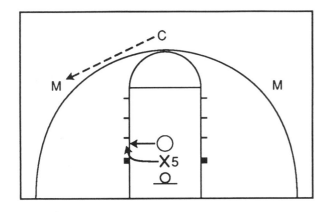

Figure 14.13   Post defense.

2-on-2: One Side

Purpose.   To teach perimeter defensive players to "dig in" on passes to the post and adjust on passes back to the perimeter. This drill also works the post defensive player on denying the pass to his man. Additionally, the offensive players are working on feeding the post and relocating for a possible jump shot.

Organization.   This drill consists of one post and one perimeter offensive player, and a corresponding defensive player

guarding each. The offense must work on one side of the court.

Procedure.   The perimeter offensive player looks to feed the post and relocate after the pass. The post offensive player must work to get open, then move effectively for the shot.

Defensively, the post player should move his feet to deny the pass into the post, and the perimeter defender should contain and pressure the ball but not get beat on the dribble. If the ball is passed into the post, the perimeter defender should dig into the post, keeping his backside to the baseline so that he can see the entire court. If the ball is passed back to the perimeter, the defender must adjust to pick up his man open.

2-on-2: Wings

Purpose.   To expose perimeter players to situations they will likely face in games when guarding the ball, when one pass away from the ball, and when more than one pass away from the ball.

Organization.   Start with an offensive player on each wing and a corresponding defender on each of them. Position yourself at the top of the key with the ball.

Procedure.   Begin the drill by dribbling to one side of the key. The two defensive players should work at denying their player the ball when they are one pass away; playing in the help side when the ball is two passes away; and playing help and recover if the ball is driven to the basket on their side (see Figure 14.14).

Coaching Point.   Eventually, you can make the drill 3-on-3, with the defense playing 22-Tough and the offense working to get open against pressure.

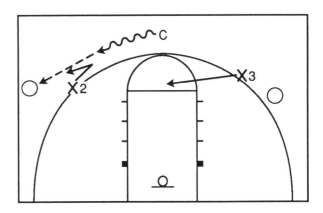

Figure 14.14   2-on-2: wings.

Perimeter-to-Post

Purpose. To teach your players each of the positions they could play while being part of a team that plays pressure defense.

Organization. Start with one offensive player and one defensive player. Start the offensive player on the wing, and position yourself at the guard spot with the ball.

Procedure. The defensive player (X2) begins by overplaying the wing. The offensive player should work to get open from the free throw line extended up to the hash mark. When you call the offensive player's name, he cuts backdoor, and the defender turns his head and denies the backdoor pass. As the cutter is going through the lane, dribble from the guard position down to the wing that was just vacated (see Figure 14.15a).

Because the defender is now more than two passes away, X2 should have both feet in the lane, seeing both the ball and his player. You can drive at any time to make sure that X2 is in position to help and recover should there be penetration when he is on the weak side.

Next, signal the offensive player to flash across the lane to the ball. As he flashes, the defender should step up the lane and deny him the ball and the position. After the offensive player flashes, he v-cuts to the ball-side block and posts up (see Figure 14.15b). The defensive player now denies the pass into the post from the wing by playing on the baseline side of the offensive player. The players then rotate from offense to defense and from defense to the end of the line.

Coaching Point. Because this drill is run 1-on-1, you can focus all of your attention on the individual and his development as a fundamentally sound defensive player.

Overmatch Drills: 5-on-4 and 6-on-4

Purpose. These two drills are designed to teach quick and proper movement within the defense. Making the defense play with one or two less players than the offense forces all of the defensive players to react quickly and correctly. Defensive players must move *on* the pass, rather than after the pass has been received. It's amazing how much quicker your defense will get

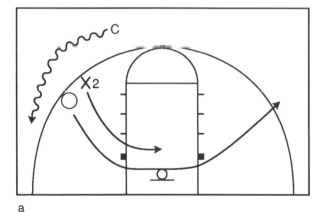

a

b

Figure 14.15 Perimeter-to-post (a) and deny the flash (b).

when playing with a numbers disadvantage. These drills will improve defenders' help and recovery skills, as well as their reaction time.

Organization. Have five offensive players face four defensive players in the halfcourt area (5-on-4). For 6-on-4, place two of the offensive players at the baseline on each side of the basket.

Procedure. Have the offense move the ball, eventually working it down to the baseline. When the baseline player gets the ball, have him drive the back of the defense. Proper rotation should take place as the defensive players help and recover to prevent the score (see Figure 14.16).

Coaching Point. Don't let defenders get in the habit of guarding an area. Instead, make them work as a unit, talking and helping as they play against the five or six offensive players.

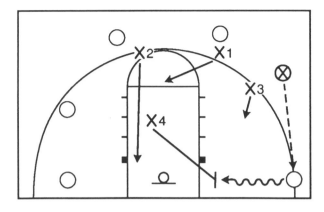

Figure 14.16 6-on-4.

Defense Against the Screen

Any time an offensive player sets a screen, the defense must talk to one another. A lack of communication results in confusion and missed assignments, which means uncontested shots for the offense.

When defending screens, I have my players follow these two rules:

- If the screen is attempted *inside the scoring area* (3-point line), get over the top of it.
- If the screen is attempted *outside the scoring area*, get through the screen by having the defender guarding the screener take a step off his player to let his teammate through.

Defensive players will not always be able to follow these rules, and that is when communication becomes especially important. At times, you may have to tell them to get over the screens even outside the scoring area if the offense is screening for a hot 3-point shooter. Obviously, you can't allow a good 3-point shooter too much room to get off his shot.

Drills for Defending a Screen

The primary purpose of these drills is to enhance communication between the defensive players who are defending against a screen. The player guarding the screener must let his teammate know the screen is

coming. And he must back off of his man, giving his teammate room to slide through the screen and stay with the player he is guarding.

I tell my players to avoid switching defenders against the screen whenever possible. I would rather each defender stay with the player he is guarding by helping and recovering.

Downscreen

Purpose. To practice communication and defensive principles against a downscreen, which frequently takes place from perimeter to post.

Organization. Begin with one offensive wing, one offensive low post, and corresponding defenders. Also, place yourself (or another coach) at the point guard spot with the ball.

Procedure. As the wing downscreens X2 to get the low-post player open on the wing, X1 should step off his man and toward the ball to give X2 room to slide through the screen. By communicating and giving each other room to move, defenders are able to work successfully against the screen (see Figure 14.17).

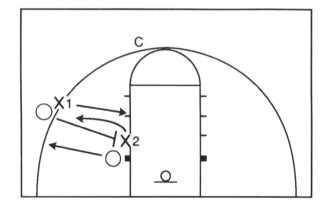

Figure 14.17 Downscreen: going over the top.

Another example of how to guard the downscreen is shown in the exchange that takes place between the weak-side guard and wing after the ball has been passed to the guard on the other side of the court. X2 and X1 must talk to each other to avoid running into each other while continuing to execute their defensive responsibilities on the weak side. Because X2 is coming up the lane and can see the entire court, he should be telling X1 what to do. X2 must move straight up the lane and into the passing lane to deny the ball (because he is now one pass away). X1 (who is now two passes away) should take a step off his player in the direction of the ball so he can take care of the weak-side defense (see Figure 14.18). The defender should *never* be more than one pass away from the player he is guarding.

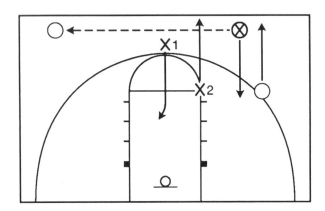

Figure 14.18   Downscreen: creating room.

Cross-Screen

Purpose.   To practice communication and defensive principles against the cross-screen, which frequently takes place between two post players.

Organization.   Begin with two low-post offensive players, corresponding defenders, and a coach on the wing with the ball. The post defender on the strong side should be denying his player the ball.

Procedure.   As I've said, your player must be able to play defense in the post as well as on the perimeter, and screens take place in the post. In defending the cross-screen, your players must communicate with each other to be successful. One post player cross-screens for the other post; X5 tells X4 what to expect. Then X4 takes one step up the lane and toward the ball to take away the high cut, and X5 defends against the low cut (see Figure 14.19). If the offensive player coming off the screen cuts high, X4 is in position to deny the pass. If he cuts low, X5 delays his cut to allow X4 to get around the screen. Player X4 must step up

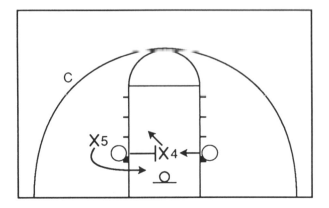

Figure 14.19   Defense vs. cross-screen.

the lane and toward the ball to insure that the screener does not flash back to the ball to be a receiver as X5 is denying the other post player the cut. As X4 recovers, X5 slides into the lane and becomes the weak-side post defender.

Coaching Point.   Remind players that the ball-side defender takes the low cut, and the help-side defender takes the high cut.

Screen on the Ball

Purpose.   To work on communication and defensive principles against a screen involving the player with the ball.

Organization.   Begin with a point guard (with the ball), a wing, and corresponding defenders.

Procedure.   If the screen occurs on the ball, the player (X3) guarding the screener should step out and hedge to stop the dribbler's penetration (see Figure 14.20a). This will allow the defender being screened (X1) time to fight over the screen and get back in front of the offensive player he is guarding, as shown in Figure 14.20b. Remind the defender who is hedging to step back off the player he is guarding, and into the path of the dribbler. He should stay low while stepping out so that he can delay the dribbler and contain the ball while his teammate gets over the screen.

Variations of the 22-Tough Defense

Two of the best variations on the 22-Tough are the Blitz Switch (26) and the Blitz Trap

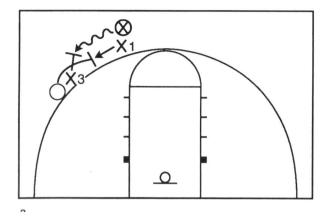

a

b

Figure 14.20 Defense vs. screen on the ball.

(25). I use them to

- create turnovers,
- control tempo,
- make strong offensive players give up the ball,
- disrupt the offensive team's patterns and timing,
- wear down the offensive players so they will not be as strong at the end of the game, and
- force weaker offensive players to handle or shoot the ball more.

Two other defenses that I'll describe later in the chapter, the Entry and Fist & Fingers defenses, are useful in certain situations. Your decision to use them should vary according to the abilities of your players, the opponent, and the game circumstances.

Preparing to Blitz Trap and Blitz Switch

When you are in 22-Tough, have the player guarding the ball as it crosses midcourt force the ball to one side and keep the drib-

bler on that side. This establishes which defenders should be denying the ball to their player, and which defenders should be off their player and in the help side. Forcing the ball to one side also creates opportunities for you to execute the Blitz Switch and Blitz Trap.

Blitz Trap—25

Let's look at an example of how a team can blitz trap an opponent. X1 plays on the dribbler's left side as he crosses midcourt. This overplay pressure forces the ballhandler to the right, where X2 is prepared to trap him. When the dribbler is three strides away from X2, X2 runs at him under control and in a defensive stance to complete the trap. As he leaves his player, X2 should begin to yell loudly to signal to his teammates that the trap is on, and the rotation should begin. This also helps to unnerve the dribbler to the point where he will sometimes pick up the dribble, thereby putting himself in an even more difficult situation.

After X1 and X2 have contained the dribbler within a certain area, they close the trap, remaining balanced and staying low to keep the ballhandler within the trap. The trap should form a "V" with the open side away from the scoring area (see Figure 14.21). Remind your players that they can maintain the trap by moving their feet, not by pushing or holding the offensive player with their hands or arms.

When the offensive player picks up the dribble, the defenders close the trap even more, keeping their feet active and cutting off the passing lanes. They keep both of

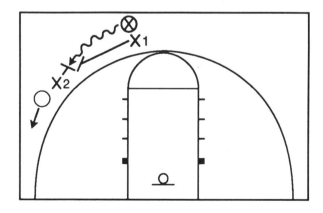

Figure 14.21 Blitz Trap: stopping the dribble.

their hands together (following the movement of the ball), and avoid the temptation to reach in and try to make a steal. Reaching would cause them to lose their balance, giving the offensive player open passing lanes. Reaching in can also be called a foul, and thus can let the offensive player off the hook.

Patience by the two players trapping the ball allows the rotation to take place. Turnovers will occur when the trap forces a hurried decision or a bad pass; the rotating players will be moving through the passing lanes to steal the ball. The defense may also force the offensive player into a violation (travel, double dribble, 5-second) or a charge.

The defenders begin their rotation as soon as they see X2 leave his player to trap the dribbler. Player X4 leaves to intercept the pass to X2's man, X5 rotates over to take the ball-side post, and X3 anticipates the off-wing going to the ball and denies him the pass (see Figure 14.22).

force enough turnovers to make up for the points they allow.

If the trap is broken with the pass or the dribble, then the defensive players must play help and recover until the defense has re-adjusted and every offensive player is being guarded. The defenders must talk and move to get back to their players as quickly as possible.

Blitz Switch—26

There are two major differences between the Blitz Switch and the Blitz Trap. First, the Blitz Switch involves only two players. The other players do not rotate to the next available receiver, although a player is encouraged to anticipate and make a steal through a passing lane if he has the angle to do so. Second, X1, instead of forming a trap with X2, will break off from the player he is guarding and pick up X2's man (see Figure 14.23).

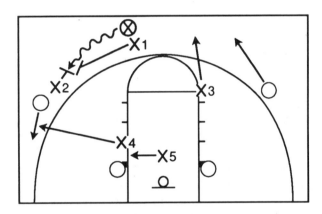

Figure 14.22   Blitz Trap: rotation.

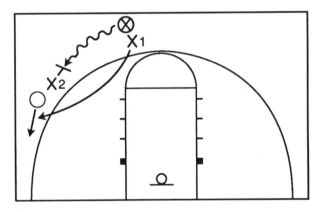

Figure 14.23   Blitz Switch.

Note that this rotation leaves open the farthest offensive player away from the trap. That's the risk you run in using the Blitz Trap defense. I take the chance that with enough pressure on the passer he will not be able to pick out the open player. If he does spot him, then your players must adjust as best they can. *Reminder*: Only a high-post defender does not get involved in the rotation.

Let your players know that because this is a gambling defense, the offense will score occasionally. However, they should also

Aside from these two principles, the Blitz Trap and the Blitz Switch are executed in much the same way. X1 overplays one of the dribbler's sides to direct the ball toward a teammate. Caution the point defender not to play so far to one side of the ballhandler that he gets sliced to the basket. He still must contain the ball. (If the point guard insists on going to the side of the overplay, X1 will simply run the switch with the defensive player on that side of the floor.)

When the dribbler is three strides away from X2, X2 runs at him and executes the

Blitz Switch. Again, he should begin to yell as he leaves his player to signal that the Blitz Switch is on. As X2 runs at the ballhandler, he should come in under control and in a defensive stance so that he does not overrun him. If he does not contain him, the purpose of the Blitz Switch is defeated.

When X2 reaches the dribbler, X1 switches off and runs through to pick up X2's player. This is very effective after the Blitz Trap has been run a few times; because the dribbler sees X2 release from his player to execute the blitz, the dribbler will attempt to dish the pass off quickly. If X1 is alert, he may be able to pick off that pass. Also, if the offensive team is beating your Blitz Trap by passing off before your players complete their rotation, the Blitz Switch can be an effective way of controlling the tempo of the game without leaving men open to be receivers.

Entry

This defense is used against a 1-4 offensive set that is trying to take advantage of your defense by spreading it out, taking away the help-side, and setting up backdoor opportunities. The purpose of the Entry defense is to eliminate the offensive team's ability to turn backdoor passes into layups; instead, it allows the completion of the first penetrating pass to the wing or high post. The completion of the pass to the wing also establishes the ball-side and help-side of the court so the defense can adjust accordingly. As soon as the first pass has been made, your team can shift back to 22-Tough (or whatever other defense you may call).

Fist & Fingers

This defense seeks to trap either the pass or the dribble as the ball is entered into the halfcourt offense. (The fullcourt version of Fist & Fingers is discussed on page 169). At times you may want your player to trap only the pass, or at other times only the dribble. Both options are possible from this defense. You can also call for your team to only trap in specific places (corners, midcourt line, below the foul line extended).

To create the trap off the pass, I often have my team play our Entry defense, which allows the completion of the first pass so the

trap can take place. The rotation is the same as when running a 25. Timing is critical if a turnover is to be created. The rotation must start as the ball is leaving the passer's hands and the nearest defensive players are beginning their attack and double team on the receiver (see Figure 14.24).

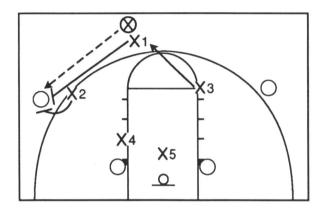

Figure 14.24   Fist & Fingers: halfcourt.

Fullcourt Defense

After teaching the fundamentals of individual and team defense, you can begin building your fullcourt team defense. Every team needs a fullcourt defense for those games when you are trailing in the closing moments and need to force a turnover. Fullcourt defenses can work to your advantage in other areas as well. They can

- control the tempo of the game to your liking,
- force the opponent to play the length of the floor when on offense,
- take advantage of your superior quickness,
- take advantage of a team that may not handle the ball well.

Fullcourt Defensive Drills

When teaching fullcourt team defense, it is wise to once again use the "break down" method and concentrate on a special phase of the defense. Do not concentrate on too much at a time. I've already described the 1-on-1 fullcourt drill (see page 147), and that is the first phase of building such a defense. The next step is the 2-on-2 drill.

2-on-2

Purpose. To teach players to apply full-court pressure defensive tactics and contest the inbounds pass.

Organization.   Use three groups of players in this drill with four players in each group, two on defense and two on offense. Use only one ball through the entire drill. When the first two offensive players have completed their trip up the court (play stops after a score, a defensive rebound, or a turnover), they switch roles with the defensive unit they just faced, and they return down court. Each group must be ready to go as soon as the group in front of it has finished. You can also divide your team in half and have one group work at each basket to get more players involved (stopping the drill at half court).

Procedure.   In this drill, position one offensive player to inbound the ball, and another at least as far back as the elbow of the foul line and on the opposite side of the court. This alignment gives the offensive players the maximum amount of room to maneuver to get the ball inbounds, thus putting pressure on the defensive players to deny the inbounds pass.

X1 lines up just off the baseline. His responsibility is to make the inbounds pass as difficult as possible by yelling, jumping up and down, moving his arms, and staying in the passing lane.

Position X2 away from his player and toward the ball. He must keep one hand in the passing lane. Positioning him in this manner allows X2 to see both the ball and his player, which is a necessity in this defensive approach. X2 should not let 2 flash across the lane. Instead, he should dictate and force him to the baseline. This is a very difficult pass to complete because of the angle and the pressure both on the ball and the receiver.

When the inbounder slaps the ball, the other offensive player makes his move to receive the pass. I do not allow the offensive team to lob the ball inbounds. In live action, there would be help in stealing these lobs. In addition, it does not help the defensive players improve if the offensive team takes the easy way out and does not force the defense to work.

X2 attempts to deny the inbounds pass. However, if the pass is successful, the inbounder clears the area by cutting in front of the player with the ball and looking for the return pass (see Figure 14.25). If the pass is not thrown, X2 then plays the ballhandler 1-on-1 up the court to the scoring area at the opposite end. Play then continues as 2-on-2 basketball until a defensive rebound, or an offensive score or turnover.

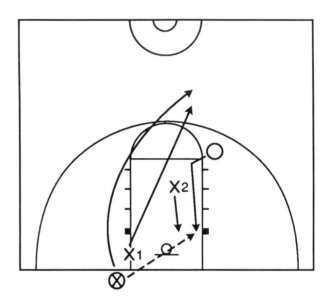

Figure 14.25   Full court: 2-on-2.

Coaching Points. It is important to emphasize putting great pressure on the inbounds pass. Once the ball is in play, the defense should continue to pressure the ball by keeping the head on the ball (as was done in the 1-on-1 drill). The dribbler should be turned as many times as possible and ultimately stopped as the defensive player closes on him. Meanwhile, the other defender should not allow his player to catch the ball.

3-on-3

Purpose. To teach fullcourt defensive pressure against teams who attack with two immediate receivers.

Organization. Use groups of six, each group containing three offensive players and three defensive players. Use one ball, and have the groups change roles when one group reaches the end of the court. You can also have players involved at both ends of the court (provided they stop at midcourt to avoid collisions).

Procedure.   The offensive unit starts with an inbounder and two players stacked at the middle of the foul line. X1 takes the inbounder, while X2 and X3 position themselves away from their men and toward the ball. The offensive player farthest from the ball breaks first, using his teammate as a screener if possible. If the first cutter cannot receiver the ball, then the other offensive player should cut in the opposite direction and look to receive the inbound pass.

X1 has the same responsibility as he did in the 2-on-2 drill. X2 and X3 should try to prevent their players from catching the ball, and to stay in proper one-pass-away position. If a screen takes place, the defenders must talk over the screen and play their men. Again, I discourage the lob pass to get the ball inbounds; the defense will not improve if the offense simply goes over the top.

If the pass is completed, the inbounder steps in and, along with the guard not receiving the ball, clears the area by running a guard in front. The defenders must work on staying between their men and the ball, as shown in Figure 14.26.

The defender guarding the ball should put aggressive pressure on the ball while

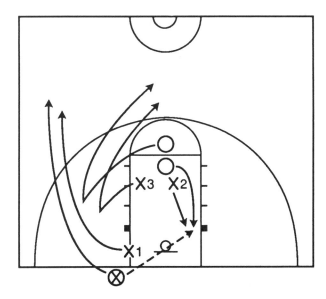

Figure 14.26   Full court: 3-on-3.

turning the offensive player as often as possible. If the ball gets across half court, they play 3-on-3 basketball.

Coaching Points.   Do not allow defenders to switch at any time during this drill. This is essential, because you never want anything coming between your defenders and the ball. To make this drill effective, work the defense against as many different alignments as you can think of.

4-on-4

Purpose.   To build one step closer to the complete fullcourt defense.

Organization.   Use three groups of four offensive and four defensive players, with the groups alternating their assignments frequently. The inbounder and the offensive player nearest to him line up using the same rules as in the fullcourt 2-on-2. The other two offensive players line up behind the midcourt line as receivers, ready to bring the ball up. Each defender gets into proper position (see Figure 14.27).

Procedure.   In this drill, X2's man is the primary receiver, and it is X2's responsibility to deny him the ball. The secondary receivers can move to receive the ball if their teammate needs help. The inbounder can attempt the lob pass in this drill to see how X3 and X4 react to the pass. There is more pressure on the defense here than in regular 5-on-5 situations because there is no defensive post player to help on the long pass.

If the pass is completed short to the player nearest the ball, the inbounder clears the area looking for a return pass. X2 must put good aggressive pressure on the ballhandler as he comes up court. When the ball crosses the midcourt line, it becomes a game of 4-on-4 basketball.

Coaching Point.   I like this drill because it puts so much pressure on X3 and X4. They must be able to react up or back to keep the ball away from their men. They should also play off their men toward the ball as if they are two passes away. In addition, they should play with their back to the sideline so they can see the entire court, including the player and the ball. This way, they can deny their player the cut to the ball if he is trying to help get the ball in bounds, and

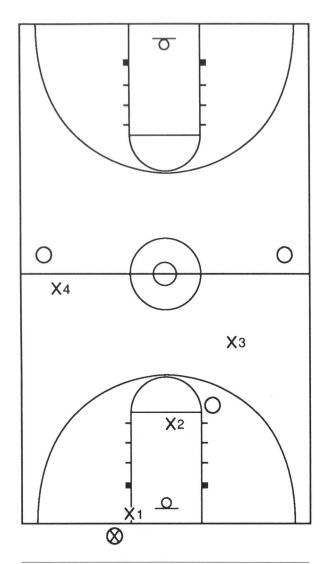

Figure 14.27   Full court: 4-on-4 alignment.

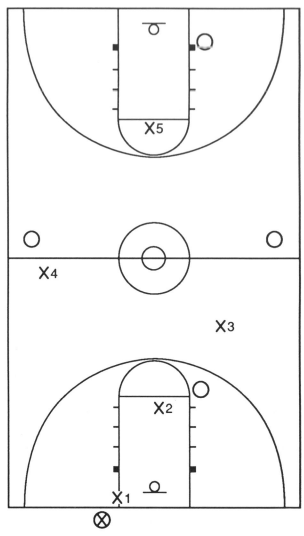

Figure 14.28   Full court: 5-on-5.

they can help pick off the lob pass to the player guarded by X2 if it is attempted.

5-on-5

Purpose.   To combine all of the elements of a fullcourt pressure defense.

Organization.   This drill is basically our 22-Tough defense in the 4 area. You can set up the offense in various alignments, depending on what type of front your opponent presents when breaking fullcourt man-to-man pressure. The alignment that I use most often is shown in Figure 14.28. This line up is the same as in the 4-on-4 drill, except add the two post players (X5 and his man) down court.

Procedure.   The responsibilities for X1, X2, X3, and X4 are the same as in the 4-on-

4 drill. X5 must play well off the low post to insure that he does not break open for a pass up court and to prevent the offensive players positioned at midcourt from catching the lob from the inbounder.

Variations of the Fullcourt 22-Tough

There are three basic variations of the 22-Tough in the 4 area. (Other variations, such as fullcourt switching and trapping will be covered next.) I refer to them with baseball terms because that seems to help players remember what the defenses are designed to do. They can be adapted to your opponent's pressure offense and style of play.

Each of these variations is simple, and all help give the standard 22-Tough in the 4 area many useful options without drastically changing the assignments of the majority of the defensive players. Also, by giving your defense a "new look," you can keep your opponents off-balance.

Shortstop

In this variation, X1, who usually guards the player inbounding the ball, plays between the ball and the receiver. X2 moves behind and on the ball side of the potential receiver, creating what is in effect a double team (see Figure 14.29).

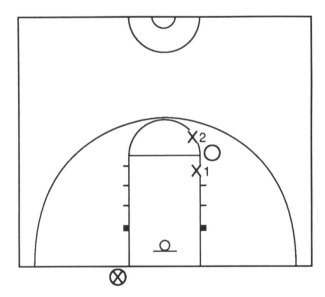

Figure 14.29 Shortstop.

If the ball should get in bounds, X1 should recover to guard the inbounder. The defense would play a normal 22-Tough in the 4 area.

This defense is particularly effective against a team with only one good ballhandler, or a team with an exceptional guard to whom you would like to deny the ball. This simple tactic is also very successful against a well-patterned ball club that depends upon a single point player to initiate the offense. When the primary receiver is double-teamed, the offense has a tendency to forgo its patterned style and play in a more hap-

hazard way. In effect, you neutralize their offensive strength.

Centerfield

This variation is designed to prevent the lob pass. The player (X1) usually guarding the inbounder plays at the head of the circle, as shown in Figure 14.30. It is X1's responsibility to pick off any medium lob. This is particularly effective when a team uses backcourt screens to break fullcourt pressure. Initially, the centerfielder should cheat to the ball side, because the backboard will prevent the inbounder from attempting the lob to the weak side.

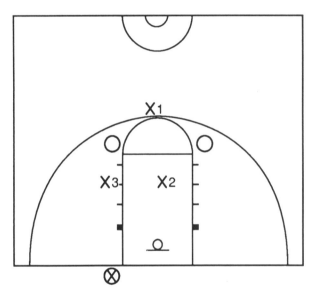

Figure 14.30 Centerfield.

The centerfielder gives 22-Tough a zone look, which often causes the offensive team to make needless and dangerous adjustments to break the press. X2 and X3 can now be even more determined about overplaying because the lob is covered.

Leftfield

The purpose of this defensive alignment is to stop the offensive team from successfully completing the fullcourt pass. X1 moves

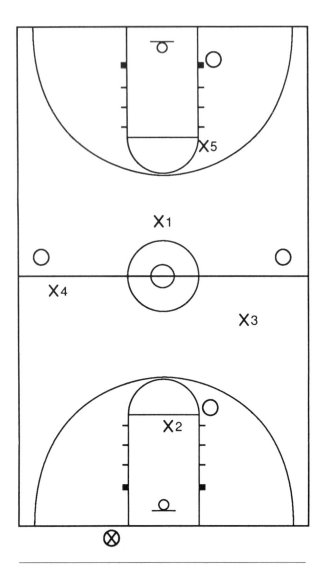

Figure 14.31 Leftfield.

to the opposite end of the court, into the middle of the 2 area (see Figure 14.31). This puts added pressure on the other four defensive players; if the pass is completed to one of their men, the press is broken by a throw back to the uncovered inbounder. Defenders can be assured, however, that they can fully overplay without worrying that the player they are guarding will break down court for the long lob.

Fullcourt Switching and Trapping Variations

As I've stated, you never want to give the offense the same look time after time. In addition to the basic variations of 22-Tough, you can also employ fullcourt blitzing and switching to disrupt the offense.

The Blitz Switch (26) can be easily executed in the 4 area. Because it is a two-player defensive tactic, there is no adjustment to be made if you apply it in the back court.

Let's look at what adjustments there would be if Blitz Trap (25) were to be run in the 4 area. If the ball were passed to the nearest offensive player, and your team was in Blitz Trap, X2 would have two options. He could force the ballhandler to the sideline for the Fan Trap, or to the middle for the Funnel Trap.

Fan Trap

X2 forces the player who received the pass to the sideline. X3 releases from his player

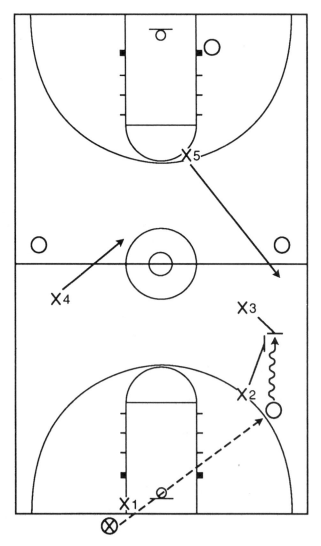

Figure 14.32 Fan Trap.

when the ballhandler is three strides away and completes the trap with X2. X5 rotates up to pick up X3's man at the midcourt line, and will take an angle that runs through the passing lane for a potential steal. X1 takes away the pass back to the inbounder, and X4 drops to play between the two deep offensive players (see Figure 14.32). X4 must remain active, read the trap, judge which receiver is most dangerous, and cheat toward that direction.

Funnel Trap

X2 forces the inbound receiver to the middle and into the trap with X1. X4 rotates up to look for a steal through the ballhandler-inbounder passing lane. X3 stays with his man, and X5 rotates up and plays between the two deep offensive players, just as X4 did in the Fan Trap (see Figure 14.33). The deep pass is left unguarded (as the defensive player cheats toward the closer receiver), but this is an extremely difficult pass to complete, especially when the passer is in the middle of an aggressive trap.

Fist & Fingers

Fist & Fingers (see page 163) can also be used as a fullcourt defense with only a few adjustments. This defense is similar to the Funnel Trap, except in this case the trap is triggered by the pass or the dribble, not just by the dribble. On the inbound pass to the

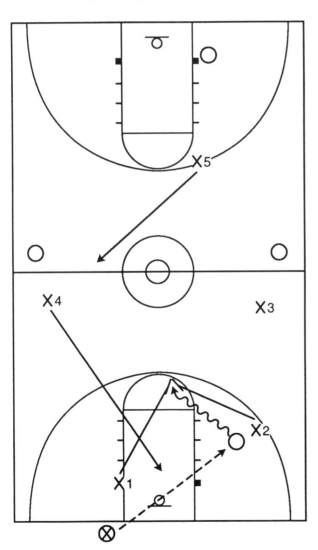

Figure 14.33 Funnel Trap.

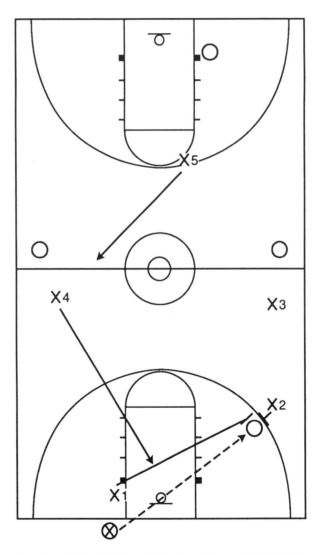

Figure 14.34 Fist & Fingers: halfcourt.

nearest receiver, X1 would leave the inbounder (or the centerfield position he may be in) to trap the ballhandler with X2. X4 would rotate again, and X5 would split the two deep offensive players while reading the trap (see Figure 14.34).

Improving Defensive Teamwork

Many of the points from "Improving Offensive Teamwork" (on pages 114-116) apply to improving defensive teamwork as well, particularly the need to go beyond the X's and O's. A difficulty in developing team defense, though, is that some players may not *want* to play defense because it is less glamorous than offense. Therefore you, as a coach, can make a difference by selling your players on the values of good individual and team defensive play.

It all goes back to what I've said before: *It's not what you coach; it's what you emphasize.* I probably emphasize the team defense more than any other phase of basketball. I tell my players that the best defensive player will always start. It may not be the most poetic statement ever uttered, but I tell them: "No defense, no play."

An occasional good-natured needle can also get a point across to a player or the team about the importance of good defense. One of my current assistants, Pat Smith, played for me before becoming an assistant of mine. He now says that I used to really get to him if he got beat, and I would say something like, "Don't worry, Pat. He's obviously a little too quick for you. But I thought you had the intelligence to be able to take better angles and cut off the quicker players." I would like to emphasize here that these needles do get a point across, but they should always be friendly and good-natured. **Never** use them to embarrass a player.

My emphasis on defense does not necessarily translate into spending more time on it than any other facet of the game. In fact, I spend more practice time on offense than defense.

 THE WIZARD'S WAY

I once attended a clinic with UCLA's John Wooden as the featured speaker. Coach Wooden asked those in attendance if they spent more time on offense or defense. About 95% of the coaches said, "Defense."

Coach Wooden said that was fine if that was what they felt was right. But he told the group that he spent more time on offense. Why? Because offense is harder to teach, and the skills are harder to develop. If you've coached for long, I'm sure you'll agree.

Almost all basketball players can become good defensive players, but not everyone has the tools to be great on offense. Also, keep in mind that when your players practice offense, half your team is playing defense. So keep an eye on the team without the ball during live practice situations. And instruct and correct players on defense as much or more than the offense they are working against.

Part V

Coaching Games

Chapter 15

Preparing for Games

The most successful basketball coaches are the ones who are best at preparing their team for each game. A well-prepared team will be confident that it has every chance to win that game as long as it plays hard, plays smart, and has fun. The bulk of this preparation is done on the practice floor by working on what your team does best and by preparing for what the opposition does best.

The Scouting Report

Scouting is an important part of preparing your team to face your next opponent. Notice I said *an* important part, not *the* important part. Our emphasis in preparation for a game is always on our own strengths,

on working even harder and getting even better at what we do best. We are more concerned with what we do offensively, defensively, and in special situations than with what our opponents do.

As I mentioned in chapter 5, John Wooden always said that he did not like to do much scouting because he felt that knowing the opponent too well made him either overconfident or petrified. And he felt that his players could sense his feelings about an upcoming game. But you can bet that the greatest coach who ever lived knew plenty about the opponent when his team took the floor.

Because I believe scouting is an important part of preparation, a rule of thumb at DeMatha is that we want to see every league opponent at least twice, three times if possible. For nonleague opponents, we feel the need to see them at least once, but preferably twice.

The Scouting Form

Before the season begins, we sit down and draw up a Master Scouting Schedule, which tells every member of our staff whom, where, and when they will be scouting. The amount of time spent on scouting is obviously dependent upon the number of assistant coaches you have available to scout.

For those of you who may be coaching alone, I recommend recruiting an interested fan or faculty member to help you with the scouting. You can make it easier on these volunteers by having a form already prepared which details the information you are looking for about the upcoming opponent. Our scouting form, shown on page 51, asks for the following information:

- Individual personnel (including height and weight) and their tendencies
- First sub in the backcourt
- First sub along the front line
- The best player to foul
- Offensive set against pressure defense
- Offensive set against halfcourt man-to-man defense
- Offensive set against halfcourt zone defense
- Delay game set
- Inbounds plays along the baseline
- Inbounds plays along the sideline
- Fullcourt pressure defense
- Halfcourt zone trap
- Man-to-man defensive look(s)
- Zone defensive look(s)
- Defensive look vs. inbounds underneath their basket
- Junk defenses (Box-and-One, etc.)
- Whether they have a player who can take over
- Match-ups that can work to our advantage/disadvantage
- What their style of play is
- What we must do to win

This information provides us with a thorough glimpse of opponents, their strengths, and their weaknesses. In short, the scouting report tells me what we must do to win.

Getting the Information

Scouting information can come from various sources. The best scouting approach is having the head coach or assistant coach actually view the game. This is the option to select when time and cost are not prohibitive. You can pick up more things in person than you can through other means.

A second method of obtaining scouting information is through the exchange of videotapes. Many high school basketball programs videotape all of their games. You can call opposing coaches before the season to see if an exchange of these tapes can be worked out. Sometimes, because of their replay potential, videotapes can help you learn even more tactical information about your opposition than would attending their games.

If you are unable to go see a particular opponent and unable to get a tape of one of its games, you then must rely on the third scouting tactic: telephone calls to other coaches who have seen or played against that team. These coaches can give you some idea of what to expect. Obviously it is better for you or your staff to actually watch a game, but telephone calls at least give you some information to help in your preparation.

I would like to emphasize once again that scouting is only one phase—and not even the most important phase—of preparing for your next opponent. It pales in comparison to season-long preparation of your team's strengths. If you adjust offenses and defenses from game to game to fit the opponent, your team may be able to do a lot of things, but none of them very well. Find a primary offense and defense that best suits your team's talents and work to perfect that. That is the best way to prepare for any opponent.

The Pregame Practice

Knowing what your opponents like to do will have some influence on your practice sessions leading up to that game. For example, if you know the opposing team likes to press a lot, you will spend a bit more time on your press offense. If you know the upcoming opponent likes to fast break, you may want to spend some time on sprinting back on defense or jumping the rebounders to prevent the outlet pass. So your points of emphasis may shift to a degree, depending on what your scouting report has told you.

I make these changes in practice subtle ones, and I do not tell the players why we are working on certain things. If I feel we need to spend a little more time working against a fullcourt press, I don't tell the players it's because our next opponent is very good at applying fullcourt pressure. We just do it, and I tell the players we are working on it because it's something we must be able to do to be a good basketball team.

Telling the players why you are working on certain phases of the game oftentimes leads to mistaken perceptions. In other words, you run the risk of building the opponent up too much or not enough. If I inform the team that we are going to face some tough fullcourt pressure, I could be intimidating my players into thinking that team is better than it is. They may think, "Well, if the coach says they're good, and we need to work on it in practice, they might be tougher than we thought. What if we can't get the ball up the court against them?" Such doubts and negative thoughts can lead to poor performance.

The opposite is also true. If I tell the team our opponent does not handle pressure very well, and that we are going to try and take advantage of that, our players may feel they are facing a weak team when that may not be the case.

So you and your staff should withhold from players your reasons for structuring your practices a certain way. It's the coaches' job to worry about why. The players have enough to worry about with execution.

We seldom mention anything specific about our next opponent until the day of the game. However, the drills we run in practice are designed to sharpen the strengths we feel will be a factor in the upcoming game.

We seldom practice our defense against an opponent's offense because our theory is that our pressure is going to force them out of their offense anyway. Sometimes, however, we must prepare for situations in which the offense will be difficult to gain command over. For example, some teams are precise enough to run an effective "Flex" offense, which has become very popular in recent years. The Flex is a baseline, screening offense that emphasizes player and ball movement. But when we have our defense work against the Flex in practices, we present it only as a good defensive drill to help in fighting over screens and giving weak-side help. Our teams then view this as a drill designed to help our defense, rather than as a preparation for a team that runs the Flex offense. (In fact, we have worked on this drill to such an extent that our offense has also become quite adept at running the Flex, and we have occasionally used it ourselves in games.)

Plan and structure your pregame practices so that you are working on the skills you feel will benefit the team the most in the upcoming game. But sell it to the players as regular practice work designed to improve your team.

Generally, I like to make the heaviest work day the practice 2 days before a game. The day before a game, I like to keep practice fairly short, so we can have fresh legs the following day. I tell the kids, "We're not going to go long, but we're going to go strong." Observe the team closely, and evaluate how it is responding. Sometimes a short practice can be more beneficial than a long one.

At practice the day before a game, we call the team together and take only about 5 minutes to go over the opposing team and its tendencies. We'll cover what they like to do offensively and defensively, and give our players a brief overview of their personnel. During this talk, I am extremely careful not to oversell the team we are about to face.

 CARR TEAM BRAINWASHED

It was the year Kenny Carr, who later became an All-American at N.C. State, a member of the 1976 Gold Medal Olympic team, and a fine NBA performer with the Portland Trailblazers, was a senior at DeMatha. We were to play in the City Championship game against a great team from Eastern High School.

Before the game, I spent about 25 minutes in front of the team talking about Eastern—how great a team they were and how awesome each and every player was. My emphasis was misguided: I placed more importance on how good *they* were and on what *they* could do than on what *we* could do. We got our brains beat out. I learned my lesson well.

Pregame Motivation

Before the game, I always hold a brief team meeting, either in the locker room when we play on the road or in a classroom when we play at home. I will walk into that room 25 minutes before the game, speak for about 5 minutes, and then leave 20 minutes for the players to loosen up. During the 5-minute session, I take the game plan out of my jacket pocket and quickly go over what we are going to do offensively and defensively, what our alignments will be in various situations, and what the match-ups will be.

READYING THE CHARGES FOR POWER

In one of the greatest high school basketball games ever played, we went up against Lew Alcindor (now Kareem Abdul-Jabbar) and Power Memorial High School. Alcindor was undefeated in his high school career, Power Memorial had won 71 games in a row, but they had beaten us by only three points the year before.

Under these conditions, my players needed simple direction, not further motivation. So, on this particular night, I walked into the locker room at the University of Maryland's Cole Field House, called the team together, and gave the following talk:

"Gentlemen, let's all get together. Offensively tonight, against their man-to-man, we're going to run the Box. If they go zone, we'll go with our 1-4 set. Any kind of pressure, it will be a two-man front.

Defensively, we're going to start with a 22-Tough, quarterbacking Feruggio to try and make the other guard handle the ball. Jump balls, we'll use our green alignment. Out of bounds, we're going to run the Line. Free throws, it'll be our Maryland alignment. Time and Score, we'll go to Four Corners to Score.

Match-ups: Whitmore—you have Alcindor, number 33. Williams—you have Toddman, number 14. Catlett—you have Brown, number 21. Wiles—you have Feruggio, number 22. Austin—you have Haughton, number 11.

Game captain. Whose turn is it to be captain? All right, Wiles. Bench captain, Petrini.

Okay, men. Real simple. We have to do a big job on both boards. We've gone over it enough.

Total front on Alcindor. Any time he catches the ball, it's got to be on lobs over our heads. We're going to get the pressure up like we've never gotten it up before.

Great crowd. Great occasion. Two great teams. Let's just make sure of one thing—that we play as hard and as smart as we can, but I want to see us have more fun than they do.

Let's go."

Underdog vs. Favorite

Unfortunately, there are always going to be fans and media people who will want to label your team as an underdog, favorite, or even-match to your opponent. But I never look at it this way. I approach each game with the mindset that we need to do certain things to be successful, no matter who we are playing.

I tell the team, "We have worked hard to get ready for this game. We are well prepared. We are in excellent shape, physically and mentally. And we are going to go out and play as hard and as smart as we can for the next 32 minutes, and we're going to have some fun."

I try to keep the approach low-key to prevent the players from falling into the trap of either feeling they must win, or playing not to lose.

If the upcoming opponent is one that I know our team feels it can easily defeat, I try to become more motivational in my approach. I think a coach has to be honest with his team. If you previously beat the team you're playing by 25 points that year, your team is not going to believe you if you try to convince them they're facing a great team. The players will see right through that.

I fear the games when we play a team we are supposed to beat handily the most because of the possibility of a letdown, a lack of intensity. You have to remind the players that they still have to prove themselves on the court, and that they didn't previously win just by showing up. This is when you have to tell the team, "I know we beat these guys by 25 points last time. They've improved a lot, and all they want is to see you come out loafing just a little bit or with the attitude that you've already got this game won. If you do, you're going to find yourselves in a real dogfight."

I would much rather play an opponent who is evenly matched with us, or even slightly better. In these cases, I know the players will be mentally sharp and play with intensity. It's when you are the heavy favorites that you really have to get the team's attention and remind everybody that they still have a game to play.

Big Games

When playing a crucial game for a championship or against an arch rival, I make minor adjustments in my pregame message to the players. In these cases, where a big crowd is expected and the motivation is already built in, I try to relax the players a little bit. I think the worst thing coaches can do before a big game is to overemphasize its importance, practice too much, and get their players too tight. The players will be wound up enough anyway from the nature of the game and what is at stake. In this situation, it is the coach's job to unwind the players and send them out on the floor in a confident frame of mind.

A perfect example of this was our game against Power Memorial. We were playing in front of 12,500 people at the University of Maryland, the first sell-out at Cole Field House. The players didn't need a Knute Rockne kind of speech to get pumped up. So I merely went over the game plan in a confident manner and told them to go out and enjoy the occasion.

Summary

You cannot work miracles before a game to ready your team. The best approach is to continuously work to improve individual and team performance in practice. However, your team will be more set to enter its next game if you apply these points of advice.

- Scouting is an important element of preparation, but not the most important part. Know your opponent's tendencies, but always work more on your strengths.
- If you have limited scouting resources, try to recruit an interested faculty member or fan to assist you.
- If you are not able to see a game of an upcoming opponent, the pertinent information can sometimes be obtained through the exchange of videotapes or through phone calls to other coaches.
- Plan your practices to work on the specific strengths of your team that you feel will be most important in the next game.
- Do not spend too much time talking about your opponent, because you run the risk of overselling or underselling that team's abilities. Keep the focus on your own team.
- If possible, keep the final workout before the game short, so the players will have fresh legs.
- Adjust your pregame talk to fit the circumstances. If you're playing a poor team, gear your talk to avoid a letdown. If you're involved in a big game, try to relax the players.

Chapter 16

Handling Game Situations

I've had coaches tell me, "Once the game starts, I stop worrying because I've done everything I can." That is the wrong attitude. Sure, preparation is important to a team's success. But you also must fulfill many responsibilities once the game is under way. It makes no difference whether your team is the favorite or underdog, playing at home or on the road, going for the league title or a .500 season. To paraphrase Gertrude Stein, "A game is a game is a game." And you've got to be ready to handle it.

Starting the Game

Once the game plan has been installed and fine-tuned in practice, your final decisions before the game will involve your starting five and the match-ups that will occur.

The Starting Five

I do not emphasize the role of starters as much as many coaches do. As I've mentioned before, I tell players, "It is not important who starts; what we really need is a lot of finishers." However, I do like to maintain as much continuity as possible in our starting five.

I never like to change my starting five after a loss because it may appear that I'm blaming the previous loss on the player who is no longer starting. So whenever I change my starting lineup, I try to do so after a victory. Also, I never make a change without calling the players involved into my office. I tell the player who will not be starting the reasons why I feel he can be more effective coming off the bench, and I try to keep his attitude positive and enthusiastic. I want him to understand we are just adjusting our strategy. I never want to create a win-lose situation with personnel changes, only win-win situations.

Explain to the player you are removing from the starting lineup that your decision may not be the right one, you just believe it is after much consideration. And despite all the knowledge and all the planning in the world, sometimes decisions just come down to gut feelings or instincts.

 "I HAD A FEELING . . ."

I remember one important league game we were playing back in the 1960s against Mackin High School. We were losing by 6 points with about 2 minutes left to go when one of our starting forwards went down with a knee injury. While I was out on the floor trying to determine how the injured player was, my assistant, Frank Fuqua, was getting our top sub at forward ready to come into the game.

After we had attended to our injured player and helped him off the floor, Frank was ready to send in that sub. I told Frank to hold up, turned to the bench, and said, "Billy Hite, get in there." Although Billy was one of the finest all-around athletes we've ever had at DeMatha and a great competitor and a clutch performer, he was only 5-11. And here I was, putting him in a forward spot in a crucial ball game.

Well, we ended up taking the game into overtime—Billy Hite made the tying basket. And in that overtime we pulled away to win easily. In a time span of about 8 minutes, Billy Hite scored 13 points.

With less than a minute to go and the game wrapped up, I turned to Frank Fuqua and said, "I just kind of felt he might be the better guy in that situation."

Frank laughed and, with a big grin on his face, said, "Oh, be quiet."

Learn to develop and trust your instincts regarding personnel decisions. They can sometimes mislead you, but I think you'll find that your instincts are right more often than they are wrong.

 THE UNTESTED SOPHOMORE

In the late '70s, we were in Lake Charles, Louisiana, playing in the Pepsi-Cola Classic. We were matched up against Wheatley High from Houston, Texas, a highly talented team with great athletes. But we had some great athletes of our own in Sidney Lowe and Derek Whittenburg, who would together go on to North Carolina State and form one of the nation's finest backcourts.

Early in the second quarter, we were enjoying a 12-point lead when Whittenburg went down heavily on his ankle. I knew there was no way Whittenburg was going to return to the game. We would discover later that he had broken a bone in his foot, and he ended up missing a big part of the season. (A few years later at N.C. State, he broke the same bone in his other foot but came back to lead the Wolfpack to the 1983 NCAA Championship.) But I never told the team that night that Derek would not be back. Instead, I told the team, "Let's see if we can keep it close until Derek gets his foot together."

I replaced Whittenburg with an untested sophomore named Bobby Ferry, who was playing in the first varsity game of his life. Before the game, I had been contemplating sending Bobby back to the junior varsity for more seasoning.

The game—one of the greatest I've ever been a part of—went into five overtimes. By the end of the fourth overtime, I had told the team about everything I could possibly think of. So during the break between the fourth and fifth overtime periods, I found myself quoting Churchill: "Gentlemen," I said, "We will stay here all night long until one of two things happens. Either we win, or they lose. We will never give in. We are going to outlast them. We will never, ever, ever give in."

Fortunately, we finished them off in that fifth overtime, the longest game I've ever coached. To this day, I don't know what I would have said if we had gone to a sixth overtime.

By the way, the sophomore I put in for Whittenburg, Bobby Ferry, scored 25 points and missed only 3 shots in his varsity debut. (He had a younger brother by the name of Danny who, fortunately, would also decide to play at DeMatha.)

Match-ups

Perhaps the most critical personnel decision for a game involves deciding on your match-ups, especially if your team plays any form of man-to-man defense. Again, I have several rules of thumb that I take into consideration when making match-up decisions.

Leading Scorer's Defensive Assignments

First, if possible, I would rather not place my leading scorer on one of the high-powered offensive players for the other team. If he's supposed to lead the way offensively for your team and also shut down the opposing team's leading scorer, then you are expecting him to control the entire game at both ends of the floor. This can make a player feel that the entire game rests on his shoulders. Even if your leading scorer is a great defensive player, outstanding play and effort at both ends are a lot to ask. Another consideration is that you do not want your leading scorer to get into early foul trouble because he's guarding the other team's ace. So, if you can, try to slide your leading scorer onto one of the opponent's lesser scorers.

Guarding the Opposition's Ballhandler

Another critical match-up is the defensive player you choose to guard the other team's ballhandler. There is a possibility that whoever guards the primary ballhandler will get into foul trouble because he will be around the ball more than the other players, and the officials are always watching the ball. So you may not want your leading scorer *or* your leading ballhandler guarding the other team's best ballhandler.

 DEFENSING KENNY

I had tough decisions to make when we played Archbishop Molloy High School from New York, featuring the great Kenny Anderson. Kenny was one of the greatest guards to ever play high school basketball, and he later led Georgia Tech to the Final Four as a freshman. We faced him twice, and both times I decided *not* to put our best ballhandler on Kenny in an attempt to avoid getting our man in foul trouble. We felt that Kenny was also such a great defensive player that we needed our best ballhandler in there at all times.

The strategy paid off. We won both games against Molloy. In the first game, John Gwynn (who later played at the University of Connecticut) made a jump shot at the buzzer (right after a basket by Anderson), and we won by 1 point. In the second game, we made two foul shots with about 4 seconds to go and won by two. We did not lose any players to fouls in either game,

and we were able to have our best ballhandler in the game at all times.

Think about potential foul trouble when assigning match-ups. You may have to decide who the most expendable players are, and then go ahead and match them up with some of the best offensive players on the other team.

As you determine your match-ups, make sure you decide on an alternate plan. If, for example, the other team's leading scorer gets red hot early, then you will be forced into a defensive switch. It may only be an individual switch, putting another player on the other team's scorer, but sometimes this can have a psychological effect on the other team. Their big scorer may think, "Uh, oh. I've been hot. Now they're putting their defensive stopper on me." If this happens, it's already been successful because you've disrupted the offensive player's focus on scoring points.

Sometimes you will have to adjust your whole defense. You may want to start trapping the man who's scoring all the points for the other team. Or you may want to try to deny him the ball and totally overplay him.

Taking Away the Opponent's Strengths

It's important to remember that you want good *team* defense. You may want to try to shut down a great player with different defenses, rather than spend the whole game trying to find a single player that can contain him.

Against Lew Alcindor, we knew one man would not be effective. So our team defensive strategy was to try to deny him the ball. We had one guy in front of him and one guy behind him at all times. He caught the ball only 11 times during that game. It was a risk on our part because we were leaving one of their players open at all times. But our feeling was and is, "Don't let their best player beat you. Make one of their lesser players beat you."

When deciding on match-ups, pay close attention to your scouting reports and try to establish what the strengths are of each of the players on the opposing team. Then, try to decide on the match-up that best takes away that strength. If one guy on their team is an awesome rebounder, try to take that away with your match-up. If another guy is a great outside shooter but doesn't penetrate well, try to take that away with your match-up.

You will never be able to take everything away from a good offensive player. What you're looking to take away is what he does best. That's why I'm often heard telling a player, "Make him beat you left-handed." The primary purpose of a match-up is to take away a player's best weapon. Try to get your players to take away the oppositions' aces; then, if they get good enough, go to work on their kings.

During the Game

A coach's job is only half over once the game begins. Ideally, you've prepared your team as well as possible. Now, you must assist your players in the execution of the game plan and provide guidance in the various circumstances that arise during game competition. You must consider

- your conduct,
- the opposing coach's conduct,
- game plan adjustments,
- personnel decisions,
- time-outs, and
- halftime.

Your Conduct

A coach's conduct in game circumstances must be beyond reproach, not only because you represent yourself, your family, and your school, but also because you are the leader of the team. You are the focal point, and your players will look to you and follow your example. If you lose your cool, your composure, or your temper, then your team will do the same. Also, the behavior of a coach can influence the behavior of the crowd.

I try to conduct myself as a gentleman at all times. Basketball, however, is an emotional sport, and there are times when those emotions will be intense. I have had a few technicals, but only a few. In 34 years of coaching, I would guess that I have yet to reach double figures in technicals. This does not mean that I'm a saint. It means that I work hard at keeping my composure, staying focused on the game, and setting the proper example for my players.

Of the technicals that have been called on me, most have been called by relatively inexperienced officials. You will find that the good, experienced officials rarely have to call a technical foul to maintain control of the game. They may simply come over to you and say, "Coach, sit down and relax and worry about coaching." It is wise to heed such advice from an official.

Generally, rookie officials are a bit nervous and insecure, and they may be quicker to resort to a technical to establish control of a game. But this is not an indictment of beginning officials. We all have to start some place; and I remember what the first year of my 10-year officiating career was like. I have the greatest respect for most officials and for the hard work and professionalism they bring to our sport. It is important, though, to know who your officials are before each game and what their reputations are. Such knowledge may help you in determining how much you can talk to an official and when it is time to leave him alone.

Opposing Coach's Conduct

It is wise not to overlook your counterpart's state of mind as the game progresses. As you know, coaches can get pretty upset, either at the way their team is playing or at the way the game is being called by the officials. Sometimes, you can use this to your advantage.

 SOMETIMES IT'S WHAT YOU DON'T SAY . . .

Early in my coaching career, we were playing one of our top conference rivals, and we could not seem to get any closer than 4 points. In the fourth quarter, we were playing about as well as we could, but we just couldn't cut any further into the lead.

I called a time-out, told the players how well they were playing, and encouraged them to keep on hustling. The head of our English department, Dr. Charles "Buck" Offutt, was standing behind the bench during that time-out. We tied the game in regulation and won it in overtime, thanks in part to a technical foul on the other team.

The next day at school, Dr. Offutt, a member of the football coaching staff, came up to me and said, "Morgan, I can't believe you called that time-out. You were never playing better when you took it, and then you didn't really have anything to say to the team during the time-out."

I said, "Buck, I took the time-out to allow the other coach to talk to his team because I knew he was emotional at that point, and that he might hurt his team rather than help it. I also figured he might pick up a technical, which he did."

So it's important to stay in control of yourself. And watch to see if you can pick up an advantage because the opposing coach is getting out of control. It may help to call a time-out and let him pick up a technical or scream at his team.

Game Plan Adjustments

I place a great deal of importance on going into each game with a comprehensive game plan of what goals we want to accomplish and how to best accomplish those goals in every conceivable situation, from inbounding plays to foul shot alignments. However, I do not feel obligated to stay with that game plan no matter what. The adjustments you make during the course of a game, although they may seem to be minor ones at the time, could determine the outcome of that game.

As I've said, your basketball coaching philosophy should allow you to be flexible enough to adjust your system to fit the talents of your players. And that flexibility should carry over to actual games. You should be able to adjust your game plan to fit the circumstances of each particular game as they develop.

Minor adjustments that help fine-tune the game plan can pay large dividends. A defensive switch or a critical substitution in a tight game may be just what it takes to put your team in the win column.

As part of the game plan, you should also have some general guidelines that dictate how you prefer to play certain situations. For example, what play do you like to run in a tie game when going for the last shot? And, at what point do you consider a player in foul trouble? When would you like to take him out, and when would you like to put him back in?

Once again, the guidelines you set are not written in stone. The game may dictate that you have to put someone who is in foul trouble back into the game earlier than you would like to. But it is smart to have these general rules of thumb to aid you in making decisions.

Wholesale changes in a game plan are not beneficial. If you are forced to throw out an entire game plan and replace it with something else, then one of two things has happened: (a) Your initial preparation was flawed, or (b) something extremely unusual has happened. It is best to stay within your arsenal and to focus on what you have worked on in practices.

I've heard stories of coaches who try to implement a brand-new offense at halftime, one that their teams have never worked on in practice. By trying to change everything in the middle of the game, you are sending the message to your players that you are panicking. So don't be surprised if they begin to panic and question their ability as well.

Personnel Decisions

Going into any game, I always have a good idea of how I want to handle my personnel in various situations. For example, if a player picks up his second foul in the first half, I generally will take him out of the game. If we can keep the game reasonably close, I would prefer not to bring him back into the game until the start of the second half. Ideally, then, the player would have three fouls to commit in the second half before disqualification. On occasion, I have swayed from this rule because of particular circumstances. If, for example, the player involved hardly ever fouls out of a game, I may put him back into the game earlier than I would otherwise.

Therefore, although your guidelines for juggling personnel should be established in your mind, they must be flexible enough to vary from game to game and opponent to opponent. For example, you should have a good idea of who your first substitute in the back court will be, as well as who your first sub in the front court will be. I always have a good idea of who I *think* that first sub in the back court will be, but sometimes the circumstances of the game may cause that to change.

That's why I keep such personnel plans private among the coaches. We do not tell the players, "Hey, Joe, you're the first sub in the back court tonight." If you have already told a certain player he will be that sub, and game conditions force a change, then you have discontented players on the bench. So I suggest that you be discreet about your personnel plans for each game; inform the other coaches, but not the players.

Time-Outs

I always like to save as many of our time-outs as possible for the end of the game. This is important for stopping the clock and setting strategy down the stretch in tight ball games. Unfortunately, though, there are instances in which you are forced to spend one before you would like to.

You may wish to call a time-out to

- correct problems in your team's execution,
- review a special play for the last shot,
- freeze an opposing free throw shooter,
- review a special last-possession defense,
- restore order in the midst of confusion,
- give the opposing team's coach more time to make a mistake, or
- rest your players without substituting.

Coaches who use time-outs effectively have an edge over those who do not. And because of the limited time available during these breaks, you must be well organized to get your message to the team as effectively and efficiently as possible. It is during these breaks that you can communicate to your team what they are doing right, what needs to be improved, and what adjustments you may have decided to make.

Time-Out Ritual

Because time-outs are so important, I have a ritual that we follow every time one is called.

1. All of the players on the floor sprint over to our bench. At this point, all of the players not in the game get up off the bench so the five coming off the floor can sit down and get water and towels.
2. While this is going on, I am formulating in my own mind what I want to say to the team. I am also checking with my assistants to see what they have noticed. By the time I've talked with the assistants and the players have gotten their water, there are only about 20 seconds left in the time-out.
3. I crouch down in front of the players and quickly tell them what we are going to do. I do not spend time telling them what they are *not* doing. I try to keep the talks during time-outs as upbeat and as positive as circumstances allow. I may say, "We've got to get on the offensive boards with more intensity," or, "We've got to make sure we do a great job of blocking out. And then once we've gotten the rebound, we want to really look to run. We've got to look up and get the ball down the floor."

Long before our first game, I tell the players that during the time-out their eyes belong to me. I want them looking directly at me. If a player is not looking directly at me, this is an indication to me that he is tired, and I will put a substitute in the game so that player will get some needed rest. Because the players know this, they always look right at me. And if they're looking at me, there's a good chance they're paying attention to what I'm saying.

I've seen some time-out situations that were not organized at all. During one game, a player from the other team actually went up into the stands and talked to his girlfriend during the time-out! This is a complete waste of an opportunity to communicate with your players. Establish a time-out ritual for your players, and demand their full attention. That way, you will take full advantage of time-out opportunities.

Halftime

Halftimes are generally 10 minutes long in high school. Once the buzzer sounds, the players head to the locker room. I leave them there to talk among themselves for the first 3 or 4 minutes. During this time, I am outside the locker room talking to my assistants and quickly going over the key statistics. I am primarily interested in how the rebounding battle is going and if any players on the other team are scoring at an unusually high level.

When I walk into the locker room, every player's eyes turn and focus on me. No matter how the game is going, I will begin my talk by making some positive comment to get their attention. As during time-outs, I do not waste my time focusing on negatives or telling the players what we are not doing. Instead, I concentrate on what we need to do in the second half to get the job done.

Approaches to Halftime Situations

If we're behind, I may say something like, "Here's what we need to do in the second half. We don't want to try to catch up all at once. We don't want to attempt to make up the 12-point deficit in the first 2 minutes. We're going to hack away at it with sound defense and good execution of our offense." Then I will get into specifics.

If it is a close battle at halftime, I will use the approach, "We're in a tight game. And the way we're going to break away from them is to do it gradually by playing sound defense, hitting the boards a little harder, and working the break."

And if we find ourselves winning at the half, I emphasize going after it even harder. So I may tell the team, "We're just going to tighten the screws, play a little better, and pull away a little bit more. What we need to

do is come out real strong in the third quarter and. . . ."

Through a good, positive approach at halftime your players should be ready to take the floor for the second half with a good idea of what they need to do. And they should have the confidence needed to do it.

Halftime Organization

Organization at halftime is crucial in communicating effectively with your team. I've been amazed at how casually some teams approach the half. I remember one time when we came out of the locker room a little earlier than usual and saw two of the opposing players already out on the floor. One was eating a hot dog, and the other was eating an ice cream cone!

As I've discussed, I let the players alone for the first 3 or 4 minutes while I talk to my assistants and formulate my thoughts. I then spend the next 3 to 4 minutes talking with the team. Finally, I try to allow about 3 minutes for players to get their thoughts together and warm-up (if they want to) before the second half starts.

Postgame Procedures

I handle postgame in the locker room in much the same way as I handle halftime. I let the players have a few minutes to themselves after the game while I meet with my assistants. I will then go in and talk to the team, *always* beginning my talk with a positive remark, whether we won or lost.

I believe it is important to keep everything positive. And in some ways it is even more important to be positive after a loss, even though the temptation may be to let out your frustrations. But remember this: Your leadership and guidance will have much more of an impact on your team after a loss than after a victory.

Winning With Class

Following a win, it is a good idea to let the players enjoy the fruits of their labors and to go ahead and celebrate. But I feel it is equally important to keep a good perspective after a win. We tell our team that winning and losing are a part of life, not just of athletics, and that if they can handle both equally well, they will be successful in whatever they do.

Part of handling winning well is to win with class. I tell our team when we are victorious that we want to have the humility of a conquering hero. That includes not taunting an opponent. Instead, we want to remember how hard we worked and all of the things we did to be successful. And we want to remember that we are going to have to work even harder to stay successful. There's an old saying that it is extremely difficult to get to the top, but it is even more difficult to stay there. One way to stay successful is to win with class.

Losing With Dignity

One thing we should always be aware of is that we really have the attention of our team following a loss. In my experiences, the players are more receptive to what the coaches have to say following a defeat.

Athletes are competitors, and competitors will be disappointed in defeat. So when you go into the locker room after a loss, you know the players will be a little down. But if the team has made a winning effort, let the players know that. Whenever your players give a winning effort, praise them for it, no matter what the outcome of the game. After a loss, help them keep their chins up and maintain a positive attitude that will carry over into the upcoming practices and games.

 LESSONS IN CLASS

The first time we played Power Memorial High School and Lew Alcindor, we came up short by 3 points. Alcindor had had an unbelievable game, scoring 39 points and grabbing 22 rebounds, all in front of almost 13,000 people. In fact, during a time-out with about 2 minutes to go, the public address announcer said to the crowd, "Ladies and Gentlemen, no matter who wins this game, I think you will all agree that we are watching the two best high school teams in America." A standing ovation followed.

But despite Alcindor's incredible game, we had taken his team right down to the wire. I told the players I had never been prouder of them, and that I had never seen a more gallant effort than the one those guys had put forth. I told them I felt really good about the game because they had left their hearts and souls out there on the floor with their tremendous effort.

After the game, Lew Alcindor led his teammates into our locker room to shake the hands of all our players. They were a classy bunch of winners.

A year later, when we turned the tables and beat Power Memorial by 3 points, I told the players that we needed to get ready to go over to the opposition's locker room and congratulate them. But they beat us to the punch. Having just seen their 71-game winning streak come to an end, here was Lew Alcindor again leading his team into our locker room to congratulate us.

Lew Alcindor and Power Memorial demonstrated to us all what it is like to win with class and to lose with class. It heightened my respect for Alcindor and for his coach, Jack Donohue, who would become the coach of the Canadian National Team. With such a combination of class and physical ability, it is no surprise that Lew Alcindor went on to become one of the greatest players our sport has ever known.

Setting the Tone

There are some teams that I love to play after they are coming off a loss. Why? Because in the locker room after the game their coach screamed and hollered at them so much that he all but guaranteed a couple more losses by destroying their confidence and their competitive spirit.

On the other hand, there are some teams I hate to play if they lost their previous game. The coaches of these teams handle losses with dignity and can rally their team and fire their players up for the next game. And this is what I try to do with our teams.

I tell the kids after a loss that I want to see them come back with the ferociousness of a wounded tiger. Telling players this helps set the tone for the next game and the practices leading up to that game.

Setting the tone for the team, after a win or a loss, is something that every coach should make an effort to do in the most positive way possible. In connection with that, I make it a point to shake the hand of every player after every game and thank them for the effort they gave.

Even after a victory, a player may be a little discouraged because he didn't feel he personally played particularly well. But you can always say, "Hey, Joe, the team did well, and that's what counts. Next game, you'll come back stronger than ever."

After a loss, most if not all of the players are going to be disappointed; you have to get them to lift their heads up. You have to set the tone by displaying the attitude, "We're coming back, and we're coming back strong."

I think one of the biggest challenges a coach faces is to pick up the spirit, enthusiasm, and confidence of a player who is very discouraged. In consequence, there is no greater reward than seeing a player whose chin was scraping the ground one day come back the next day with renewed vigor. How do you accomplish that? There's no magic answer. Just believe in the player, care about how he's feeling, and always be positive.

Not a Time for Strategy

In my postgame comments I never spend any time going over tactical problems or adjustments. I have found over the years that it is just a waste of time to do so, whether following a win or loss. The players are either so elated over a win or so dejected over a loss that they will not be able to fully absorb any tactical information at that point.

Tactical information should not be your first concern at that point anyway. The players' attitudes and mental well-being should occupy your time and efforts. You don't want them to be too high after a win, or too low after a loss. Immediately after the game is the time when you can be most influential in helping them maintain an even keel. Save the tactical information for the following practice.

Besides keeping everything positive, the only other thing that needs to be mentioned after a game is the upcoming opponent. All you need to say is something like, "Fellows, our next game is against Central on Friday, and we're really going to have to be ready." Such a statement can help keep the players focused. After a loss, the upcoming game is an opportunity to redeem themselves. After a win, the mention of the next game serves as a reminder that there is still work to be done.

Summary

- Try to keep some continuity in your starting five. Avoid making changes after a loss, because it looks as if you are blaming the player who is no longer starting.
- Use your scouting reports to decide on match-ups, with the goal of any match-up being to take away the other team's strengths. Make them beat you "left-handed."
- Critical match-ups include who will guard the other team's leading scorer and ballhandler. When deciding on these match-ups, consider other factors as well, such as potential foul trouble.
- Become involved with the game. Don't just be a spectator.
- As the leader of the team, the coach must display exemplary conduct at all times. Coaches who lose their cool will have teams who do the same thing.
- Make minor adjustments in your game plan as dictated by game conditions. Never try to put in a new system during a game without having a chance to work on it in practice.
- Have general guidelines in mind as to how you want to handle personnel in all situations.
- Remember that sometimes you just have to trust your instincts.
- Try to use your time-outs as sparingly as possible so you will have enough for crucial points in the game.
- Organize your time-out procedures to maximize use of the limited time available to your team.

- Keep talks during time-outs, at halftime, and after the game as positive as possible.
- Try to keep your players' emotions as level as possible, not too high and not too low.
- Learn to handle winning and losing with equal class and dignity.
- Avoid discussing tactics with your team immediately following a game. Save it for the next practice.

Part VI

Coaching Evaluation

Chapter 17

Evaluating Players

To become a successful basketball coach, you must have the resources and ability to evaluate your players, yourself, your assistants, and your overall program. You want these evaluations to be thorough and honest. Therefore, everyone involved must be open-minded enough to give and receive constructive criticism, assured that the evaluation process is for the good of the program. And one of the most difficult evaluations you'll make as a coach involves deciding which players will make the cut and what positions those players will play.

Summer Evaluation

We are fortunate at DeMatha to have an extensive summer league program that allows my assistants to work with our players. Furthermore, it allows me to watch some of the players in action before practices begin on November 8. This gives us a big advantage in that we do not have to evaluate the players based on only a week or two of practice performances.

The summer leagues in June, July, and early August provide tough competition at the varsity and junior varsity levels. My assistants are the coaches of these teams, and whenever possible I attend these games and sit in the stands to observe and evaluate. Legally, I am allowed to coach these teams if I choose to do so. But I think the players hear enough from me during the actual season; they're better off receiving instruction from staff members who will give them similar, but not the same, coaching. In addition, these games give my assistant coaches a chance to run the show, which is valuable experience for them and for me.

For high school basketball players to become the best they can be, it is important that they play basketball in the summer. Summer leagues and summer camps are available all over the country, and your players should be taking advantage of those opportunities to play more ball. In some cases, coaching staffs may not be allowed to coach the summer teams. When this is the case, I recommend that you at least try to observe your players. And if that is not possible, try to stay in touch with your players through frequent phone calls or postcards.

Our focus during the summer leagues is on observing the players and assisting them in their development. Before these leagues begin, I meet with my assistants and organize a detailed playing schedule for all of the players who will be competing. The varsity team is in two different leagues, and we start a different group of five in each of those leagues. This way, everybody learns how to start, everybody learns how to come off the bench, and many learn how to be finishers. It makes the kids better players, and it lets the coaching staff see how the players react in different situations.

During the course of the summer, I pull aside various players and chat with them, passing along some of the things I think they need to work on. I also go and speak to the team after each game that I attend. But I wait until after the head coach that night has made his comments. The postgame talks I give are very brief and are just pep talks to tell the guys they are doing a good job and should keep working hard.

After the final summer game, I make it a point to talk with the summer league participants and have them give the coaches a round of applause for working with them all summer. I tell the players to take a little bit of time off and maybe enjoy a family vacation.

But I remind the players that once school starts in September, it's time to get back to work for tryouts that begin in November. I stress to them that what they do between the beginning of school and the beginning of tryouts will probably determine whether they make the team. And if they do make the team, what they have done in that time will probably determine what kind of year they are going to have.

The Fall Meeting

The school year begins in late August or early September. Around the middle of September, I suggest that you hold what I call a Fall Meeting. Perhaps you will want to have three different meetings, one each for the freshmen, junior varsity (JV), and varsity teams. If your program is similar to ours, the varsity meeting room will be packed with young men who dream of making the team.

I open that meeting with motivational remarks, talk about how the summer league went, and go over our schedule for the upcoming season. Second, I introduce our academic advisor and remind the players that we will be checking on their academic progress every 2 weeks. I tell the candidates quite bluntly that if there is a tough choice as to who will make the team, we will go with the better student. I also educate the players on college eligibility requirements and tell them of importance of the SAT prep courses and exams.

I then have the players fill out pertinent information about themselves on index cards (see Figure 17.1). This includes their class schedule, so we will know where to find a player any time we need to get ahold of him.

We announce to the players that there will be open gym on Monday, Wednesday, and Friday for juniors and seniors; the gym will be available to freshmen and sophomores on Tuesday and Thursday. These open gyms are *not* organized practices, but merely an opportunity for the players to run and play in the gym as they work to get in shape. Legally, I am allowed to attend these gym sessions as long as I provide no instruction and do not organize anything.

I rarely attend open gym because I do not want the players to feel they are trying out. We are simply providing them with the facility where they can play games, work on their shooting, or do whatever they feel like. One of the great benefits to an open gym is that the leaders of the team begin to emerge as they take charge of the time available.

Also at the Fall Meeting, I stress to the candidates the importance of being a member of the student body. I give the example (that I mentioned earlier) of James Brown, now a CBS sportscaster, who always had a

Player Information Card

Name _____

Address _____

Phone _____

Year in school _____

Where you began the 9th grade _____

Height _____   Weight _____

Birthdate (month-date-year) _____

Age as of today _____

Shoe size _____

Jacket size: XL   L   M   S

What team did you play on last year?

(Put class schedule on back of card)

Figure 17.1 Player information card.

friendly smile and "hello" for everyone at the school. He had plenty of ability as well, as evidenced by a great basketball career at Harvard and briefly in the NBA; but it was his pleasant and outgoing demeanor that made James one of the most popular players to ever go through DeMatha.

As we close the meeting, I remind the players that they are expected to report in shape and that *all* spots are open. I tell the candidates that there have been expected big contributors who became complacent and, unexpectedly, were beaten out by newcomers who had worked harder and improved more. I say this to encourage all candidates to come out and give it their best shot, because you never know what may happen when someone is given a chance. And I can promise them that they will get a fair chance.

 A CHANCE WAS ALL HE NEEDED

I gave such a talk at the Fall Meeting in 1969. In the back of the room, a freshman named Adrian Dantley was listening. Little did I dream that he would make the varsity, much less become a starter, in his freshman year. Adrian is the only player in DeMatha history to be a 4-year starter. He went on to become a high school and college All-American and an NBA All-Star.

Dantley and other "surprises" serve as a reminder to me to avoid predetermining who will make the squad. We have to keep an open mind when evaluating our players for the upcoming season. When we say that all spots are open, we've got to really mean it. Almost every year, you'll find that someone you did not figure to start will end up cracking the first five.

Fall Evaluations

At the Fall Meeting, I hand out the Fall Evaluation sheets for the players to fill out (see Figure 17.2). We encourage them to take their time and think about what they put on the form. One of the most important elements of the form is the section where we ask the player to write down his academic and athletic goals for the year. These

---

Player's Fall Evaluation

Name: _____   Address: _____

_____

Phone: _____   Year in school: _____   Height: _____   Weight: _____

1. Where do you see yourself on the team (role)?

2. What did you do this summer to make yourself a better student?

3. What did you do this summer to make yourself a better player?

4. What grade would you give yourself for your total effort to improve as a basketball player this summer? Circle one.

   Excellent   Very good   Good (average)   Below average   Poor

5. What do you plan on doing between now and November to make yourself a better player?

6. What weaknesses have become strengths since last May?

7. What do you think will be the strengths/weaknesses of this year's team?

8. List separately the following:
   a. Your academic goals for the year:

   b. Your athletic goals for the year:

Figure 17.2   Player's fall evaluation form.

should be realistic, challenging targets to which the player is strongly committed—a promise to himself. I encourage them to take their goal-setting seriously.

Later on in the year, if a player is not doing as well academically as he should be, I might call him into the office, read back to him what his academic goals for the year were, and try to see what the problem might be. The same is true of athletic goals. If a certain player says his goal is to become an outstanding defensive player, but he's just not getting the job done, I will do the same thing: talk with him and remind him what his goals for the year were. Sometimes a little reminder is all it takes. In other instances, I may work with the player to revise his goals and aim for things that may be more attainable. Impossible goals will diminish, not increase, a player's efforts.

Preseason Evaluations

Practice begins in early November. Typically, you'll use this time to see how players stack up against one another. Our first 3 days of practice are practically identical. First we have players perform stretching exercises and warm-up drills. Then we hold scrimmages and simply watch the players play.

I have a rule that I will give every player at least 3 days of tryouts. I feel that these 3 days of scrimmaging are the best way to accurately evaluate a player. It gives the coaches a chance to watch the players under different conditions. We also have our managers keep statistics of all the scrimmages, which aid us in our evaluation of the players. We do not videotape these scrimmages and review the tapes to select the team. I think it's important to get a feel for the kind of players you have, and videotape does not capture all of the intensity and activity that occurs on the court.

We generally have about 40 students try out for the varsity team. I divide the candidates into five-player teams and have them scrimmage each other. I will move players from one team to another in an attempt to balance things as much as possible.

Balanced teams accomplish two things: (a) They afford the coaches a better opportunity to find that diamond in the rough, and (b) they are more fair to the players involved. When the teams are evenly balanced, it is easier to spot those players that rise above the other players' level of play. This allows you to make a better determination about a player's skills. It doesn't do anyone any good to have your five projected starters playing against five players who are likely to get cut.

I do not necessarily have the team selected after the 3 days of scrimmaging. In fact, I may let only a few guys go at that point. But by that time, I do have a foundation upon which to evaluate the remaining players. Generally, I try to have my 12- to 15-player team picked by the 10th practice. I prefer to have it done sooner than that, but I want to allow myself enough time to get all the information I need to make the proper personnel decisions.

Making the Cut

With DeMatha basketball, the kids usually start with the freshman team, work their way up to the junior varsity, and then try out for the varsity. Because of this system, it is unlikely that a very good player will slip through the cracks. Our largest turnout is always for the freshman team, which sometimes has 75 to 100 candidates try out. In this case, we run three separate practices for a few days, dividing the players alphabetically into teams for easier evaluation.

When you have a lot of candidates for your team, it can seem overwhelming to try and give each one a good look. But you will make the best decisions for your program and for the individuals trying out if you are willing to work hard and make the time to watch closely during the selection process.

Making cuts should not be an arbitrary decision. You can't just think someone looks like a player and decide on that basis. Sure, sometimes your instincts give you a feeling about a certain athlete. But you need more than that to go on.

One of the biggest mistakes coaches make is to pick players by what I call the "eyeball test." Some coaches assume that if someone *looks* like a player, then he must *be* a player, and they keep him on the team.

I recommend staying away from the eyeball test. Instead, judge players by their per-

---

Cutting Criteria

When deciding whether or not to keep a player, consider these points:

- What kind of person the player is
- What kind of student the athlete is
- How quick the player is
- What kind of shooter the player is
- What kind of competitor the player is
- What kind of ballhandler the player is
- What kind of passer the player is
- How the player gets along with teammates
- How coachable the player appears to be
- How high the player can jump
- How fast the player can run

---

formance. I've always said, "Don't play potential, play performance." And, similarly, "Don't keep potential, keep performance."

That does not mean you're mistaken if you keep some players who show potential but have failed to perform consistently. You can work with them to try to develop them. It is wise to keep such players as long as they have good attitudes, are coachable, and are willing to work hard to develop their potential. But, for the majority of your roster, keep players who perform and not those who *may* develop their potential.

The Hardest Part of Coaching

After the 3 days of scrimmaging and evaluating are completed, I then sit down with the rest of the staff to face what is the most difficult aspect of coaching. Together, we make the tough decisions about who we will keep and not keep on the team. Cutting players is really the only part of my job that I have found to be disagreeable. When young men have dreams of playing varsity basketball and give their all during the tryouts, it is very difficult for me to tell them they are not going to make it.

For each player I am going to cut, I take the time to speak with them individually in my office. I don't believe in posting lists that indicate who made the team or who got cut. I think that is a cruel, cold way of cutting players. When the player comes into my office, I start off by thanking him for coming out for the team and making such a great effort. I try my best to help the player keep things in perspective, tell him that life is a lot bigger than basketball, and generally just try to ease his disappointment as best I can.

If the players cut are not seniors, I invite them to come back for the team next year. But no matter what year they are in school, I encourage them to play in some of the local leagues, and I tell them that basketball is a great sport that can be played at a lot of different levels. I try to help the young men handle the fact that they are not going to make the school's team and emphasize that there are playing and coaching opportunities elsewhere.

Most players are able to take getting cut fairly well. Many of them are smart enough to see it coming. Understandably, all are disappointed, and some shed a few tears.

Maybe it is good that I was never a great player. Using myself as an example, I point out to the players I cut that there comes a time in everyone's life when the basketball will be taken out of their hands. And I try to get the young man to focus on the positives in his life.

I may say something like, "You are a great student. You get along well with people. And I know you are going to be a real success in life. But you're not going to win every game you play, and this is a great experience for you. My last year of organized basketball was after my first year of junior college. And I accepted that, just as you have to accept this. But what you have to do is go on and have the greatest year you can. You can continue to play basketball and have fun at it, and I hope you'll come out and support the team."

Giving Kids a Second Chance

As hard as we may try not to make mistakes when cutting players, it inevitably happens. And that is the basis for another rule of mine. If, after a player has been cut, he truly feels he did not get a fair look, did not perform as well as he's capable of, or that the coaches just plain made a mistake, then he must wait one day and then come talk to me. I will give him another look. You might be surprised at how this can keep you from missing a potentially great player.

 ALL-CITY ALMOST OUT

When I was coaching JV football at St. John's High School, I cut a young man named Fred Eskew. He came back to talk to me and told me he thought I had made a mistake, so I agreed to give him another chance.

Boy, was he right—I had made a big mistake. He went on to become a three-time All-Metropolitan player at St. John's. He proved to me that my assessments are never 100% correct. And I've become more open to players' positions ever since.

Putting Players in Positions

As I mentioned in chapter 7, I prefer to assign players to only two positions: the perimeter and the post. Perimeter players, who face the basket, include guards, small forwards, and swing players. The post players, who play with their back to the basket, include power forwards and centers. I am not sold on the designations of big guard, point guard, small forward, power forward, and center. As you have seen in previous chapters, I do assign numbers to players for alignment purposes. But in my way of thinking, there are two types of players on the floor rather than five.

Looking for Complete Players

I like to have as many complete basketball players as I can. These are players who possess, to some degree, all the necessary skills on the court. I am not satisfied with someone who can only rebound, or only dribble, or only shoot from outside of 15 feet. To be a basketball player, you must possess all of the skills required of you while you are on the floor.

However, it is the coach's job to put players in positions that best utilize their strengths. If the best position for a player is playing facing the basket, make him a perimeter player. If he's stronger with his back to the basket, make him a post player. Of course, it's ideal when a player can play either position.

 A COACH'S DREAM

Every coach should at least once be blessed with a player having all-around skills. I was when Danny Ferry attended DeMatha.

I remember one year when we played Archbishop Carroll High School for the league championship. Carroll featured Derrick Lewis, who went on to a successful career at Maryland and to pro ball in Europe. The inside match-up between Derrick and Danny was virtually dead even. But Danny was talented enough that he was able to pull away from the basket, and the odds shifted to his favor. Danny was just a little too quick for Derrick, and had a good outside shot that very few post players were able to move out to the perimeter and defend.

Putting Your Team in Position

Obviously, game situations often dictate certain coaching strategies. For example, if late in the game the other team is pressing, you will want the ball in the hands of your best ballhandler. At that stage of the game, you will call for an offense that keeps the best dribbler and passer in control of the ball. While I do not necessarily designate a point guard, I make sure that we are equipped to handle this and many other situations.

You can also prepare by knowing in advance the combination of five players that you will put on the floor in all those various situations. You should identify your best starting team, your best ballhandling team (consisting of a combination of your five best ballhandlers and foul shooters), your best rebounding team, your best pressing team, and so forth.

WATCH YOUR WALLET AROUND THIS TEAM

We call one of our special situation teams, the all-out pressing team, the "Pick Pockets." And over the years, they've earned their name.

In one game against Long Island Lutheran, we found ourselves down by 23 points going into the last quarter. I inserted the "Pick Pockets" and told them that we couldn't let the other team get the ball over half court. They did their job—in a hurry! Then, with a minute to go in the game, we put in our ball-control team to protect our 4-point lead.

In a similar situation, we found ourselves down by 15 after the first quarter against Paint Branch High School. Once again we turned to the "Pick Pockets," and at the half we led by 13 points. That's a 28-point turn around in one quarter!

I use these examples to illustrate that a coach has to know what five players will make up the best team that you need on the floor in a particular situation. If you decide this ahead of time, you can get the most out of your team in each circumstance you face.

Evaluating Practices

As I told you in Part II, I break our entire season down into a master season plan, monthly plan, weekly plan, and daily plan. When drawing up these long- and short-term practice plans, I always ask for the help of my staff. I have a practice plan for every practice that I have ever had at DeMatha High School.

Keeping records over the long term can be of particular help when evaluating the different squads from year to year. I can go back into the records if I'm interested in knowing where the team was at a certain point in the season the year before. Also, I can go back through the records and find teams that had similar talent as my present team. I use that information to help in deciding what to do in practice with my current team, knowing what has worked with past teams.

The more organized you are, the better coach you will be, and the better your team will be. As with everything in life, organization can be achieved through hard work. I suggest that you keep a written record of almost everything (practice plans, scouting reports, player files, and so forth) and a filing system that allows you to find what you are looking for without too much trouble.

Part of being organized is knowing what you want to accomplish for the season and for that particular month, week, and day. A high level of organization allows you to get the most out of every minute you spend out on the floor. As the old saying goes, "It's not the hours you put into something that counts. It's what you put into the hours." And what you put into your hours with the team should be well planned in advance.

Practice Observations

The primary thing to look for during practice is how hard the players are working. I'm a believer in the coaching commandment, "As they practice, so shall they play." So I want my players out there giving it their all in practice as well as in games.

I pay particular attention to my best players to make sure they are out there working their hardest. Sometimes the very talented players can be so successful going at 90% speed, that they fail to push themselves and do not improve.

It should be the ambition of every player to take himself to the next level. The way to get to that level is to practice as hard as you possibly can. So keep a sharp eye on all of your players to make sure they are not just going through the motions. I tell the players that every single day they are either going to get a little bit better or take a little step backward. There is no such thing as standing still. The only way to steadily improve is to give your best effort each day.

Assistant Input

I am fortunate to have two full-time assistants who help a great deal in observing and evaluating practices. We sit down and draw up that day's plan before we ever take the floor so we all know what we want to accomplish and look for. The assistant who works with the post players will concentrate on them, and the assistant who works with the perimeter players will be watching them. I keep an overall perspective on the practice.

After the practice is over and the team has been dismissed, I again meet with my assistants. We discuss the practice and look over the statistics that were kept by the team managers. The form on which we draw up our daily practice plan (see page 57) includes a section at the end for comments about that particular practice. This is our opportunity to record what we did

well that day and what we need to work on. We then proceed to draw up the plan for the next day's practice.

The next day's practice plan should not necessarily depend on the success of the previous day's practice. Instead, pay more attention to your plan for that week. If you fluctuate daily, your players are likely to be similarly inconsistent. When you're guided by your weekly plan, which was taken from the monthly plan, you'll be on course to meet the objectives outlined in your season plan.

Videotape

I frequently have one of the managers videotape practices, but only when I have a specific purpose in mind. Sometimes I'll videotape a drill to illustrate a point to one player. For example, I may tell a player that he's not running the lane as well as he thinks he is. If I can show him on film what I am talking about, he cannot disagree.

 **CANDID CAMERA**

Eddie Fogler, the coach at Vanderbilt University, played under Dean Smith at North Carolina University. He told me of a time when Coach Smith was really getting on him for not hustling. Eddie said he knew that he was going full speed and really working hard and that Coach Smith was wrong. But one film session convinced Eddie that Dean Smith was right. Pictures don't lie. Sometimes a player needs to see for himself what the coach is talking about for it to register.

I cannot emphasize enough the importance of evaluating every single practice. How you practice is how you play. And through these daily evaluations you can determine if you are on course toward playing as you envisioned in your long-term plans.

Evaluating Games

To ensure that you observe games as fully as you can, assign all of your coaches to watch specific things at certain times of the game. This should begin during the 20-minute warm-up, with one of your assistants monitoring players' execution of the pregame routine just to make sure everything is going smoothly. At the same time, another coach should make sure the score-keeper has the correct lineup with the correct numbers in the official book.

 A WIN—NOT BY THE BOOK

When we played in St. John's in 1978, our star guard, Dutch Morley, had a great first half. Unfortunately, prior to the game our score-keeper had inadvertently put the wrong number in the book for Dutch. The very attentive St. John's scorekeeper noticed the mistake and pointed it out to the referee. We were assessed a technical.

St. John's made the foul shot, then scored on the subsequent possession. We were fortunate to hold on and beat that very tough St. John's team. But imagine how everybody, especially our scorekeeper, would have felt had an inadvertent mistake like that cost us the game and given us our only loss of the season.

Game Duties

Once the game starts, every coach should perform an assigned role. As the head coach, my job is to observe the overall offensive and defensive picture of the game.

One of my assistants is assigned the role of sitting right next to me on the bench and taking notes on all the comments I make. He will jot down what I say as the game goes on, and I may want to refer to his notes for use during time-outs, halftime, or the next day in practice.

Generally, my comments are related to phases of the game that I feel need improvement. I may say things like, "Joe just gave up the baseline," or, "We're not changing ends of the floor," or, "We're not looking up against their zone press." All of my verbal observations are written down by my assistant, and they provide us with a running account of significant individual and team performance concerns during the game.

My other assistant is busy keeping track of the number of fouls on players from both teams, as well as the time-out situation. This assistant is responsible for letting me know immediately if one of our players picks up his second foul in the first half. He will also let me know if someone from the other team is getting into foul trouble. For example, if the other team's best rebounder picks up his third foul, my assistant should let me know. We then might try to work the ball inside, force that player to play defense, and possibly help him pick up his fourth foul. (But if he gives us the easy basket, we'll take that, too.)

The coach who keeps the fouls and time-outs is also responsible for watching the opposing team's huddle during those time-outs to see what substitutions the other team is making. He notifies me of any changes that are made during the time-out so that we have an opportunity to counteract their move with one of our own. Many teams have sneaked in a sub or two during time-outs and have gotten a cheap basket because the defending team didn't make the adjustment to the new personnel on the floor.

As part of his assignment in keeping an eye on the opposition, this assistant is also responsible for getting involved in any meetings during a time-out that the other coaches may be having with the officials. I want our team to be represented in all such meetings to make sure the opponent does not gain an unfair advantage. Although good officials go out of their way to make sure both teams are represented, I want an assistant coach to make sure we're a part of any discussions taking place.

As I have said, during practices one of my assistants coaches perimeter players, and the other works with the post players. During games, in addition to the other duties I've described, the two assistants carefully observe the players they coach in practices.

I encourage my assistants' input at all times throughout the games, and sometimes ask their opinion on trends in the game. But I make sure they tell *me* what they see and not the players. Meanwhile, I keep the bigger picture in mind and make any corrections I think are necessary. A rule we have is that there must be only one voice coming from the bench, and that voice is mine. Players on the floor can't benefit from three different coaches yelling three different things to them.

I strongly recommend that you really get into the game. Don't just be a spectator out there. As a coach, you've got to get a feel for games. Your assistants help you keep track of things, but you may not fully appreciate the meaning of what they tell you if you are removed from the nuances of the action. It's easy to become just a spectator, especially when things are going well. If you hit three or four fast breaks in a row, the tendency is to jump up and down and cheer. But before you lead the cheering section, you should reflect upon and understand *why* your team was able to get those easy scoring opportunities.

We have one of our managers keeping stats, along with our faculty moderator. Another manager is our scorekeeper and keeps the book. A third manager videotapes the game. And the fourth manager, our student trainer, is on the bench to help with injuries and to provide water during time-outs.

Postgame Evaluation

With all the feedback I get, I have a pretty good record of what happened out on the floor once the game is completed. I have a list of my comments, the statistics, the time-out and foul charts, and a videotape of the game. In addition, as soon as possible after the game, my coaches and I meet and write down everything we can remember about the game.

From all of these information sources, we determine what we need to do as a result. We'll talk about what we need to work on the next day and whether there will be any change to our weekly or daily plan. I believe it is important to do these things right after the game when your memory of the game is still sharp.

At practice the next day, the first thing we do is go over a synopsis I've prepared from the preceding game. Win or lose, I have players walk through the trouble spots to try and help them understand my analysis. This helps players know why certain things worked or didn't work, and how they can improve their performance.

Summary

- If possible, get your players into summer leagues. It will make them better players, and give you more information to evaluate.
- Tell candidates for your team that all spots are open during try-outs, and make it be the truth.
- Have your players write down their academic and athletic goals at the start of each year.
- You may benefit from spending the first few days of practice just scrimmaging to get a good look at the candidates.
- Don't make arbitrary cuts based on casual observations. Arm yourself with specific information to make these decisions.
- Take time to speak individually with the players you are cutting.
- You may want to have a procedure whereby any player who is cut can be given a second look.
- All players should be versatile on the court, but put them in positions that best utilize their strengths.
- Identify your best five-player units for meeting various game conditions (i.e., your best ballhandling team, your best rebounding team, etc.).
- Draw up a practice plan daily and stick to it.
- Watch practices to make sure your players are working hard.
- Meet with your assistants to evaluate every practice.
- Videotape practices when you have a need to.
- Assign duties to your assistants and managers to insure careful observation and recordkeeping at all games.
- Meet with your assistants as soon as possible after games to evaluate and analyze.
- At the first practice after a game, take the time to walk through and demonstrate the points you wish to cover from your analysis of the previous game.

Chapter 18

Evaluating Your Program

A coach's job is not over when the season ends; it just changes. Rather than working hands-on with players, you will be evaluating and planning for the future. In many ways, the work you do after the season determines whether your program improves the following year. It's not enough to just sit back at the end of the year and say, "Boy, we had a great year. Wasn't it wonderful?" Or, "We had a lousy year, and we'll have to do better next year."

Postseason Evaluation

No matter what kind of season you had, you need to sit down and thoroughly evaluate your program. What you want to find out is where you were, how you did with what you had, and where you are going. As I've men-

tioned, there is no progress without change. But all change is not necessarily progress. It is the evaluation process that will allow you to discover what needs to be changed and what needs to be left alone.

Senior Feedback

The first step I recommend in analyzing your program is to have your graduating seniors write out their thoughts on the program. Tell the seniors that you are not looking for flowery accolades, but substantive ideas and criticisms that they believe will improve your program. It should be a private, personal evaluation by the seniors; for it to be helpful, they must be completely honest.

Through the years, I have gotten tremendous feedback from our graduating students. If I have a specific concern, I may ask them for their thoughts on that subject. Their responses may not always be what you want to hear, but realize that their insights can be for the good of the program. And it is not always negative; what the seniors like about the program also comes through in these evaluations. But whether it's positive or negative, getting input from your graduating seniors is a great way to begin your program evaluation.

Assistant Coaches' Input

I also ask all of my coaches for a written evaluation of the past season. I learned a long time ago from George Allen, the late, great coach of the NFL's Rams and Redskins, that if you really want someone's opinion, get it in writing.

If you call a meeting of all of the people associated with your program, there's a chance that only the outspoken among them will voice their thoughts, thus excluding some potentially valuable information from the quieter types. In writing, though, chances are better that what is on the paper will accurately represent that person's thoughts.

Evaluation of Assistants' Performance

At the same time, you should evaluate your staff. Again, I suggest that you do this in writing. Then sit down with each member of the staff and go over that evaluation with him. Tell each of them what you honestly see as his strengths and weaknesses, and what he can do to improve as a coach.

I have been blessed to have assistants who are interested in improving themselves and are receptive to constructive criticism, attitudes which help make these sessions valuable. In fact, there are 16 former DeMatha assistants now coaching at the collegiate level, seven of whom are Division I head coaches. I think each of them would say these yearly evaluations in some way contributed to his growth as a coach.

Purpose of Evaluations

The evaluations should be completed for positive reasons, primarily so that all of the players and all of the coaches (including the head coach) can grow. From examining the strengths and weaknesses of the coaches and the overall program, I can get a pretty good picture of what I'm doing well or not doing well.

As the head coach, I view myself as the teacher. But, as the saying goes, sometimes the teacher learns more than the student. That may be particularly true in coaching. From these evaluations, we can learn quite a bit about ourselves as head coaches and about the kind of program we are running.

I also spend some time evaluating my own performance of the past season. I go over the season and examine things I did not get done, or things I did that I shouldn't have done. And I try to decide what I need to change.

When conducting evaluations, we must be honest with ourselves and with others. We must be open-minded and flexible enough to incorporate changes that are for the good of the kids and the good of the program.

Postseason Player Evaluations

My assistants and I evaluate our personnel the same way we evaluate ourselves and our program. We have each player submit a written evaluation of himself to the coaching staff. I will then meet individually with each player and discuss with him his own and the coaches' evaluations. At these meetings, I will share with each player the things that the coaching staff believes he needs to do to become a better basketball player. I remind each player that individual evaluations continue throughout the year, and that he will undergo the same process during summer league play.

I also give the players their off-season workout plans *in writing*. When they have a written copy of the complete program, you eliminate the possibility that something may be forgotten. And if they lose the written form, we have it on record and can give them another copy without having to sit down and go through the evaluation process all over again.

I can't emphasize enough how important these postseason evaluations can be to your players and your program. I've talked earlier about Bill Langloh, who was a guard for DeMatha in the 1960s. In one of these meetings with Bill, I told him I thought he was a half-step too slow to play big-time Division I basketball. He asked what he could do to correct that, and I prescribed a quickness program involving jumping rope, running hills and steps, and similar activities.

As a result of that meeting, for one entire summer Bill spent 30 minutes a day, 5 days a week, working on his quickness. Did it pay off? Bill Langloh went on to become a 4-year starter at the University of Virginia and led the Cavaliers to their first ACC title. That might never have happened if we hadn't spent those 30 minutes talking during our evaluation meeting.

Adrian Dantley is another example. When we talked at the end of his first year, Adrian said he wanted to lose weight and gain strength. We went up the road to the University of Maryland, checked into its weight program, and Adrian got to work. Although small at 6-5, the strength training habits he developed in high school helped him be a great inside force at both the collegiate and professional levels.

Building for the Future

It has often been said about the DeMatha program, "They never rebuild. They just reload." This can be true of any program if you have lower levels of the overall program, such as freshman and junior varsity teams, that contribute consistently to the varsity. If you have a basic structure to your program that allows players to develop as they work their way up to the varsity, you can continue to run your program without missing too much of a beat.

Evaluations are a big part of this. They can allow you to streamline and change the program, even as you adjust your style of play to the personnel in your system each year. Frequent evaluations can help the program to evolve and demonstrate a growth pattern, and can help to eliminate overhauls of the system every couple of years.

This is not to say you won't have differences to deal with. Every player, team, and year will be different. But analyzing and evaluating each situation as to how it was handled, what the result was, and how it could be improved are the keys to building and maintaining a successful program.

One reminder: Conduct all of your evaluations and make any resulting adjustments within the framework of your own personality and philosophy. There are no magic coaching formulas that you can apply to a group of players for guaranteed success.

John Wooden's UCLA teams played one style of ball, game in and game out. Still, he admired North Carolina coach Dean Smith because he could teach so many different things and teach them all well. Smith, whose teams play multiple offenses and defenses, is one of the greatest coaches of all time. Yet so is John Wooden. Smith and Wooden are different people with different styles who are both among the best ever in our profession. As I said, the only way to succeed is by going about your work in a manner that is consistent with your personality and philosophy.

So be yourself at all times. Work hard at being a good coach. Listen to what people have to say and be open-minded enough to consider new ideas. Keep your program in perspective. Constantly reevaluate your program and incorporate positive changes. But most of all, have fun. If you do, you'll build a successful program that will win its share of games and, more importantly, produce young people who are well-prepared for life—who will one day say they were proud to have you as a coach.

Summary

- At the end of the season, honestly evaluate all phases of your program.
- Have graduating seniors provide you with a written assessment of your program, the positives and negatives they saw while part of the program.

- Conduct all of your evaluations in two parts: a written assessment followed by a one-on-one talk.
- Have your assistant coaches submit a written evaluation.
- Be open-minded enough to evaluate yourself and honestly consider what new ideas may emerge during evaluations.
- For underclassmen, provide them with written workout programs structured to promote their development over the summer.
- Make all evaluations and adjustments within the framework of your personality and coaching philosophy.
- Have fun and be genuine in your efforts to promote the development of your program and the student-athletes who are in it.

Appendix A
Motivational Messages

Players as Models

There are little eyes upon you,
And they're watching night and day;
There are little ears that quickly
Take in every word you say;
There are little hands all eager
To do anything you do;
And a little boy who's dreaming
Of the day he'll be like you.

You're the little fellow's idol;
You're the wisest of the wise,
In this little mind about you,
No suspicions rise.
He believes in you devoutly,
Holds that all you say and do;
He will say and do, in your way,
When he's a grown-up like you.

There's a wide-eyed little fellow,
Who believes you're always right,
And his ears are always open,
And he watches day and night;
You are setting an example
Every day in all you do,
For the little boy who's waiting
To grow up to be like you.

Coaches as Models

No written word,
No oral plea,
Can tell our players
What they should be;
Nor all the books
On the shelves,
It's what their coaches
Are themselves.

You're writing the gospel,
A chapter each day,
By the deeds that you do
And the words that you say.
Men read what you write,
Whether faithless or true;
Say, what is the gospel
According to you?

205

On Winning and Losing

When the Great Scorer comes to mark against your name,
He'll ask not whether you won or lost, but how you played the game.

—Grantland Rice

Effort and Success

In the battle of life it is not the critics who count; not the man who points out how the strong man stumbled, or where the doer of a deed could have done better. The credit belongs to the man who is actually in the arena; whose face is marred by dust and sweat and blood; who strives valiantly; who errs and comes short again and again because there is no effort without error and shortcoming; who does actually strive to do the deeds; who knows the great enthusiasms, the great devotion, spends himself in a worthy cause; who at best knows in the end the triumph of high achievement; and who at worst if he fails, at least fails daring greatly, so that his place shall never be with those cold and timid souls who have tasted neither victory or defeat.

—Theodore Roosevelt

Principles to Live and Coach By

- *Players are working with you, not for you.*
- *Be interested in finding the best way, not your own way.*
- *It is the little things that make the big things happen; life is just one small victory after another.*
- *There is no progress without change. Yet all change is not progress.*
- *Be yourself. Don't compare yourself to others.*
- *When you disagree, do so without being disagreeable. Keep emotions under control.*
- *Never discipline to punish; discipline to teach.*
- *Don't let what you can't do interfere with what you can do. Don't be affected by what you cannot control.*
- *Base decisions on performance, not potential.*
- *Team accomplishments are more important than individual achievements. Always exhaust "We" before "I."*

—Morgan Wootten

The Big 5 for Coaches

1. *Our goal must be to provide a wholesome environment in which young men or women can develop themselves spiritually, socially, and academically.*
2. *As coaches, we should be the kind of coach we would want our sons or daughters to play for.*
3. *We must never lose sight of the fact that basketball is a game and it should be fun. We should never put winning ahead of the individual.*
4. *Because basketball is a great teaching situation, we must use this opportunity to educate the young men or women on our teams. We must prepare them for the many decisions they will be making that will have long-range effects on the quality of their lives.*
5. *This is the bottom line: Are we doing all we can to make our players' sport experience as rewarding as possible?*

—Morgan Wootten

Appendix B

Sample Monthly Practice Plan

						November						
	8	9	10	11	12	13	14	15	16	17	18	19
Stretching	✔	✔	✔	✔	✔	✔		✔	✔	✔	✔	✔
Comments	✔	✔	✔	✔	✔	✔		✔	✔	✔	✔	✔
Warm-up ☆	✔	✔	✔	✔	✔	✔		✔	✔	✔	✔	✔
Big 3 Drills ☆☆	✔	✔	✔	✔	✔	✔		✔	✔	✔	✔	✔
Stance/Steps	✔	✔										
Screening		✔										
Shooting Stations	✔	✔	✔	✔	✔	✔						✔
Rebounding Drills												
Post/Perim. Stations												✔
Free Throws/Sprints	✔	✔	✔	✔	✔	✔		✔	✔	✔	✔	✔
1-on-1 Full Court	✔	✔	✔	✔	✔	✔		✔	✔	✔	✔	✔
1-on-1 Half Court	✔											
1-on-1 Station							O					✔
2-on-2 Full Court				✔	✔	✔		✔	✔			✔
2-on-2 Stations		✔	✔	✔	✔	✔	F					
3-on-3 Full Court				✔	✔	✔		✔				
4-on-4 Full Court					✔		F	✔				
5-on-5 Full Court					✔			✔				
"21"												
Scrimmage	✔	✔	✔						✔		✔	
Dry Run All (5-on-0)												
Offense:												
Fast Break												
Stations												
Change												
Man-to-Man Half Court				✔	✔	✔					✔	
Four Corners								✔				
Zone Stations								✔	✔	✔	✔	
Zone Half Court								✔	✔	✔		
Drift									✔			
Release												✔
Out-of-Bounds Plays												
Line				✔								
Box 1			✔				O					
Box 2			✔									
Box 3						✔	F					
Box Out						✔						
Stack Options							F				✔	
Wide												✔
Color											✔	
Vs. 43												
Time and Score									✔			
Victory					✔							
Ladder									✔			
Deep											✔	
8 Play												✔

(Cont.)

					November							
	8	9	10	11	12	13	14	15	16	17	18	19

Defense:

Drills

	8	9	10	11	12	13	14	15	16	17	18	19
Forward/Guard Overplay	✓	✓	✓							✓		✓
Horseshoe Drill			✓							✓		✓
Fogler Drill				✓	✓	✓				✓		✓
Recovery												
Intercept Drill												
Explain # System				✓								
22-Tough				✓			O					
Halfcourt Man-to-Man							F	✓	✓		✓	✓
25-Blitz Trap					✓			✓	✓			
26-Blitz Switch							F	✓	✓			
Zone Sets												✓
2-2-1 Zone Press						✓		✓	✓			
33 in the 2 Area										✓		
33 in the 3 Area												
44 Zone to 43 Trap									✓			
Vs. O.B. Plays												
Closing Comments	✓	✓	✓	✓	✓	✓		✓	✓	✓	✓	✓

☆Warm-up includes single exchange passing drill, fullcourt layup drill, and 10 free throws in a row.

☆☆Big 3 includes 3-on-2/2-on-1 drill, recognition drill, and 5 two-shot free throw attempts.

Note. The ✓ indicates that this practice component is emphasized or first taught. A skill or strategy will be practiced in most practices subsequent to its introduction; therefore, the absence of a ✓ should not be interpreted as an omission.

						November						Dec
	20	21	22	23	24	25	26	27	28	29	30	1
Stretching	✓		✓	✓	✓		✓	✓		✓	✓	
Comments					✓			✓		✓	✓	
Warm-up ☆	✓	O	✓	✓	✓	O	✓	✓	O	✓	✓	G
Big 3 Drills ☆☆					✓			✓		✓	✓	
Stance/Steps		F				F			F			A
Screening												
Shooting Stations		F			✓	F		✓	F	✓	✓	M
Rebounding Drills								✓				
Post/Perim. Stations					✓							E
Free Throws/Sprints					✓			✓		✓	✓	
1-on-1 Full Court					✓			✓		✓	✓	
1-on-1 Half Court												
1-on-1 Station												
2-on-2 Full Court								✓		✓	✓	
2-on-2 Stations												
3-on-3 Full Court										✓	✓	
4-on-4 Full Court											✓	
5-on-5 Full Court											✓	
"21"						O			O		✓	G
Scrimmage	✓		✓	✓			✓					
Dry Run All (5-on-0)						F			F		✓	A
Offense:												
Fast Break						F			F			M
Stations								✓				
Change								✓				E
Man-to-Man Half Court					✓					✓		
Four Corners												
Zone Stations								✓		✓	✓	
Zone Half Court					✓			✓		✓		
Drift												
Release												
Out-of-Bounds Plays												
Line					✓							
Box 1												
Box 2												G
Box 3												
Box Out						O			O			A
Stack Options												
Wide						F			F			M
Color												
Vs. 43						F			F	✓		E
Time and Score					✓			✓				
Victory												
Ladder												
Deep												
8 Play												

(Cont.)

	20	21	22	23	24	November 25	26	27	28	29	30	Dec 1
Defense:												
Drills												
Forward/Guard Overplay					✔					✔		
Horseshoe Drill					✔					✔		
Fogler Drill					✔					✔		
Recovery										✔		
Intercept Drill										✔		G
Explain # System												
22-Tough						O			O			A
Halfcourt Man-to-Man												
25-Blitz Trap						F			F			M
26-Blitz Switch												
Zone Sets						F			F			E
33 in the 2 Area											✔	
33 in the 3 Area										✔		
44 Zone to 43 Trap												
Vs. O.B. Plays								✔				
Closing Comments					✔			✔		✔	✔	

☆Warm-up includes single exchange passing drill, fullcourt layup drill, and 10 free throws in a row.

☆☆Big 3 includes 3-on-2/2-on-1 drill, recognition drill, and 5 two-shot free throw attempts.

Note. The ✔ indicates that this practice component is emphasized or first taught. A skill or strategy will be practiced in most practices subsequent to its introduction; therefore, the absence of a ✔ should not be interpreted as an omission.

Index

About the Author

Morgan Wootten has been the head basketball coach at DeMatha Catholic High School in Hyattsville, MD, since 1956. His 88% win record is one of the highest in high school basketball history. Another great achievement is the fact that more than 175 of Wootten's players have been offered an athletic or academic college scholarship. Many of his former players have gone on to play in the National Basketball Association. Wootten is also a developer of future coaches—seven of his former assistants have gone on to become Division I head coaches.

In 1991, Wootten became the only high school coach to receive the Naismith Memorial Basketball Hall of Fame's most prestigious single honor, the John W. Bunn award. The previous year (1990), Wootten was se-lected as the top teacher-coach of all sports in America by the Disney Television Channel. During his coaching career, Wootten has been named National Coach of the Year 5 times and Washington, DC, Area Coach of the Year more than 20 times. He is a charter member of the Washington Metro Basketball Hall of Fame. Wootten has served as chairman of the player Selection Committee for the McDonald's High School All-American Basketball Game since its inception.

During the off-season, Wootten runs his own camp and speaks at basketball clinics and seminars worldwide. He has also written five books and produced three instructional tapes. He and his wife, Kathy, reside in Hyattsville. In his spare time, he enjoys reading, golfing, and traveling.

Dave Gilbert, who assisted Wootten in preparing the manuscript, is a sports journalist in Washington, DC. He is chief announcer for a sports production firm, and a veteran play-by-play announcer of college basketball games. Gilbert has also written and produced a variety of sports programs broadcast on Washington radio and television stations.